LONGMAN EXAM SKILLS

Proficiency
Use of English

Fiona Scott-Barrett

CONTENTS MAP

EXAM FACTFILE

Certificate of Proficiency in English Paper 3: Use of English	
takes	1 hour 30 minutes
is answered	on a separate answer sheet
includes	a total of 44 questions
is marked	out of a weighted final total of 40 marks (adjusted from a raw score of 75 marks as described in more detail below) or a fifth of the overall total of 200 marks for the whole Proficiency exam

Paper 3 contains 5 sections:

Part	Consists of:	Tests:	Marks
1	a cloze test with fifteen gaps.	your knowledge of grammar and vocabulary.	One mark for each correct answer.
2	a text containing ten gaps. Each gap must be filled with a word formed from the stem provided.	your knowledge of vocabulary and word formation.	One mark for each correct answer.
3	six questions each containing three sentences with a gap in them. The missing word is the same for the three sentences. Candidates must find one word which fits all three sentences.	your knowledge of vocabulary (phrasal verbs, collocations, set phrases, etc.).	Two marks for each correctly answered question.
4	eight sentences which must be transformed using a given word.	your knowledge of grammar and vocabulary.	Two marks for each correct answer.
5	• two texts on which you answer a total of four questions. • a summary-writing task based on the two texts.	• your awareness of the use of language in a text. • your ability to extract relevant information from texts and write a short summary.	• Two marks for each correct answer. • Up to a total of fourteen marks.

TIMING AND EXAM TECHNIQUE

As you can see from the Exam factfile opposite, there is a total of one and a half hours allocated to Paper 3 Use of English. In order to use this time efficiently:

- Remember that the total time includes the time you need to transfer your answers to the answer sheets at the end of the test. Allow about ten minutes for this.
- Allow roughly the same proportion of time for each part of the test as the marks that are allocated to it. This means:
  Parts 1 and 2 together should take up about 25 minutes.
  Parts 3 and 4 should together take 25 to 30 minutes.
  Part 5 should take about 25 minutes.
  This will leave you time for checking and transferring your answers at the end.
- Do the parts that you find the easiest first.
- Don't waste time struggling over a question that is giving you difficulty. Leave it, move on to the next question or part of the test and come back to the troublesome questions in any spare time you have at the end of the test.
- If two questions from different parts of the test are tricky, spend more time on the one that is worth more marks.
- Don't write two alternative answers for questions 1 to 43 – even if one is correct, they will both be marked wrong.
- Don't leave any of the questions 1 to 43 unanswered – even a guess might turn out to be lucky!

Introduction

Part 1: Cloze test

What you have to do

- You read a text which contains sixteen gaps.
- The first will have been completed for you as an example.
- You must put **one** word only in each remaining gap. Sometimes more than one word could logically fit in the gap. In this case choose only one of them. If you write two words, both will be marked wrong even if one is correct.
- You may make notes on the question sheet but all answers must be transferred to the answer sheet before you hand the papers in.
- As your answers to this section will be checked by computer, you **must** write them in capital letters.

Strategy building I

Always read the whole text before you start filling any gaps.
This will help you to get an overall understanding of its main arguments. In addition, some gaps may test not only your understanding of a sentence, but of the whole text. For example, the phrase '*in .... respects*' could be commenting on a whole text and you may not know until you've read it all which of the choices – '*some*', '*many*' or '*all*' are all possible – would be the most appropriate to fill this gap.

Task
Read the whole text about earthquake prediction on page 7 opposite. What conclusion does it come to? Having read the whole text, what word would you put in gap 13?

Strategy building II

Always study the text before and after each gap carefully.
Knowing how the gaps relate to the surrounding text can help you guess what kind of word you need to write. For example, among other possibilities, the gap might:

- form part of a phrasal verb.
  The company was set ***up*** *ten years ago.*
  We ***set*** *off early in the morning.*

- test your knowledge of dependent prepositions.
  a sharp decline ***in*** *sales; insisted* ***on*** *being*

- form part of a set phrase.
  first and ***foremost****;* ***above*** *all;* ***on*** *the whole*

- connect two ideas.
  The French enjoy this ***while*** *to the British it is...*
  ... on the ***other*** *hand ...*

- refer to earlier or later parts of the text.
  ... ***such*** *examples are ...; ...* ***which*** *is considered to be ...*
  ... ***these*** *are not ...; ...* ***it*** *is likely that ...*
  In the case of reference words, the gap may relate to an idea expressed one or more sentences earlier.

- test your knowledge of collocation (which words are naturally used together).
  ... they ***reached*** *the* ***conclusion*** *that ...; ...* ***place*** *an* ***order*** *for ...*

Tasks

1 Look again at the text about earthquake prediction below.

1. One of the gaps forms part of a phrasal verb. Which one? ....
2. Three of the gaps test your knowledge of dependent prepositions. Which ones? ....
3. Three of the gaps form part of set phrases. Which ones? ....
4. Two gaps form part of connecting phrases. Which ones? ....
5. One gap refers to an earlier part of the text. Which one? ....
6. One gap forms part of a verb-noun collocation. Which one? ....

2 Now complete the gaps you identified in Task 1 with a suitable word.

3 Complete the remaining three gaps. Read the surrounding text to help you find what words should go in each gap.

Practice

For questions 1 – 15, read the text below and think of the word which best fits each space. Use only **one** word in each space. There is an example at the beginning (0).

Example:

0	O	F													

Earthquake prediction

If scientists were able to warn governments **(0)** ...of.... an impending earthquake, even if only a few hours **(1)** .... advance, lives might be saved and international rescue workers could be at the scene of the disaster by the time it happened, instead of heading **(2)** .... their local airports several hours after the event.

(3) .... it is, seismologists have long been able to predict roughly where earthquakes will happen, but they are still **(4)** .... from knowing how to forecast exactly when **(5)** .... may strike. The one and **(6)** .... successful prediction in recorded history was for the 1975 earthquake in Haicheng, China. In the months preceding the earthquake changes **(7)** .... land elevation and ground water levels, widespread reports of peculiar animal behaviour, and many foreshocks had **(8)** .... to a low-level warning. As a **(9)** .... of an increase in foreshock activity, an evacuation warning was **(10)** .... the day before a magnitude 7.3 earthquake. Unfortunately, in **(11)** .... of their success in 1975, the Chinese failed to predict the Tangshan earthquake the following year, which **(12)** .... an appalling 250,000 fatalities.

Since **(13)** .... completely reliable method of prediction has been found, most governments now focus **(14)** .... mitigating the effects of earthquakes once they strike **(15)** .... than attempting to forecast them.

Part 2: Word formation

What you have to do

- You read a text which contains eleven gaps.
- The first will have been completed for you as an example.
- You must put **one** word only in each remaining gap. This word must be formed from the stem word given in capitals at the end of the line where the gap appears.
- You may make notes on the question sheet but all answers must be transferred to the answer sheet before you hand the papers in.
- As your answers to this section will be checked by computer, you **must** write them in capital letters.

Strategy building I

Always read the whole text before you start filling any gaps.
This will help you to get an overall understanding of its main arguments. In addition, as with the cloze passage, some gaps may test not only your understanding of a sentence, but of the whole text.

Strategy building II

Identify the part of speech needed to fill each gap.
Look at the words immediately before and after each gap to guide you. For example in the text on page 9 opposite:

- Gap 16 is preceded by the possessive pronoun '*its*', therefore the word you need in the gap must be a noun.
- Gap 18 is preceded by the verb '*be*' and there is no article, therefore the word you need in the gap must be an adjective.
- Gap 22 precedes and qualifies the adjective '*remote*', therefore the word you need in the gap must be an adverb.

Tasks

1 Read the whole of the text about Isabella Bird on page 9.

2 Go through the remaining gaps one by one and identify what part of speech is needed in each gap.

Strategy building III

Read the surrounding text carefully for clues to the meaning of the word that must be fitted in the gap.
For example, gap 21 in the text about Isabella Bird could be filled either with the noun '*sleepiness*' or '*sleeplessness*'. However, the word '*plagued*' in the same sentence implies that this was a recurrent and unwanted problem, rather than a temporary state, therefore '*sleeplessness*' would be the more appropriate choice.

Tasks

1 Read the sentence containing gap 18. Two adjectives can be formed from the word '*value*'. What are they? Which of the two would be more appropriate to collocate with the word '*skills*' in the same sentence?

2 Read the sentence containing gap 23. Four verbs can be formed from the stem '*count*', but only one would be a synonym for '(*The books in which she) told tales of (her journeys)*... .' What is the verb you need?

Strategy building IV

Be aware that more than one transformation may be needed.
For example, the stem *chant* could be transformed up to four times.

1 By adding a verb prefix – *enchant*
2 By adding a negative prefix – *disenchant*
3 By adding a noun suffix or adjective suffix – *disenchantment / disenchanted*
4 By adding an adverb suffix – *disenchantedly*

Tasks

1 Go through the text about Isabella Bird and identify all the gaps where more than one transformation is needed.

2 Now complete the whole task.

Practice

For questions 16 – 25, read the text below. Use the word given in capitals at the end of some of the lines to form a word that fits in the space in the same line. There is an example at the beginning (0).

Example:

0	S	T	I	F	L	I	N	G	L	Y						

Isabella Bird

Life in Victorian Britain was **(0)** ..stiflingly.. dull for many women and a few reacted against its **(16)** .... by seeking freedom and adventure in travel. Although she had an otherwise conventional **(17)** ...., Isabella Bird (1831 – 1904) learnt two skills in childhood which proved to be **(18)** .... when she grew up. As she was a frail child, a doctor recommended frequent excursions **(19)** .... so Isabella learnt to ride and her clergyman father took her with him on trips round his parish. On these rides he taught her to be **(20)** .... and exact in her description of nature and people, attributes which made her later travel writings successful.

STIFLE
RESTRICT
BRING
VALUE
DOOR
OBSERVE

At the age of 18 Isabella travelled to the Scottish Highlands to aid her recovery from an operation. From then on, her life followed a pattern of periods at home plagued by back pain, headaches, and **(21)** ...., interspersed with periods of adventurous travel to **(22)** .... remote and exotic locations.

SLEEP
INCREASE

The books in which she **(23)** .... her journeys met with success and the **(24)** .... from these supplemented a modest inheritance from her mother and allowed her to finance further travels. Her achievements were **(25)** .... recognised in 1892 when she and fourteen other ladies were the first women to be invited to join the Royal Geographical Society.

COUNT
COME
OFFICE

Part 3: Gapped sentences

What you have to do

- This part consists of six questions. Each question is made up of three separate sentences.
- An example is also given at the start of the task.
- You must identify **one** word which could fit in all three of the sentences in each question.
- You may make notes on the question sheet but all answers must be transferred to the answer sheet before you hand the papers in.
- As your answers to this section will be checked by computer, you **must** write them in capital letters.

Strategy building I

Identify the part of speech needed to fill each gap.
The gapped word in each of the three sentences may form part of an idiom, set phrase, phrasal verb or collocation, but will nevertheless always be the same part of speech.

Tasks

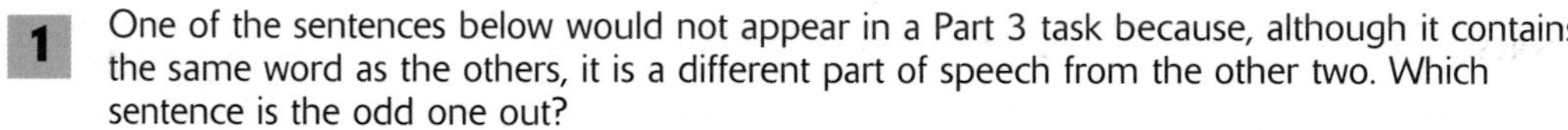

1 One of the sentences below would not appear in a Part 3 task because, although it contains the same word as the others, it is a different part of speech from the other two. Which sentence is the odd one out?

- ○ Unemployment has *hit* record levels.
- ○ People are queuing up to see the latest Hollywood *hit*.
- ○ He *hit* his younger brother with his tennis racquet.

2 Identify what part of speech is needed to fill the gaps in sentences 26 – 31 on page 11 opposite.

Strategy building II

Start with the sentence you find easiest in each group of three.
Find as many possibilities as you can to fill that gap, then eliminate those which do not fit the other sentences.

Example

- ○ Bruce sent his steak back because it was ....
- ○ They felt very anxious when their car broke down in a .... area of the town.
- ○ The company spokesman had to answer a lot of .... questions about the forthcoming takeover.

The first sentence could be completed by the adjectives *overdone, underdone, overcooked, undercooked, tasteless, revolting, tough* or *disgusting*. Of these adjectives, the last three could perhaps be applied to the second sentence but neither *revolting* nor *disgusting* would be likely to apply to questions about a company takeover. Thus the only word that would logically complete all three sentences is *tough*.

Task
Apply the same approach to answering questions 26 – 31 on page 11.

Practice

For questions 26 – 31, think of **one** word only which can be used appropriately in all three sentences. Here is an example (0).

Example:

- The young man devoted his life to the .... of pleasure.
- I have to admit that hill walking is a .... which doesn't interest me at all.
- The flustered mother ran out of the supermarket in hot .... of her absconding toddler.

0	P	U	R	S	U	I	T									

26

- Tom was unable to sit his exams as he was .... up with a bad bout of flu.
- The government minister has .... himself open to criticism by his careless and prejudiced remarks.
- My English teacher always .... great stress on correct pronunciation.

27

- They live in a log cabin .... in the forest.
- Their father was so .... in thought that he didn't even notice the children had come home.
- He took a .... breath before beginning to recite the poem.

28

- I have to catch an early .... to Paris.
- She broke her leg after falling down a .... of stairs.
- The children took .... when they saw the schoolteacher, his face red with anger, striding across the playground towards them.

29

- Her spirits .... as the weeks went by and her brother still failed to return home.
- The ship .... without trace soon after entering the area known as the Bermuda Triangle.
- As soon as she got home, Martha .... into her favourite armchair with a sigh of relief.

30

- It isn't Anna's .... to speak to strangers on trains.
- When that night-club refused me entrance because I wasn't wearing a tie, I decided to take my .... elsewhere.
- In larger cities, the old French .... of going home from work for lunch is dying out.

31

- I'd make a very poor nurse as I can't .... the sight of blood.
- Please don't .... on ceremony, just help yourselves to anything you want to drink.
- The letters GB on the back of a car .... for Great Britain.

Part 4: Key word transformations

What you have to do

- This part consists of eight questions. Each question is made up of a prompt sentence, a key word and a gapped sentence of which only the beginning and end are given.
- An example is given at the start of the task.
- You must complete the gapped sentence so that it has a similar meaning to the prompt sentence. You **must** include the key word in your sentence and you **must not** change it in any way.
- You may write no fewer than three and no more than eight words, including the key word. Contractions e.g. *wouldn't* counts as two words.
- You may make notes on the question sheet but all answers must be transferred to the answer sheet before you hand the papers in.

Strategy building I

Follow the instructions carefully.
Read '*What you have to do*' again and the instructions and example for Part 4 on page 13.

Task
Two sample answers to Part 4 questions are given below. Each is grammatically correct, but would not be awarded the full marks available. Identify what is wrong with each of the sample answers.

1 If my cooker's working again by then, I'll have you over to dinner on Friday.
repaired
Provided *that I've finished repairing the cooker by* then, I'll have you over to dinner on Friday.

2 The product launch is unlikely to be successful unless it is planned in great detail.
essential
Detailed *planning is absolutely essential to ensure the success of* the product launch.

Strategy building II

Be aware that more than one change to the prompt sentence may be needed.
For example, the correct answer to question 1 above involves:

- Changing verb tense and voice. *is working again* ➡ *has been repaired*
- Identifying a synonymous word/phrase. *If* ➡ *Provided* ***that***

This results in the correct answer:
Provided *that the cooker has been repaired by* then, I'll have you over to dinner on Friday.

The correct answer to question 2 above involves:

- Changing a verb to a noun. *planned* ➡ *planning*
- Changing an adjective to a noun. *successful* ➡ *success*
- Identifying two dependent prepositions. *essential* ***to*** and *success* ***of***

This results in the correct answer:
Detailed *planning is essential to the success of* the product launch.

Task

1 Identify what kinds of changes will need to be made to sentences 32 to 39 on page 13 opposite.

2 Rewrite the sentences.

Practice

For questions 32 – 39, complete the second sentence so that it has a similar meaning to the first sentence, using the word given. **Do not change the word given**. You must use between three and eight words, including the word given. Here is an example (0).

Example:

0 The company's profits appear to be improving significantly this year.
evidence
The company's .... this year.

0	profits show evidence of significant improvement

32 She's forever warning her husband about driving too fast, but he pays no attention.
often
No .... her husband about driving too fast, he pays no attention.

33 She emigrated immediately after gaining her degree.
graduated
No .... abroad.

34 Phil stopped being so unrealistic when he lost his job.
brought
The .... earth.

35 She got her licence because her father helped her learn to drive.
assistance
But .... passed her driving test.

36 It wasn't Susan's fault that the dog chewed your slipper.
blame
Susan's .... your slipper.

37 You must not enter this area unless you are wearing protective clothing.
strictly
Entry to this area .... who is not wearing protective clothing.

38 My father persuaded me to learn another foreign language.
talked
It was .... another foreign language.

39 She'd only just got dressed when the first of the guests arrived.
dressing
No sooner .... the first of the guests arrived.

Part 5: Summary task

What you have to do

- This part consists of five questions based on two texts. The first four of these (questions 40 – 43) involve answering two questions on each of the texts. More details are given below.
- To answer question 44 you must identify relevant information from both texts and write a short text (between 50 and 70 words) summarising this information.
- You may make notes on the question sheet but all answers must be transferred to the answer sheet before you hand the papers in.

Detailed look at the task: Questions 40 to 43

These questions usually test four different skills.

1 Explaining the meaning of words or phrases in the texts.
2 Recognising forward and backward reference.
3 Identifying words or phrases and their function in the texts.
4 Answering questions on the content of the texts.

Task
Match the questions below to the skills (1 – 4 above) that they are testing.

a What problem could be solved by the measures described in lines 6 to 7? ☐
b Which phrase in paragraph ... indicates ...? ☐
c What is meant by the phrase ...? ☐
d What image of ... does the writer create? ☐
e What exactly does the phrase ... in line 5 describe? ☐
f What is the writer's opinion of ...? ☐
g Which two words reflect the need for ... mentioned in the first text? ☐
h What does the word ... mean in this context? ☐

Each of these skills are dealt with separately and in detail in Units 1 to 4 (pages 30 – 31, 42 – 43, 54 – 55 and 74 – 75) of this book.

Detailed look at the task: Question 44

Two elements are involved in this question.

1 Identifying the relevant content points.

- There will be four of these distributed between the two texts.
- Correct identification of each point will gain you one mark.
- Units 5 and 6 (pages 87 and 99) of this book deal with this skill in detail.

2 Rephrasing and linking these points into a concise but comprehensive summary.

- Up to ten marks can be awarded for this task.
- Your summary must be between 50 and 70 words long.
- Marks will be deducted if it is substantially longer than this.
- Units 7 and 10 (pages 119 and 163) of this book deal in detail with the skill of writing a short summary.
- Practice of this skill, with varying degrees of guidance, is given in Units 8, 9, 11, 12, 13, 14 and 15 as well as in the five Practice tests.

Exam tips

- The texts will have a similar theme, but present slightly different viewpoints or aspects of the topic. Always read through both texts quickly before looking at the questions, and identify what topic they both deal with.
- It is not necessary to write complete sentences in answer to questions 40 to 43. In some cases one or two words or a short phrase may be enough.
- Questions 40 to 43 carry a total of eight marks, in contrast to a possible total of fourteen for question 44, and involve much less writing. It is therefore worth spending some time on answering them correctly.
- If you are having trouble with the summary-writing section or don't have time to complete a clean second draft, you will at least gain some points if you have correctly identified some or all of the content points and link them into a simple text with basic connectors (e.g. *and, but*).

Practice

1 Skim-read these two texts. In terms of subject-matter, what do they have in common?

Text 1

At present, scientists simply do not know the right criteria for consistently making a clone of an animal. So far five species have been cloned – cattle, sheep, pigs, goats and mice – but at a grim price. For example, with cattle, a total of 8,919 eggs from cows have been used to create cloned embryos, of which only 71 live calves were born. More than a quarter of these were alarmingly larger than normal, some had serious mental abnormalities and many were found to have underdeveloped lungs. 26 of them died young, making an overall success rate of about one in 200 eggs. There is no reason to assume that the success rate for humans would be any better and the disappointment and pain caused by miscarriages, abnormalities and early deaths would undoubtedly be much greater.

Cogent though these arguments against human reproductive cloning are, the prospect of success is even more alarming. Imagine this scenario: a young boy grows up in the shadow of a gifted brother killed in a car accident. At each stage in his life, the achievements of his deceased sibling are held up to him and his own failings are constantly ridiculed. Normally such a child would protest that he should not have to live up to unreal expectations. But this boy cannot, for he is a clone, created from a cell taken from his brother's body. Or consider the situation in which a person creates a clone of himself or herself to overcome infertility. A child created this way would be the identical genetic copy of his father (or mother). So how would he react if his parent succumbed prematurely to an illness of genetic origin? Such worries may once have seemed fanciful and remote, but, according to Ian Wilmut, creator of the world's first cloned mammal, Dolly the sheep, the issue is so pressing as to demand a national debate among psychologists and biologists.

Text 2

Though less celebrated than Dolly, the birth of Polly, the second cloned sheep created by Ian Wilmut, is far more ominous. With Polly, Wilmut's team customised a human gene into a sheep cell and then cloned the sheep, making it the first truly "designer animal". Using the clone as a "standard model", scientists can now produce endless variations tailored to suit the requirements of their clients. There is little doubt that, in the not too distant future, proponents of human cloning will be clamouring for the right to extend customised cloning to humans as well. At first glance, there seems to be a humanitarian argument on their side – prospective parents would want to spare their cloned offspring from a genetic predisposition for life-threatening diseases, such as strokes or cancer, and thus would ask for those genes to be eliminated from the donor cell. But where should the client, or the law, draw the line? What if the parent knew he or she was likely to pass on a genetic predisposition for depression or dyslexia, or even for a body shape they happen to dislike? Such questions must be resolved before we start playing God with our genes.

Furthermore, if customised cloning became widely accepted and practised, how would people regard children who weren't cloned and customised to design specifications? What about children born with disabilities, or even those who did not fit the accepted norms of cloned beauty, health or intelligence? Would society view such children with tolerance or come to see them as errors in the genetic code – in short, as defective products? If that were to happen, we might lose the most precious gift of all, the human capacity to empathise with each other. When we empathise with another human being, it's because we feel and experience their vulnerability, their frailties and their unique struggle to claim their humanity. But, in a world that comes to expect perfection in its offspring, can empathy really survive?

2 Read the rubric below. Then re-read the two texts, underlining or highlighting any points in them you think are relevant to the summary-writing task.

In a paragraph of between 50 and 70 words, summarise, in your own words as far as possible, the arguments against reproducing humans by cloning.

3 Eight potential content points are listed below. Work with a partner and decide which four best summarise the arguments in the texts.

More than four of the points may be true, but you must choose the four that, taken together, best summarise ***all*** *the ideas / examples in the texts.*

1. Clones will have the same genetic predispositions towards illnesses or mental problems as their donors.
2. Clones might well be under great psychological pressure.
3. Cloning has a low success rate and a high cost in terms of miscarriages, abnormalities and deaths.
4. Cloning raises ethical problems concerning the type and extent of genetic customisation that should be allowed.
5. Customised cloning risks creating an underclass of non-cloned children who may not be accepted as they do not conform to society's standards.
6. Empathy cannot survive in a world that worships perfection.
7. Humans suffer more than animals do.
8. Parents will have higher expectations of clones than of non-cloned children.

Reminder: One mark will be given in the exam for each correctly identified content point.

4 Now arrange your resulting four content points in a logical order.

5 The summary you write should:

- be the correct length (between 50 and 70 words).
- be well-organised.
- be grammatically accurate.
- not include too many words or phrases copied from the texts.

Model summaries

Four model summaries are given below. Each of them is grammatically accurate, but most display some other faults. Use the checklist opposite to help you assess each model.

A

Cloning is dangerous and lots of embryos and children would die. Even if the process was successful, a clone's life would be blighted by living in the shadow of its predecessor or by knowing what illnesses it would develop later. Worst of all, so-called 'designer cloning' might create an underclass of children who had not been cloned.

B

The cloning technique is not properly developed yet so the disappointment and pain caused by miscarriages, abnormalities and early deaths would be great. A child created this way would be the identical genetic copy of his parent and would react badly if his parent died young from an illness of genetic origin. Parents who wanted to spare their offspring from this kind of problem would not know where to draw the line. Also, they might look down on non-cloned children that were born with disabilities.

C

Cloning currently results in an unacceptably high number of miscarriages and congenital defects and, even if humans were successfully cloned, they would probably have severe psychological problems. Worse still, if 'designer cloning' became the norm, it would raise serious ethical issues about the extent and type of customisation carried out. It might also create a society in which non-cloned people were looked down on as being sub-standard.

D

Cloning has a low success rate and causes a lot of abnormalities and deaths. Clones would be under psychological pressure. Cloning raises ethical problems concerning the type and extent of customization. Customised cloning risks creating an underclass of non-cloned children. They might not be accepted by the clones.

Checklist

Is the summary the right length?	A	B	C	D
Yes				
No – too long				
No – too short				
Are all four content points included?	A	B	C	D
Yes				
No				
Have the ideas from the texts been rephrased in the writer's own words?	A	B	C	D
Yes, mainly				
Hardly at all				
Are the ideas linked together coherently into a short paragraph?	A	B	C	D
Yes				
No – just a list of points				

6 Based on your completed checklist, which model summary do you think would receive the highest marks?

Skills review

- Write the first draft of your summary, based on the rephrased content points.
- Count the number of words you have used.
- Check that you have not included unnecessary details.
- Check that you have not copied sections of the original texts word for word.
- Where possible, use noun + noun compounds to shorten sentences.
- Where possible, use verbs or phrases which convey meaning succinctly, e.g.
  genetic encoding rather than *everyone's genetic code will be recorded*
  investigate why rather than *try to find out the reasons for*
- Cut out any superfluous words.
- Check your final number of words and write a clean copy of your paraphrased summary.

1 People and relationships

Grammar
- Present and future tenses

Vocabulary
- Phrasal verbs: relationships
- Word formation: noun suffixes
- Idioms and set phrases

Summary
- Identifying words and phrases in the text

Grammar: Present and future tenses

Grammar overview

Present simple

We use the Present simple:

1 to talk about habitual actions, often with adverbs of frequency
*He frequently **responds** angrily to even the slightest criticism.*

2 to talk about definite arrangements in the future
*The Parent Teachers Association meeting **begins** at 7 o'clock.*

3 to talk about permanent states
*A good relationship **combines** love, trust and friendship.*

4 to describe a permanent truth
*Emotional and physical changes in adolescence **mean** that teenagers often **behave** unpredictably.*

5 when we are relating a story or telling a joke
*'Initially, the hero **decides** to seek out his real mother after years of separation.'*

6 in newspaper headlines
*Minister **attacks** social services in child poverty scandal.*

Present continuous

We use the Present continuous:

1 to talk about an activity which is in progress at the present time
*In Britain, the number of children who live with step-parents **is rising**.*

2 to talk about a temporary activity
*Their mother's in hospital so the twins **are staying** with their grandparents.*

3 to talk about our plans or arrangements for the future
*I can't meet up with you on Friday afternoon as **I'm seeing** my mother-in-law then.*

4 to talk about an activity which is in progress as we speak
***I'm cooking** lunch for the kids, can I call you back later?*

Will

We use *will*:

1 to make predictions and offers
*According to research, a child with high self-esteem at the age of ten **will be** more successful in later life.*

***I'll try** to persuade your father to give you the money.*

2 to talk about decisions we make at the moment of speaking
***I'll forgive** you for your hypocritical behaviour considering your apology.*

3 to describe known facts
*The clocks **will change** in the last week of October.*

Be going to	
We use *be going to*: **1** to describe our intentions for a future time *I* ***am going to try*** *and exercise self-control when I come face to face with the school bully who caused me such pain as a child.* **2** to talk about actions which we have planned or organised for the future *My cousins and I* ***are going to hold*** *a surprise birthday party for our grandmother.*	**3** to make predictions about the future based on evidence we have in the present *The children are highly vulnerable and their parents' decision to separate* ***is going to*** *cause them great distress.*
Future perfect	
We use the Future perfect: **1** to talk about an action which will be finished by a certain point in the future *My grandparents* ***will have been married*** *for 50 years next April.*	**2** to talk about an activity which continues over a certain period of time and which will be finished by a certain time in the future *By the time the election results are announced the presidential candidates* ***will have been campaigning*** *for three months solid.* **3** to make assumptions about the present *Don't phone her at this time of night;* ***she'll have gone*** *to bed by now.*

Advanced grammar points

Grammar point 1

Look at the six verbs in the dialogue below. Some of them are in the wrong form of the present tense. Decide which ones, and why they are wrong. Then correct them.

Father: **(1)** Do you cook lunch Clare? **(2)** I'm expecting your mother will be pleased. You never **(3)** help in the kitchen.
Daughter: No, Dad. Mum **(4)** is making some soup. **(5)** I'm just tasting it. **(6)** It's tasting really delicious.

Verbs which refer to states rather than activities are rarely used with continuous tenses. Some of the most common are:

- Verbs of the senses and perception: *see, taste, smell, sound, hear, notice, perceive*
- Verbs describing emotional states: *like, want, abhor, love, wish, adore, detest*
- Verbs relating to mental states and attitudes: *think, believe, feel, know, suspect, consider, recall, regard, agree, appreciate, presume, reckon, understand, seem*
- Other verbs: *be, belong, consist of, have, owe, own, matter*

However, some verbs from the lists above can be used with a continuous tense. This transforms their meaning from a description of a state to a reference to an activity with a definite beginning and end, for example:

This ***tastes*** *good.* (state)
I'm tasting *the soup to see if it's got enough salt.* (activity)
I ***consider*** *£40 a ludicrous price to pay for a child's skirt.* (state)
I'm considering *whether or not to apply for that job I saw in the paper.* (activity)

Some of these verbs have a different meaning altogether if used with a continuous tense, for example:

I ***see*** *you finally got round to doing up your kitchen.* (perceive visually – state)
*She used to go out with John, but she****'s seeing*** *a guy from her work these days.* (go out with – activity)
I ***have*** *a Fiat Punto.* (own – state)
I'm having *my lunch now; could you call back later?* (eat – activity)
At work she ***appears*** *to be very confident, but I think she's shy with strangers.* (seem – state)
*He****'s appearing*** *in a production of 'Romeo and Juliet' at the King's Theatre.* (act – activity)

Grammar point 2

One of the two sentences below is incorrect. Which one, and what is wrong with it?

1 You're always wiping your nose on your sleeve; couldn't you use a tissue?
2 You're never blowing your nose.

- *Always, forever* or *continually* can be used with the present continuous tense in the positive form to indicate that the speaker finds another person's habit or repeated action annoying.
  *She's **forever borrowing** my things without asking me.*

- However, the simple present is chosen if the sentence is in the negative or interrogative form.
  *She **never asks** before borrowing my things.*
  *Why **don't** you **ask** before you borrow my things?*

Practice A

Complete the sentences with the correct present tense form of the verb in brackets.

1 Don't disturb your father at the moment – he .... (think) about a problem he's got at work.

2 I used to enjoy chatting to Jane, but these days she .... (forever complain) about something or other.

3 I .... (suspect) that my daughter's new friends .... (have) a bad effect on her schoolwork.

4 We .... (have) salmon for supper, but I .... (presume) you .... (not want) any, Tom, since you .... (abhor) fish in any form.

5 And while we're on the subject of mistakes, I .... (recall) you telling me that it would take me only ten minutes to get to town, and I arrived an hour late for an important meeting.

6 A: He always .... (wear) jeans and a T-shirt, even when he .... (entertain) clients.
B: Well, he's the boss, he can do what he .... (want).
A: True, but what .... (annoy) me is that his T-shirt .... (always come out of) his trousers so he .... (continually tuck) it back in.

7 A: What on earth .... (you do)?
B: I .... (smell) the meat. I think it might have gone off.
A: Let me try. No, I .... (not think) so. It .... (smell) fine to me.

8 A: Don't interrupt, dear. You .... (always interrupt) me when I .... (talk) to my friends. It's not polite.
B: It .... (not matter). She .... (seem) to me to be a very well-behaved child.

9 A: Look! .... (you see) that couple at the table over there?
B: Yes, it's Steve and Gloria.
A: Surely they .... (not see) each other again? I heard they'd had a fight.
B: Well, judging from the way they .... (look) at each other, they .... (appear) to be back together again.

Grammar point 3

All the sentences below relate to future time. Match each sentence to its function.

Sentence	Function
1 All Proficiency students are to report to the principal at ten o'clock.	**a** referring to an event in the immediate future.
2 The plane is due to arrive at 16.45.	**b** making a formal request
3 I'm about to go down to the shops.	**c** making a prediction
4 School fees are sure to go up.	**d** referring to an event which is expected to happen at a particular time.

- Future forms with the infinitive.
  am/is/are to (go/see) *am/is/are about to* (go/see) *am/is/are due to* (go/see)
- Making predictions using the infinitive.
  am/is/are sure/certain/bound/likely/unlikely to (go/see)
- Making predictions using constructions with *will*.
  It's likely/possible/probable/unlikely that (prices) *will* (rise/go up)
  I'm sure/certain that (prices) *will* + (rise/go up)
  I doubt whether/if (prices) *will* (rise/go up)
  I expect (that) (prices) *will* (rise/go up)

Practice B

Match each sentence 1–3 to a sentence a-c which has a similar meaning.

1 It's likely that fuel prices will rise this year.
2 Fuel prices are unlikely to rise this year.
3 I'm sure that fuel prices will rise this year.

a I doubt if fuel prices will rise this year.
b Fuel prices are bound to rise this year.
c I expect fuel prices will rise this year.

Practice C

Complete the second sentence so that it has a similar meaning to the first sentence, using the word given. Do not change the word given. You must use between three and eight words, including the word given.

1 I think Carol's unlikely to pass her driving test at the first attempt.
whether
I .... her driving test at the first attempt.

2 I'm certain that Anne will come to the party tonight.
sure
Anne .... to the party tonight.

3 I can't chat now, as I'm on the point of departing for the airport.
leave
I can't chat now, as I'm .... the airport.

4 I've ordered a taxi and I expect it will be here any minute now.
due
The taxi .... arrive any minute now.

5 Please note that all guests must leave their room key at reception when they leave the hotel.
are
All .... their room key at reception when they leave the hotel.

Use your English

Work with a partner. Discuss current and future trends in your country in *two* of the topic areas below. Then together prepare a very short talk (less than a minute) on each of the two topics to give to the whole class. Try to use a range of appropriate structures. A model is given on the following page.

- Use of the Internet at home.
- Relationships between parents and children.
- Teenagers' social life and free time.
- Trends in education.
- Shopping habits.

Model

In our opinion, the Internet is not very well-established here yet, and only a few people have an Internet connection at home. However, a lot of cybercafes are opening up, and they're very popular, especially with young people. It's likely that these young people will encourage their parents to buy them computers for home use and, since the costs of hardware are coming down all the time, domestic use of the Internet is bound to increase.

Practice D

Read the whole text below then complete the gaps by writing the appropriate form of the verb in the margin.
Choose from these tenses – Present simple / continuous, *going to* + verb, Future simple / continuous *, Future perfect simple *

You might want to study the uses of the tenses marked with an asterisk again in this unit, Grammar overview, pages 20–21.

It happens every October. I'll be sitting on a train on a rainy Friday afternoon and I **(1)** .... up and see that almost everyone else in the carriage is old enough to be my mother. Some of these women **(2)** .... at their watches and sighing a lot, as if to brace themselves for an ordeal. Others **(3)** .... on duty for the school half-term holiday. They **(4)** .... two or three school-aged children with them, the younger ones settled with colouring books and crayons and matching bags of crisps. And, as always, I **(5)** .... like saying to one of them 'Would you like to come and be our grandmother too?' You see, grandparents **(6)** .... into two categories these days – the doting and the disappearing. Some of the doting ones **(7)** .... their grandchildren up from school every day. Others are on duty less frequently but are quite happy to drop everything and rush round to baby-sit when their working daughter or daughter-in-law **(8)** .... them at 7.00 am to say that a grandchild is sick .
But that is only half the story. Not once in my 22 years of working motherhood have either my parents or my in-laws offered to baby-sit. When asked why, they say 'We **(9)** .... too many of our friends being taken advantage of. They raised their own families and now they **(10)** .... up their grandchildren. By the time they're seventy, they **(11)** .... half their lives looking after children.' My children **(12)** .... entirely. In fact, that's what they **(13)** .... most about their grandparents – they're so much fun. They **(14)** .... their grandchildren like burdens or mouths to feed, but like fascinating friends. When they can squeeze in a visit, they **(15)** .... Monopoly with the children with real enthusiasm or get out a globe to show them all the countries they **(16)** .... on their next holiday. As I write this, my own parents **(17)** .... in the Far East on a month's holiday and my children **(18)** .... to getting postcards from Thailand, Singapore and Indonesia. I am resigned to the fact that they **(19)** .... grandparents of the doting variety. But I **(20)** .... their verve and hope that I will be as adventurous as they are when I reach their age.

	Verb
(1)	LOOK
(2)	GLANCE
(3)	ALREADY BE
(4)	HAVE
(5)	FEEL
(6)	FALL
(7)	PICK
(8)	PHONE
(9)	SEE
(10)	BRING
(11)	SPEND
(12)	AGREE
(13)	APPRECIATE
(14)	NOT TREAT
(15)	PLAY
(16)	VISIT
(17)	TRAVEL
(18)	LOOK FORWARD
(19)	NEVER BE
(20)	ADMIRE

Vocabulary

Phrasal verbs: relationships

1 Read the whole text of the monologue below, then match each phrasal verb in bold to a definition.

'You know, she had such a friendly, open face that I (1) **took to** Katie the very first time I met her and we've been best friends since then. We've only (2) **fallen out with** each other on one occasion, it happened when we both (3) **fell for** the same boy at school ... he had the most gorgeous big brown eyes. But he comes from a posh suburb and Katie and I both live in a tower block, so he (4) **looked down on** both of us, and so anyway he didn't (5) **come between** us for long. Katie and I (6) **made up** after that quarrel and have (7) **got along with** each other perfectly since then. You know, my dad can be horrible sometimes – he has a tendency to (8) **lash out at** me when he's angry, I don't mean he hits me or anything, but he says cruel things and he likes to (9) **put me down** especially in front of his friends, saying I'm useless because I don't know how to cook and clean, that sort of thing. A lot of the time, I can (10) **put up with** his behaviour, but sometimes, I'm feeling, like, sensitive, and it really (11) **gets me down**. So that's when I get on the phone, because I know I can (12) **turn to** Katie for comfort, she's always kind and understanding, like, I know she won't (13) **let me down**, she always has time for me.'

- **a** to cause trouble between two or more people ☐
- **b** to suddenly speak angrily to someone or to try to hit someone ☐
- **c** to like someone or something from the beginning ☐
- **d** to express a low opinion of someone and thus make them feel hurt ☐
- **e** to have a good relationship ☐
- **f** to quarrel ☐
- **g** to bear or tolerate something ☐
- **h** to fall in love with or be very attracted to someone ☐
- **i** to make someone feel sad ☐
- **j** to become friends again after a fight or disagreement ☐
- **k** to hold a poor opinion of someone ☐
- **l** to cause someone to be disappointed ☐
- **m** to go to someone for help ☐

2 The two phrasal verbs below have opposite meanings to two of the phrasal verbs in the passage.

look up to ≠ .... take against ≠ ....

3 The fifteen phrasal verbs above can be used in four different patterns. Look again at the text and complete the chart. Follow the examples given.

Pattern	Phrasal verbs
verb + preposition + noun/nounphrase/pronoun	took to Katie, ... take against sb, ...
verb + noun/noun phrase/pronoun + adverb	put me down, ...
verb + adverb + preposition + noun/noun phrase/pronoun	look up to sb, ...
verb + adverb + preposition + noun/noun phrase/pronoun **or** verb + adverb (without an object)	make up with Katie, ... Katie and I made up, ...

4 Rephrase the parts of these sentences in bold by using phrasal verbs from the chart above. Add appropriate nouns, noun phrases or pronouns if necessary.

1 It was a bit embarrassing at the dinner party as Mark kept **making rude remarks about his wife** in front of us all.

2 I always got the impression that she **thought she was superior to** us.

3 I didn't mean to do it, but I lost my temper and **said some very rude things to** the kids.

4 I have always **admired and respected** my father.

5 I would probably have married him, but my mother **disapproved of him and destroyed our relationship**.

6 Maybe you don't like him, but I've always **had a friendly relationship with** Jim.

7 I heard that they **had a fight** last week, but I believe they've **become friendly again** since.

8 For some reason, I **took an instant dislike to** him from the moment we met.

9 She promised to show up on time today for a change, but as usual she **didn't** – she was half an hour late and we missed the start of the film.

10 That tall man with the loud voice over there is exactly the type that my sister **is usually attracted to**.

11 I can no longer **stand** the noise my neighbours make every night.

5 Many of these phrasal verbs have more than one meaning. With a partner, choose two phrasal verbs from the list below and, using a dictionary, find one other meaning for each verb. Then write your own sentences to illustrate these alternative meanings. When all pairs are ready, take turns to read your sentences aloud. The rest of the class must suggest definitions based on the sentences they hear.

get on with	**turn to**	**take to**	**make up**	**lash out**	**fall out**

Example: *'I'm amazed she* ***fell for*** *Tony's story about losing his wallet on the bus; she should know that he says that every time he needs to borrow money.'*

Answer: *'It means to be deceived or tricked by someone or something.'*

Study tip

When recording new phrasal verbs at home, you can organise them:

- by topic area (as in this book).
- alphabetically according to the verb.
- according to the preposition or adverb (e.g. all phrasal verbs with *out* together).

Try experimenting with the different methods and see which one works best for you.

Word formation: noun suffixes

6 Many nouns can be formed by adding a suffix to another noun, or a verb or adjective. Nine suffixes which are frequently used to create abstract nouns (nouns which are not people, places or objects) are listed in the chart below, with some examples. Which would you guess is the most commonly used suffix?

Suffix	Nouns
- ance/-ence	tolerance, independence, ...
- cy	infancy, ...
- dom	wisdom, ...
- hood	motherhood, ...
- ity	sanity, ...
- ment	encouragement, ...
- ness	thoughtfulness, ...
- tion	concentration, ...
- ure	exposure, ...

7 Work with a partner. Together think of one more abstract noun to add to each category. Then share your ideas with the rest of the class, and add their words to your list.

8 Complete the gaps in the text with a noun formed from the word given in the margin. The first one has been done as an example.

Important social changes are taking place in the areas of **(0)** ...marriage... and the family. There is a global **(1)** .... going on in how we think of ourselves and how we form ties and **(2)** .... with others.	MARRY REVOLVE CONNECT
What most people call the traditional family was in fact a transitional phase in family **(3)** .... in the 1950s. By then the idea that romantic love was the best **(4)** .... for marriage had replaced the concept of marriage as an economic contract. The family has since changed further.	DEVELOP FOUND
In the traditional family the married couple was only one part of the family system. Ties with children and other relatives were equally important in day-to-day **(5)** .... Today the couple is at the core of what the family is. While statistically marriage is still the norm, for most people its **(6)** .... has completely changed. Although marriage promotes the **(7)** .... of a relationship by making a public declaration of **(8)** ...., it is now the quality of the couple's relationship which is considered the most important element.	EXIST SIGNIFY STABLE COMMIT
A couple has its own exclusive history. It is a unit based upon emotional communication or **(9)** .... Communication is both the means of establishing the tie in the first place and the basis for ensuring continuing **(10)** .... in the relationship.	INTIMATE HAPPY

Idioms and set phrases

9 Think of **one** word which can be used to complete all three sentences in each group below. Follow the example.

- The young man devoted his life to the *pursuit* of pleasure.
- I have to admit that hill walking is a *pursuit* which doesn't interest me at all.
- The flustered mother ran out of the supermarket in hot *pursuit* of her absconding toddler.

Do the easiest sentence in each group of three first. Use a dictionary to help you check if the word you've chosen also fits in the other sentences.

1

- I waited years to do it, but I finally .... my own back on him for his disloyalty to me.
- Loud noise is something that has always .... on my nerves.
- The party was a great success as all the guests .... on like a house on fire.

2

- She has a gift for .... out the best in people.
- I don't like her high and mighty attitude; she needs .... down a peg or two.
- I hope you don't mind me .... my mother here with me.

3

- I must have upset her, as she usually chats happily to me, but today she .... me dead when we met in the street.
- Don't .... a lot, please; it's just a trim that I want.
- He was so enraged by his nephew's behaviour that he .... him off without a penny.

4

- I have to admit that with John and me it was .... at first sight.
- There is little .... lost between me and my next-door neighbour.
- I'm hoping it's just a case of puppy ...., as I'm certainly not letting my son get married at the age of sixteen.

5

- Take good .... of my daughter; she's the only one I've got.
- There are over 600 children in .... our town, of whom ten per cent are in the local children's home.
- I don't .... what you say; I believe I'm old enough to make my own decisions.

10 Underline or highlight the idioms in exercise 9 opposite then match them to the definitions below. Follow the example. The third sentence in questions 2 and 5, and the second sentence in question 3 are not included.

I waited years to do it, but I finally <u>got my own back</u> on him for his disloyalty to me.

a	refuse to give someone any more money	☐
b	have an unfriendly or hostile relationship with	☐
c	look after well	☐
d	refuse to speak to	☐
e	annoy someone	☐
f	take revenge on	1a
g	to be made to act more humbly	☐
h	being looked after in a home or by foster parents	☐
i	love which appears the moment two people meet	☐
j	have a very good relationship or have a lot of fun together	☐
k	make other people behave well	☐
l	love or infatuation exhibited by a very young person	☐

Cloze

11 Read the whole text below then complete the gaps by writing **one** word in each space. The first one has been done as an example.

I don't know why we fathers put up **(0)** ....with.......... it – women these days want men to help them take care **(1)** .... the children, but at the same time they refuse to let us get on with the task. The phone rings when a mother is in the middle of dressing the baby, so she asks her husband to finish the job. But instead of being glad that she can **(2)** .... to him for help, she sighs loudly over his efforts and puts **(3)** .... down by immediately changing the child's outfit. This kind of behaviour is unlikely to bring **(4)** .... the best in a new father. At best it undermines his already shaky confidence; at worst it can lead to a situation where little **(5)** .... is lost between husband and wife and he seeks to **(6)** .... his own back on her by refusing to help at all.

When our son was born, it was love at first **(7)** .... for me, but my wife's firm belief in her superior talent for babycare made it hard for me to **(8)** .... to my role as a father. Now that he is three years old, I am at last allowed to take our son to the park or play ball alone with him in the garden and, happily, we get on **(9)** .... a house on fire. But there were many occasions in the first three years when my wife's high-handed attitude really got me **(10)** .... If women really want equality in their relationships, then they must allow men the equality to learn from their own mistakes when it comes to raising children.

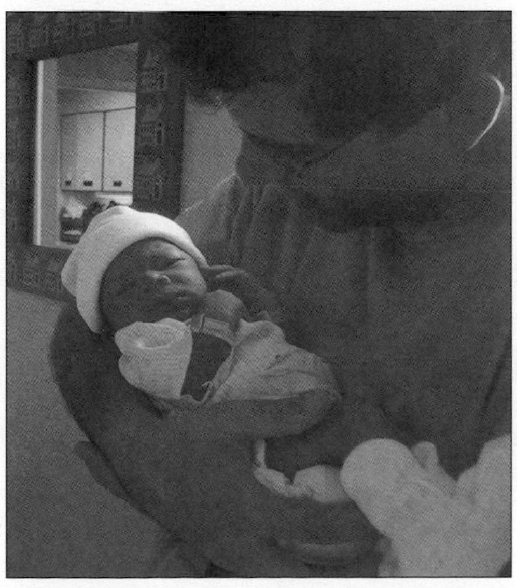

Summary

Reading

1 Skim-read these two texts. In terms of subject-matter, what do they have in common?

Text 1

A government survey recently found that 2,000 children in England and Wales were waiting to be adopted and 1,200 families wanted to adopt them. Yet under the current adoption structure, a third of those children waiting for a new home remain in the care of local authorities for more than three years.

In a bid to speed up the process a national adoption register is to be set up, matching children with potential parents. The register, covering England and Wales, will co-ordinate current systems, which critics say have left too many children languishing in care rather than being placed with adoptive parents.

Social services departments are widely supposed to be slow and obstructive in offering children in care the opportunity of a fresh start with an adoptive family. In their defence, social services directors say their critics have a hopelessly rosy view of the adoption scene. Far from thousands of bouncing babies and tottering toddlers being kept from would-be adopters, as some imagine, children in care are a much more complex and challenging group. Many children awaiting adoption have emotional or behavioural difficulties, disabilities or are accompanied by a brother or sister who must be adopted with them.

Text 2

Anita is two years old and in council care. Her general health is good, she has no behavioural difficulties and she has eyes like saucers. That those eyes cannot see, however, is one of her multiple disabilities. She can move her hands and legs, but is otherwise immobile. She is very passive, but will respond to loud noise. She doesn't smile, but she does express contentment with a facial expression, say the adoption people at Brent council in north London, who are looking for a loving family to take her on.

While Anita may be at the extreme end of the spectrum, most of those being looked after by local authorities come with considerable baggage. As one London social services director puts it: 'The people who want to adopt babies outnumber the babies by 1,000 to one. The people who want to adopt our children are outnumbered by the children probably three to one.'

Children in care are not, either, especially young. The average age is over 10 and fewer than 20% are under five. More than 40% are aged 10-15 and 18% are over 16. A strapping adolescent is not often exactly what the potential adopter had in mind.

Skills development: Identifying words and phrases in the texts

2 Read quickly through the questions in the tinted boxes opposite and say which of them:

1 require you to cross-refer between two parts of a text or two texts?
2 require you to look at one section of text only?

3 Now answer the questions, using the clues below each question to help you.

Question 1: *Which phrase in Text 1, paragraph 3 indicates that most people have an unrealistic idea of what adoption involves?*

1 The key part of the question is underlined here: 'most people have an unrealistic idea of what adoption involves'. Think of synonyms for the word 'idea' (e.g. *notion*). Can you find any of these synonyms in this paragraph? Underline it/them.

2 Is any synonym preceded by an adjective or adverb and adjective combination? Does this adjective or combination have a meaning similar to 'unrealistic'?

3 Can you now identify the phrase?

Question 2: *Which phrase in Text 2, paragraph 1 describes an attractive feature of the child, Anita?*

1 Underline the key part of the question.

2 A number of features of the child are described. Go through each in turn, deciding if it is neutral, negative or could be considered attractive. You should be left with one only. What is it?

Question 3: *Which word in Text 1, paragraph 2 reinforces the point made in paragraph 1 of the same text about the length of time children spend in care?*

1 Re-read what is said about children in care in paragraph 1. Is it a positive or negative comment?

2 Find the words 'children' and 'in care' in paragraph 2 and underline them. Is there any other word nearby in this sentence which might also convey a negative comment?

Question 4: *Which phrase in Text 2, paragraph 2, reflects the problems mentioned in lines 14 to 15 of Text 1?*

1 Re-read lines 14 – 15 in Text 1. Who has these problems?

2 Search in paragraph 2 of Text 2 for references to the same group of people. Underline them.

3 Are any of these references followed by a phrase which, used metaphorically, could mean 'a lot of problems'? What is the phrase?

Skills review

When answering questions of this type that require you to look at one section of text only:

- Underline key words in the question.
- Look for synonyms for the key words or for words with similar/related meanings.
- If in doubt, check each possible phrase in the paragraph by a process of elimination.

When answering questions of this type that require you to cross-refer between two parts of a text or two texts:

- First read the section which is being referred to.
- Then look at the relevant other section of the text or of the other text.
- Search for and underline words in the target paragraph which are the same as or similar to words in the reference lines/paragraph.
- Look at words and phrases that come immediately before or after the words you have underlined.

4 Now answer these questions.

1 Which phrase in Text 1 paragraph 3 emphasises the fact that most people who want to adopt would prefer very young children?

2 Which word in Text 1, paragraph 3 echoes the idea that social workers are responsible for children 'being kept from would-be adopters' in the same paragraph?

3 Which phrase in Text 2, paragraph 3 refers to the 10 – 15 age group mentioned in the same paragraph?

2 Society and social development

Grammar
- Past and perfect tenses

Vocabulary
- Phrasal verbs and set phrases: crime and punishment
- Verbs followed by *-ing* clauses
- Word formation: negative prefixes

Summary
- Identifying what is being referred to

Grammar: Past and perfect tenses

Grammar overview

Past simple

We use the Past simple:

1 to talk about an action which was completed at a specific time in the past
*The original study, **carried out** in 1996, focused on the problems of stress at work.*

2 to talk about habitual actions in the past
*Every month my grandfather **sent** me a parcel containing gifts, puzzles and children's magazines.*

3 to describe states in the past
*As a child she **felt** very isolated because of her disability.*

▶ This tense is associated with a number of time expressions such as ***a week ago, last year, yesterday, in 1995*** etc.

Past continuous

We use the Past continuous:

1 to talk about an activity in progress at a particular time in the past
*I **was living** in Paris when I met my husband.*

2 to talk about an activity in progress in the past which was interrupted by another action
*The Minister **was conducting** an enquiry into road safety when the accident happened.*

3 to talk about two activities which were in progress simultaneously – the two clauses are often linked by *while*
*The secretarial staff **were collecting** the relevant information **while** the administrator **was preparing** the report.*

4 to set the scene at the beginning of a narrative
*The sun **was rising** and a light wind **was blowing** as the children set off from home for the last time.*

5 with *always* to express criticism of somebody's annoying habits in the past
*She **was always turning** up late to rehearsals.*

▶ We do not use the past continuous to talk about habitual actions in the past.
~~*We were camping on my grandparents' farm every summer.*~~

Present perfect simple

We use the Present perfect simple:

1 to talk about recent events – we often use *just* for emphasis
*The headmaster **has just announced** his resignation.*

2 to talk about an action which took place at an unspecified time in the past
*In most European countries people **have given up** wearing traditional dress, except on special occasions.*

3 to talk about an action which took place at an unspecified time in the past and which has an obvious result in the present
*Heavy rain **has caused** widespread flooding and traffic chaos.*

4 with state verbs to describe a situation lasting up to the present moment
*The gulf between rich and poor **has become** wider over the last two decades.*

5 with the phrase *It's the first time … / It's the only time …*
***It's the first time** that the government **has tackled** the problem of violent crime.*

▶ This tense is associated with a number of time expressions such as ***already, ever, for, in the last few days, just, never, recently, since, so far, still*** and ***yet***. We never use the Present perfect with a definite time reference.
~~*I've lived in Paris in 1989.*~~

Present perfect continuous

We use the Present perfect continuous:

1 to talk about an activity lasting up to and including the present moment.
*Campaigners **have been protesting** about overcrowding and poor conditions in prisons for many years.*

2 to talk about an activity which has not yet been completed
***I've been working** on this project for a month and it's still not ready.*

3 to talk about an activity which has only just been completed
*My son **has been revising** for his exams all summer so now he's taking a well-earned rest.*

4 to talk about an activity which we have repeated over a certain period of time
***I've been visiting** a physiotherapist for some months now in the hope of curing my back problems.*

▶ Present perfect simple v. Present perfect continuous
The Present perfect simple emphasises the completion of an action the consequences of which often affect the present time. The Present perfect continuous is used to emphasise the duration of an activity.

▶ Some state verbs may be used in the Present perfect simple or continuous with no difference in meaning.
***Have you felt** this way for long?*
***Have you been feeling** this way for long?*

Past perfect simple

We use the Past perfect simple:

1 to talk about an activity which was completed at a time before a certain point in the past
*By the time Mozart was five years old he **had already composed** his first concerto.*

▶ This tense is not used simply to describe actions which took place a long time ago. It must be used in contrast to another past event.

▶ It is associated with a number of time expressions such as ***by the time, until, when, before*** and ***after***. Unlike the Present perfect tense, definite time references may be used – ***in 1989, when I was 11 years old*** etc.

Past perfect continuous

We use the Past perfect continuous:

1 to talk about a continuing activity which took place before a certain point in the past
*She **had been writing** for twenty years before her first novel was published.*

2 in the same way that we use the Present perfect continuous and simple to emphasis duration
***I'd been revising** for several months but I still wasn't ready for the exam.*
*The house was in a terrible mess because John **had been re-painting** the walls.*

▶ Like the Present perfect continuous this tense emphasises the duration of an activity rather than its completion. Some verbs which refer to states rather than activities do not have a continuous form. (See Unit 1, Advanced grammar points, page 21.)

Advanced grammar points

Grammar point 1

1 Match the beginnings of the two sentences below to the ending which would logically complete each one.

1	I was thinking of visiting my aunt at Easter	**a**	but then my uncle fell ill.
2	I was going to visit my aunt at Easter	**b**	but your idea sounds more fun

2 Which beginning above has the same meaning as the ones below?

- I had hoped to visit my aunt at Easter.
- I'd been intending to visit my aunt at Easter.
- I was planning to visit my aunt.

- Plans which were made in the past but were not fulfilled, or will not be fulfilled, can be expressed with *was going to*, or the Past perfect or Past continuous form of verbs such as *mean, hope, expect, plan* and *intend.*
- To talk about possible plans for the future *was/were thinking of* + *ing* is used.
  *I **was thinking of going** skiing next weekend.*

Grammar point 2

One of the sentences below is incorrect. Which one is it and what is wrong with it?

1 When I was a child I used to love going for long walks in the country.
2 When I was a child I would love going for long walks in the country.
3 When I was a child my mother and I used to go for long walks in the country.
4 When I was a child my mother and I would go for long walks in the country.

Both *used to* + verb and *would* + verb can be used to describe habits and routines in the past. However, only *used to* + verb can be used to talk about states in the past.

Grammar point 3

What time period do the words in italics below refer to – the past, the present or the future?

1 Yes, it's a nice dress, but I *was looking* for something a bit more up-to-date actually.
2 We *were wondering* if you'd like to go out for a drink.
3 I *was thinking* – would it be better to meet up a bit earlier?

The Past continuous is often used with a present meaning to make suggestions, requests or mild criticisms sound more polite.

Practice A

Circle the more appropriate verb to fill each gap below. If both are equally suitable, circle **both.**

A: Yes, can I help you?
B: Ehm .. actually (1) .... for the accounts manager. Is this not his office?
A: You're right, it (2) .... be. But we've been moved around and he's up on the third floor now.

1	**a** I'd been looking	**b** I was looking	**c** both
2	**a** used to	**b** would	**c** both

A: Anne, I know you're an opera fan, and, well, (3) .... if you'd like to go and see 'Carmen' together?
B: That's very kind of you George. When did you have in mind?
A: How about Friday? Are you doing anything then?
B: Well, (4) .... over to see my sister, but I can do that any time.

3	**a** I was thinking	**b** I was wondering	**c** both
4	**a** I was going to go	**b** I was thinking of going	**c** both

A: Did you have a good Christmas?
B: No, it was pretty disappointing actually. I (5) .... to my grandparents' place on Christmas Day. We (6) .... go there when I was a child and I have wonderful memories of how we (7) .... roast chestnuts on their open fire. I (8) .... adore that smell!
Anyway, Grandad fell and broke his hip on Christmas Eve, so I spent most of that week at the hospital with him.

5	**a** I'd been planning to go	**b** I was thinking of going	**c** both
6	**a** would	**b** used to	**c** both
7	**a** would	**b** used to	**c** both
8	**a** would	**b** used to	**c** both

Grammar point 4

One of the sentences below is incorrect. Which one is it and what is wrong with it?

1 Since I left college, I've lived and worked in four different European countries.

2 Since I lived here, there hasn't been a day when the water hasn't been cut off.

- When since is used to link a state to a point or event in the past, it is followed by the Past simple.
  I've known her since we ***were*** *five years old.*
- When it is used to link two states that have both existed for the same period, it is followed by Present perfect. *As long as* is sometimes used instead of *since* in this situation.
  We've been best friends ***since / as long as*** *we****'ve known*** *each other.*

Practice B

Complete the sentences with the Present perfect or Past simple form of the verbs in brackets.

1. Since he .... (move) to France his French .... (improve) a lot.
2. He .... (become) an ardent wine lover since he .... (live) in France.
3. No doubt greed and jealousy .... (exist) as long as mankind .... (do).
4. Since I .... (know) her, she .... (always use) the same old battered handbag.
5. I .... (always wear) flat shoes since I .... (fall) off a pair of platform shoes and .... (sprain) my ankle.
6. Since we .... (be) neighbours he .... (never even offer) me a cup of tea.
7. I'm sure he .... (never clean) the car as long as he .... (own) it.
8. I .... (become) a much better cook since I .... (be married) to a chef.
9. She .... (only learn) to cook since she .... (get married).
10. Since they .... (be) here they .... (never stop) complaining.

Practice C

Read the whole text below, then complete the gaps by writing the appropriate form of the verb in the margin. Choose from the following tenses – Present simple, Past simple, Past continuous, Present perfect simple, Past perfect simple and Future simple. The first one has been done as an example.

In 1900, we **(0)** ..knew.. our place. Since then, ordinary people	**KNOW**
(1) .... to unite in common cause, and parliaments and palaces no longer	**LEARN**
(2) .... politics. The twentieth century, perhaps more than any other,	**MONOPOLISE**
(3) .... the century of the activist, when political initiative passed to the	**BE**
streets and factories. Flashes of popular involvement **(4)** .... in previous	**EXIST**
eras but only in localised or short-lived forms. But by 1900 the spread of	
industry, ideology and voting itself **(5)** .... to the democratisation not	**LEAD**
only of forms of government, but also of participation in the political process.	
In Britain, the suffragettes **(6)** .... this change. Their struggle for votes for	**EPITOMISE**
women **(7)** .... techniques – from demonstrations and lobbying to acts of	**INVOLVE**
self-sacrifice and civil disobedience – that **(8)** .... a template for mass	**REMAIN**
campaigning to this day. But activism **(9)** ...., more than anything, a	**BE**
creation of the working-class movement whose power **(10)** .... in the	**SWELL**
years around the First World War. By the 1930s, millions across the world	
(11) .... a network of trade unions, co-ops, workers' libraries and	**JOIN**
socialist or communist parties. At the same time, Hitler and Mussolini	
(12) .... an inverted parody of these movements with their own mass	**FASHION**
parties, women's, youth and labour organisations. The left-wing activists	
later **(13)** .... an important role in the armed resistance movements in	**PLAY**
Nazi-occupied Europe.	
The immediate political impact of 1968, the 20th century's ultimate year of	
activism, **(14)** .... less significant than the wider spirit of revolt it	**BE**
(15) .... for a generation. The civil-rights activism of Martin Luther King	**FUEL**
and others **(16)** .... racist segregation in the southern US states. In the	**ALREADY DEFEAT**
wake of 1968, campaigns on race, gender and the environment **(17)** ....,	**MULTIPLY**
while the peace and anti-nuclear movements **(18)** .... in the early 80s.	**PEAK**
By the 1980s, activism directed towards wider political change **(19)**	**BEGIN**
to decline, as resurgent market ideology **(20)** .... to convince people they	**SEEK**
were consumers first, citizens second. During the 90s, political activism	
(21) .... even weaker and more fragmented. Nowadays the word activist	**GREW**
(22) .... a term of abuse, even within social-democratic parties built on	**BECOME**
activism. It **(23)** .... to be seen if once again as so often before, politics	**REMAIN**
(24) .... a specialised function reserved for elites, or whether forcing the	**BECOME**
genie of political participation back into the bottle **(25)** .... to be an	**PROVE**
impossible task.	

Vocabulary

Phrasal verbs and set phrases: crime and punishment

1 The fifteen newspaper headlines below all contain phrasal verbs or set phrases related in some way to crime and punishment. Match each headline to a definition.

1. Terrorists **blow up** hijacked plane. ☐
2. Intruders **break in** to stately home. ☐
3. Three prisoners **break out from** high-security jail. ☐
4. Jury expected to **bring in verdict on** alleged serial killer today. ☐
5. Company director **brought up on charges of** embezzlement. ☐
6. Hit and run driver to **come before** magistrates today. ☐
7. Pensioners **done out of** life savings by bogus insurance salesman. ☐
8. Company director **got away with** fraud for ten years. ☐
9. Masked woman **holds up** bank. ☐
10. Teenage hooligan **let off** on account of his age. ☐
11. Thieves **make off with** paintings worth over £10 million. ☐
12. Missing financier may be **on the run** from tax officials. ☐
13. Twelve youths **pulled in** after city-centre brawl. ☐
14. Serial killer **sent down** for twenty years. ☐
15. Hundreds of pensioners **taken in** by con man. ☐
16. Escaped prisoner **turns** himself **in**. ☐

a steal
b rob while using a weapon
c enter a building by force, usually in order to steal something
d cause to explode
e be deceived/cheated and thus lose money
f be tricked
g be arrested
h appear in court
i be accused of
j give a judgement as to whether someone is guilty or innocent
k be sent to prison
l be allowed to go unpunished
m go to/surrender to the police of your own accord
n be hiding from the police or other authorities
o manage to commit a crime without being detected
p escape from

2 The phrasal verbs below have the same meanings as two phrasal verbs in the headlines. Find the verbs in the headlines.

give oneself up = ...
get/make away with = ...

3 Complete each gap in this extract from a newspaper article with a suitable verb, adverb or preposition. The first one has been done as an example.

Escaped prisoner Dean Parsons finally gave himself (0) ...up..... this morning after a dramatic twelve-hour siege during which he threatened to (1) .... himself and his female hostage up with a hand grenade. Parsons, who was serving an eight-year sentence for holding (2) .... a Post Office and making (3) .... with five thousand pounds, had (4) .... out of Peterhead prison eleven days previously. The hostage is believed to be Kelly McAlister, Parson's former girlfriend, and the occupant of the flat where the siege took place.

Three years ago, when Parsons first came (5) .... the court for armed robbery, McAlister was brought (6) .... on charges of being an accomplice to the crime. However, when the jury brought their verdict (7) ...., McAlister was let (8) .... for lack of evidence. After he was sentenced, Parsons was led from the dock shouting 'You should have (9) .... her down too. It was her idea in the first place!'

It is not yet known where or how Parsons spent his first ten days (10) .... the run, but last night neighbours of McAlister's phoned the police to report sounds of someone breaking (11) .... next door. The police arrived to find ....

Verbs followed by *-ing* clauses

Many verbs related to crime, punishment and apology are followed by present or perfect gerunds, often in combination with a preposition, for example:

> *She accused him* ***of stealing*** (present gerund) *her wallet.*
> *She accused him* ***of having stolen*** (perfect gerund) *her wallet.*
> *He was accused* ***of stealing/having stolen*** *a wallet containing £80.*

4 All the verbs below are followed by gerunds, and some are used with prepositions. Two are used without prepositions. Put each verb in the correct part of the chart. Follow the example.

accuse	**acquit**	**admit**	**apologise**	**arrest**	**blame**	**convict**	**charge**
confess	**deny**	**forgive**	**punish**	**regret**	**repent**	**suspect**	

no preposition	for	of	to	with
....	....	*accuse,*	....	....
....	....	....	....	....
....	....	....	....	....
....	....	....	....	....
....	....	....	....	....
....	....	....	....	....

5 In addition, some verb + adjective collocations related to the same topic areas are also followed by prepositions and *-ing* forms. Add these to the correct part of the chart above:

feel/be held responsible	**plead guilty**	**be found innocent/guilty**

6 Five verbs in exercise 4 can be also be used with *that* clauses, for example:

> *She admitted* ***to having taken*** *a necklace from the shop without paying for it. or*
> *She admitted* ***that she had taken*** *a necklace from the shop without paying for it.*

Which are the other four verbs that can be used in this way?

Study tip

When you record new vocabulary it is a good idea to also write down the grammatical structure that follows a word, for example,

acquit someone/*be acquitted* **of** + ing

This is particularly helpful for Part 4 of the Use of English paper and will also improve your accuracy for other papers, such as Speaking and Writing.

7 Complete the second sentence so that it has a similar meaning to the first sentence, using the word given. Do not change the word given. You must use between three and eight words, including the word given.

1 Now that he was older, Liam wished that he had not wasted his youth on gambling.
regretted
Now that he was older, Liam .... his youth on gambling.

2 The witness said it was untrue that she had a romantic relationship with the defendant.
denied
The witness .... involved with the defendant.

3 The jury ruled that the defendant had not murdered his wife.
acquitted
The defendant .... his wife.

4 The jury ruled that the defendant had not murdered his wife.
innocent
The defendant .... his wife.

5 The woman admitted that she had been driving while drunk.
pled/pleaded
The woman .... drunk driving.

6 The woman admitted that she had been driving while drunk.
confessed
The woman .... driven while drunk.

7 The police have pulled in five men whom they think are drug dealers.
suspected
The police have pulled in five men .... drug dealers.

8 The police have pulled in five men whom they think are drug dealers.
arrested
Five men .... drug dealing.

9 The police have charged a woman with stealing jewellery worth over £7,000.
accused
The woman .... jewellery worth over £7,000.

10 The police have charged a woman with stealing jewellery worth over £7,000.
brought
The woman .... theft.

11 The accountant persuaded nearly 200 people to invest a total of £20,000 in non-existent companies.
done
Nearly 200 people .... a total of £20,000 by the accountant.

12 The accountant persuaded nearly 200 people to invest a total of £20,000 in non-existent companies.
taken
Nearly 200 people .... the accountant's scheme.

Word formation: negative prefixes

8 The prefixes below can be added to nouns, adjectives or verbs to change their meaning to a negative one. Match each set of prefixes to the meaning they convey.

Prefixes

1 **anti/anti-** as in *anti-racism*

2 **dis/im/in/un-** as in *disbelieve, impersonal, incapacity* or *unhappy*

3 **mal/mis-** as in *malfunction* or *mismatched*

Meanings

a bad(ly) or wrong(ly)

b not/the opposite of

c against

9 Put the words below in the correct part of the chart, adding the prefix that would be used to give the word a negative meaning. The first three have been done as examples.

appear	**comfortable**	**government**	**polite**
balance	**conduct**	**grateful**	**plausible**
balanced	**desirable**	**inform**	**practice**
behave	**do**	**interest**	**satisfied**
capable	**eligible**	**obedience**	**septic**
colonial	**experience**	**mature**	**tolerant**
comfort	**formation**	**mobile**	**trustworthy**

anti-/anti-	....
dis-	disappear, ...
im-	imbalance, ...
in-	....
mal-	....
mis-	....
un-	unbalanced, ...

Use your English

Work with a partner. Choose two words from the chart above. Write two sentences, each including one of the words you have chosen. The sentences should not be definitions, but should illustrate the meaning of the word. When all pairs are ready, take turns to read your sentences aloud, saying 'beep' instead of the word. The rest of the class must guess what the missing word is.

Example: *I thought it was very 'beep' of him to leave the party without thanking the hostess.*

Answer: ***impolite***

10 The prefix *im-* does not always have a negative meaning. What meaning does it convey when put in front of these words?

migrate	**plant**	**peril**	**port**	**prison**

11 Using a dictionary, check the exact meaning of the five words created by adding the prefix *im-* in exercise 10 above.

12 Complete the gaps in the text with a word formed from the word given in the margin. All the words you need to write contain negative prefixes. The first one has been done as an example.

Complaining can be used constructively, for example to draw attention to **(0)** inefficiency, but all too often in western society it consists of **(1)** .... moaning and groaning which leads to **(2)** .... and unnecessary arguments within relationships. EFFICIENT SOCIAL TRUST

So it is refreshing to live in a society where people do not complain. Kiribati consists of thirty-three small islands located in the Central Pacific. By western standards, the islanders' diet is plain and monotonous, but, thanks to plentiful fish, none of the islanders suffer from **(3)** .... Feasts are popular social occasions, but if the fish is underdone or the rice proves to be **(4)** ...., nobody complains. Similarly, in restaurants, if the waiter brings the wrong dish or the bill is **(5)** ...., the error is pointed out with a calm smile, not a surly frown. Ships frequently leave hours later than scheduled, yet the passengers wait with none of the signs of **(6)** .... which would be loudly evident elsewhere. NUTRITION EDIBLE CALCULATE PATIENT

Other traits of the Kiribati people complement this **(7)** .... to complain. Teachers find it difficult to get their pupils to answer questions in class because it is culturally **(8)** .... to show yourselves to be better than those around you. Competition is not exactly frowned upon in this society, but it is refreshingly **(9)** .... Western tennis stars, well-known for their **(10)** .... behaviour on court, could learn a lot from one young finalist here who, despite being the better player, deliberately lost the match as his opponent was an older and more respected member of the village. INCLINE ACCEPT CHARACTER MODEST

Gapped sentences

13 Think of **one** word which can be used to complete all three sentences in each group below. Follow the example.

- The young man devoted his life to the *pursuit* of pleasure.
- I have to admit that hill walking is a *pursuit* which doesn't interest me at all.
- The flustered mother ran out of the supermarket in hot *pursuit* of her absconding toddler.

All the words in this section have appeared earlier in this unit, but not necessarily in the same context or in the same form (for example, you may have studied the verb, but need to use a noun here).

1

- She is well-known for her strong religious ....
- My parents taught me to have the courage of my own .... and not to give in to persuasion by people I didn't respect.
- The defendant has asked for two other .... for shoplifting to be taken into account.

2

- Tony is rather lacking in .... graces, but when he unwinds he can be quite interesting to talk to.
- Elephants are .... animals and tend to congregate in groups.
- Increased .... mobility has blurred the lines between the middle and upper classes in Britain.

3

- The manager .... a severe headache as his reason for not attending the meeting.
- The accused .... not guilty to armed robbery.
- Paul .... with his father to buy him a motorbike for his birthday.

4

- We decided to settle out of .... to avoid the publicity and expense of a trial.
- Famous artists used to hold .... in this cafe, and students, models and admirers would come to share a beer and listen to them talk about art.
- The ball hit the back of the .... and bounced back over the net.

5

- The way she said that to me, it sounded more like a .... of abuse than an endearment.
- At the end of the autumn .... the junior class will be putting on a pantomime.
- The prospects for employment in the long .... are uncertain, but we can offer a range of temporary jobs at the moment.

6

- Taking lots of vitamin C is believed to increase your .... to colds and flu.
- Her uncle was a famous member of the .... during the war.
- The government's proposals for cutting back on social spending have met with a lot of .... from both politicians and charities.

7

- The government today announced a new .... to encourage reading among young people.
- I'm not very satisfied with my new secretary as she refuses to use her own .... and is always asking me to give her instructions.
- The home team took the .... early in the match, forcing the other side to play a mainly defensive game.

14 Using a dictionary, check the exact meaning of any words, phrases or usages that were unfamiliar to you. With a partner, write your own sentences to illustrate the usage and meaning of the new items.

Summary

Reading

1 Skim-read these two texts. In terms of subject-matter, what do they have in common?

Text 1

As once pointed out in a Beatles' song, money can't buy you love. Recent research from both sides of the Atlantic indicates that it doesn't guarantee happiness either. A book published in America claims that two decades of rapidly increasing affluence and lavish spending have not made anyone any happier. Goods and services that were once considered luxuries – a car, an annual holiday in the sun, a bigger house – have now become expectations. Their absence is a source of dissatisfaction.

Meanwhile, a British study of 39,000 people from eight nations concluded that 25-year-olds were three times more likely to suffer from depression now than fifty years ago, despite the fact that people in these countries are markedly better off nowadays. Drug use, violent crimes and compulsive behaviour are all on the increase, as is the suicide rate.

It is difficult to pinpoint one specific cause of this misery. Although western societies in general are richer, the gulf between rich and poor is growing; divorce is like an emotional world war; unemployment reduces people's sense of self-esteem and purpose. In general, we seem to feel let down by our own aspirations. Even when we succeed, we feel that we have failed.

Text 2

The affluent of the western world live in a therapy culture; even those of us who have not lain on the couch are soaked in the language of self-consciousness, fulfilment, self-knowledge. We indulge in introspection, looking inside ourselves for the reasons for our pain and dissatisfaction. Our lives have become journeys of self-discovery and our ambition is to find happiness along the way. Yet happiness remains hard to pin down. We know when we're unhappy, irritable, angry or depressed, but we usually only realise we were happy when it's already become a memory.

Perhaps we are going about this quest the wrong way. In all the research into happiness, what emerges is that when people say they are happy, they are almost always caught up in activity. Employed people are far more likely to be happy than the unemployed, which is only partly to do with income. Eccentrics are contented because they become so engrossed with their obsessive pursuits. Cheerful children are those who disappear into their play. It is in these moments of euphoric forgetfulness, when we are no longer dwelling upon ourselves, that we find what we cannot ever grasp when we are consciously trying to do so.

Skills development: Identifying what is being referred to

2 Answer the questions in the tinted boxes, using the clues to help you. They all relate to Text 1.

***Question 1:** What doesn't guarantee happiness? (line 2)*

1 Find and underline the phrase 'doesn't guarantee happiness'. What word comes immediately before this phrase?

2 The word you have found is a pronoun. It must therefore refer to a noun which has appeared earlier in the text. Is it a pronoun that relates to singular or plural nouns?

3 Underline all possible nouns earlier in the text that, grammatically, this pronoun could refer to. Which of the four is the one you want?

***Question 2:** What is 'a source of dissatisfaction' in western society? (line 6)*

1 Find and underline the key phrase. What words appear immediately before it?

2 One of these words is a noun. Can you think of another way to say this?

3 There is also a pronoun. Does it refers to a singular or plural noun?

4 Search for nouns that appear earlier in the text which would match this pronoun grammatically. Underline the nouns.

5 There is a relative clause describing the nouns you have underlined. Can you paraphrase it using one adjective?

6 Combine your answers to clues 2, 4 and 5 to answer Question 2.

***Question 3:** What exactly does the phrase 'this misery' describe? (line 11)*

1 Look earlier in the text for any nouns that are synonyms of 'misery'. Underline them.

2 Check that the nouns you have underlined are synonyms of 'misery', not examples of how misery can affect people. You should be left with one possible word only.

3 In the same section of the text that you have identified this word, find the people who suffer from 'misery'.

4 Combine your answers to clues 2 and 4 to answer Question 3.

Skills review

When answering questions of this type, use these strategies to help you:

- **Underline the phrase you've been given in the question and look at the words immediately before it.**
- **Search backwards through the text for nouns that would match pronouns, determiners or phrases you've underlined, for example *it, this, that, these, those, its, their, such problems, of this type, such as these.***
- **Search backwards through the text for nouns that are synonyms of nouns you've underlined.**
- **Rephrase and condense your answers where possible, but not so much that they completely alter the original meaning.**
- **Remember that it is not necessary to answer using a complete sentence**

3 Now answer these questions on Text 2:

1 Whose lives have become 'journeys of self-discovery'? (line 5)

2 What are people going about in the wrong way? (line 9)

3 What exactly does the phrase 'these moments of euphoric forgetfulness' describe? (lines 14 and 15)

3 Lifestyles, social and national customs

Grammar
- Adjectives and adverbs

Vocabulary
- Collocations: pairs of adjectives and adverbs
- Similes
- Word formation: adjectives ending in *-ful* and *-ic*

Summary
- Explaining the meaning of words or phrases

Grammar: Adjectives and adverbs

Grammar overview

Position of adjectives

- Adjectives normally appear before the nouns they describe or after link verbs (*appear, be, become, feel, get, look, taste, sound, smell* etc.).
  *It's a **simple** problem to solve.*
  *The problem seems **simple**.*

- Many adjectives may be used in both positions, some may be used in only one position or the other, and some change their meaning depending on their position.
  *I'm **sorry*** (= sad, regretful) *to hear about your brother's accident.*
  *The tramp was a **sorry*** (= pitiful) *sight in his tattered clothes and battered hat.*

- If there are several adjectives in a sentence they can be listed in this order.

number	judgement	dimensions	colour	origin	material	
three	–	*small*	*brown*	–	*china*	*teapots*
several	*beautiful*	–	–	*Greek*	*leather*	*bags*

Comparison of adjectives

Basic form		Comparative forms		Superlative forms
simple	→	*simpler/less simple*	→	*the simplest/the least simple*
pretty	→	*prettier/less pretty*	→	*the prettiest/the least pretty*
typical	→	*more/less typical*	→	*the most/the least typical*

Adjective forms

- Some adjectives end in *-ly* but should not be confused with adverbs. Some examples of this kind are: *brotherly, chilly, comely, costly, deadly, ghastly,* etc.

- Some adjectives have two forms, one ending in *-ed* and one in *-ing*.
  *The children were very **excited** about the carnival.*
  *We saw an **amusing** comedy at the theatre.*
  Some examples of this kind are: *fascinated – fascinating, enthralled – enthralling, surprised – surprising, amazed – amazing,* etc.

(not) as … as and *not so … as*

*Their house is **as large as** ours.*

*Today's lecture **wasn't so interesting as** last week's.*

So, such, too and *enough*

*The cake smells **so delicious that** I'd like to eat it immediately.*

*It was **such an interesting book that** I read it twice.*

*She feels **too old to** go to discos these days.*

*That child is **(not) old enough** to dress himself.*

Adverb forms

- The majority of adverbs are formed by adding the suffixes *–ly* or *–ally* to adjectives and making spelling changes where necessary: *simple – simply, pretty – prettily, typical – typically, dramatic – dramatically,* etc.
- Some adverbs have the same form as the related adjective.
  *She's a **hard** worker.* *She works **hard**.*
  *He's an **early** riser.* *He gets up **early**.*
- Others may have two forms which differ in meaning.
  *The pylon towered **high** above the skyline.* (place)
  *I think **highly** of my art teacher.* (manner)
  *The film was **pretty** good.* (modifying an adjective)
  *The child smiled **prettily**.* (manner)
  Further examples of this kind are: *hard – hardly, late – lately, direct – directly, deep – deeply, wrong – wrongly, sharp – sharply, scarce – scarcely*

Comparison of adverbs

Basic form		Comparative forms		Superlative forms
simply	→	*more/less simply*	→	*the most/the least simply*
typically	→	*more/less typically*	→	*the most/the least typically*

▶ A few adverbs have *–er* comparative forms.
*The plane arrived **earlier** than expected.*
*He runs **faster** than I do.*

Adverbs used before comparative adjectives

Adverbs of this type give information about the **degree of difference** between two things which are being compared.
*The company's performance has been **significantly** better this year than last year.*
*Prices in supermarkets are **marginally** higher here than in Britain.*
Other adverbs of this kind are: *far, rather, infinitely, much,* etc.

Adverbs used before past participles

Some adverbs can be used before the past participle of a verb. The resulting collocation functions as an adjective. Many of these combinations feature the adverb *well* and may be spelt with or without a hyphen.

*a **smartly dressed** woman*
*a **well known** politician*
*a **well-paid (well paid)** job*
*a **badly behaved** child*
***highly polished** shoes*

Advanced grammar points

Grammar point 1

Two of the sentences below are incorrect. Which ones, and what is wrong with them?

1 I thought the food was quite delicious.
2 I thought the food was fairly delicious.
3 I thought the food was quite tasty.
4 I thought the food was fairly tasty.
5 I thought the food was somewhat tasty.

- Some adjectives in English, e.g. *good, tasty* (known as 'weak gradable adjectives') can describe a range of feelings, states or judgements. These can be modified by adverbs such as *fairly, quite, very* and *extremely*.

not very tasty fairly tasty tasty very tasty exceedingly tasty

- When used with these adjectives, *quite* means the same as *fairly*. The adverb *somewhat* can also modify weak gradable adjectives, but is generally only used with ones which have a negative meaning, e.g. *somewhat tasteless, somewhat annoying*.
- Others express only very strong feelings, states or judgements:

revolting freezing delicious boiling

- These can be modified by adverbs such as *absolutely, completely, totally* or *utterly*. When used with these adjectives, *quite* means the same as *absolutely*.

Practice A

Circle the adjectives in the lists below which are weak gradable adjectives. If necessary, use a dictionary to help you and/or to check the meaning of any adjectives in these lists which are unfamiliar to you.

1 angry, annoyed, furious, irritated, outraged
2 delightful, enjoyable, exceptional, impeccable, nice, outstanding, perfect, pleasant
3 astounded, dumbfounded, surprised, staggered
4 courteous, kind, polite, sympathetic
5 aggressive, bad-tempered, loathsome, rude, unpleasant

Practice B

Choose which adverbs can fill each gap. Two or three of them may be possible in each sentence.

1 She is usually .... courteous to strangers.
a quite **b** exceedingly **c** absolutely **d** somewhat

2 I was .... dumbfounded to hear that he had left his wife.
a quite **b** very **c** utterly **d** somewhat

3 I'm surprised you like him so much; I've always found him .... rude.
a somewhat **b** very **c** totally **d** extremely

4 Your son's behaviour at the party was .... impeccable.
a not very **b** rather **c** absolutely **d** quite

5 I find the thought of eating snails .... unpleasant.
a fairly **b** absolutely **c** somewhat **d** utterly

6 She was .... outraged when she learnt that he'd been lying to her.
a fairly **b** totally **c** extremely **d** completely

Grammar point 2

Two of the sentences below express similar meanings. Which ones?

1 The more he drinks, the less he talks.
2 He drinks a lot but doesn't talk very much.
3 When he's drinking he becomes more and more silent.

Double comparatives can be formed with adjectives, adverbs or a mixture of both, and show that one action or activity leads to or is linked to the other, eg:

The faster *I ran,* ***the more breathless*** *I became.*
The angrier *John gets,* ***the quieter*** *his wife becomes.*

Practice C

Rephrase the sentences below using double comparatives. Use the word(s) given in brackets in the first half of the new sentence. Follow the example.

As she grows up, your daughter is becoming increasingly beautiful. (older)
The older your daughter gets, the more beautiful she becomes.

1 He kept on playing and got more and more tired. (longer)
....

2 If you finish typing that report quickly, you may go home early. (sooner)
....

3 When I start eating chocolate biscuits, I find I want more and more. (more)
....

4 He becomes clumsier and clumsier when he gets very tired. (more tired)
....

5 I like Sam less and less each time I see him. (more often)
....

Grammar point 3

Rewrite the words in b below so that they are in the correct order and have the same meaning as clause a.

a He was such a convincing liar that everyone was taken in by his stories.
b liar/convincing/so/he/was/a that everyone was taken in by his stories.

In written English, the structure so + adjective + *a/an* + noun + *is/was* + *he/she/it* + *that* can be used to emphasise an adjective, for example:
***So charming a woman is she** that everyone who meets her likes her.*

Note: this structure is possible only with singular, countable nouns. For other examples of structures using *so* and adjectives see this unit, Grammar overview, page 44, Unit 9, Advanced grammar points, page 134, and Unit 14, Grammar overview page 208.

Grammar point 4

Which of the sentences below:

1 describes a general preference?
2 describes what the speaker would like to do at the time of speaking?
3 can be used in both of the above situations?

a I would rather eat out than go to the cinema.
b I would prefer to eat out than go to the cinema.
c I prefer eating out to going to the cinema.

A general preference can be expressed by:

- *prefer* + *ing* form + *to* + *ing* form
  *I **prefer learning** languages **to studying** science subjects.*
  would rather/would sooner + verb + *than* + verb
  *My sister **would sooner die than** be seen out without her make-up on.*
  *Most kids **would rather play than** do their homework.*

A specific preference time at the time of speaking can be expressed by:

- *would prefer to* + verb + *rather than*
  *I **would prefer to** go to a French restaurant **(rather) than** an Indian one.*
- *would rather/would sooner* + verb + *than*
  *I **would rather go** to a French restaurant **than** an Indian one.*

Practice D

Complete the second sentence so that it has a similar meaning to the first sentence, using the word given. Do not change the word given. You must use between three and eight words, including the word given.

1 It was such a boring film that I fell asleep in the middle of it.
dull
So .... that I fell asleep in the middle of it.

2 It has its drawbacks, but in general I would rather work at home than spend hours commuting.
prefer
Despite its drawbacks, I .... hours commuting.

3 As he gets older, Tim is becoming increasingly tight-fisted.
more
The .... becomes.

4 Ruth never asks anyone for a loan as she doesn't like to admit she has financial problems.
proud
Ruth .... her money.

5 I thought his behaviour at the party last night was absolutely outrageous.
shocking
I thought he behaved .... at the party last night.

6 The biscuits tasted so peculiar that I took them back to the shop.
such
The biscuits .... that I took them back to the shop.

7 Sandra enjoys driving fast but when she does so her passengers get frightened.
the
The .... passengers become.

8 My husband and I prefer travelling by ship to going on long-haul flights.
sooner
My husband and I .... long-haul flights.

9 I would have thought their daughter was too immature to be living on her own.
enough
I'm surprised they .... to be living on her own.

10 He is a complete hypocrite; in public he condemns smokers, yet he smokes a packet a day himself.
that
So .... in public he condemns smokers, while smoking a packet a day himself.

Practice E

Complete the gaps in the text with one word only. The first one has been done as an example.

One of the fastest growing areas **(0)** .....of..... business training nowadays is intercultural training. I recently attended a seminar of this type and, although parts of it were **(1)** .... interesting, in general I found it was not practical **(2)** .... to be really useful in a day-to-day sense. I have always believed that experience is the **(3)** .... teacher. In fact, I think that perhaps **(4)** .... most enjoyable way to study cultural diversity is to observe what, when and how other nations eat.

On my last visit to the United States I spent a weekend with a family I know. Like many other American families they always keep their fridge **(5)** .... stocked so that any member of the family can help themselves to food if and when they feel hungry. Only once during my visit did the **(6)** .... family sit down together to eat a cooked meal, and my hostess explained that this was a special event in my honour as normally they were all **(7)** .... busy at weekends with social or sporting events **(8)** .... eat together. In my view, experiences like these tell us **(9)** .... about the role of family life and attitudes to time in America **(10)** .... any seminar could do.

Vocabulary

Collocations: pairs of adjectives and adverbs

Several phrases in English consist of pairs of adjectives or adverbs linked with *and*. These are 'fixed collocations' – i.e., the same pair of words always occur together, and other combinations are not acceptable.

1 Match the words in the two columns to make commonly-used phrases. The first one has been done as an example.

1	back and	h	**a**	truly
2	cut and		**b**	tested
3	fair and		**c**	square
4	fast and		**d**	sound
5	hard and		**e**	on
6	high and		**f**	mild
7	meek and		**g**	furious
8	off and		**h**	forth
9	over and		**i**	fast
10	safe and		**j**	dry
11	tried and		**k**	dried
12	well and		**l**	above

2 Use the phrases from exercise 1 to complete the sentences below. If necessary, use a dictionary to help you.

1 I can't believe that Charlotte lost her temper last night – she's normally so ....!

2 In many Mediterranean countries the custom of walking .... along the seafront or main street is still a well-established habit on summer evenings.

3 Kath and Bill have been seeing each other .... for the last five years, but neither of them seems to want to make a permanent commitment to the other.

4 Although there are no .... rules for doing business in other countries, politeness and respect for other people's customs will never go amiss.

5 I think I'm usually pretty good at doing crossword puzzles, but I must admit I was .... baffled by the one in *The Times* yesterday.

6 All staff who are sent to work abroad will receive a special allowance .... their normal salary.

7 There's absolutely no point in arguing any more, because the chairman has made up his mind and the decision is ....

8 If you don't want to go out with her any longer, why don't you just tell her so ....? It will hurt her much less in the long run than pretending that you're still keen on her when you're not.

9 The strike has left thousands of holidaymakers ...., without any means of getting home to their jobs or families.

10 Since the new management took over, developments in the company have been coming so .... that it's hard to keep up with the changes.

11 I think we should stick to the .... methods of doing this, since they've been proved to work; there's no point in modifying a system just for the sake of change.

12 The two missing climbers were found this morning, ... despite spending ten hours overnight in deep snow without a tent.

Study tip

Effective use of a good English-English dictionary, for example the *Longman Dictionary of Contemporary English*, will not only help you find the meaning of new phrases, but also help you to enlarge your vocabulary. For example, if you want to check the meaning of a phrase which consists of a pair of adjectives or adverbs:

- try looking up the first word in the pair, i.e. for *safe and sound*, look up *safe*. You will find a definition and an example, e.g.: *safe and sound* = unharmed, especially after being in danger: *The missing children were found* ***safe and sound.***
- you will also find other expressions containing the word *safe* and other words that it is often used with , e.g.:
  be in safe hands = to be with someone who will look after you very well: *I needed to know my kids* ***were in safe hands.***
  a safe place/a safe journey/a safe investment/a safe subject of conversation
- you may also find cross-references to other expressions containing the word *safe*, e.g.: see also *play it safe.*

3  Look up these pairs of words in an English-English dictionary and answer the questions below.

first and foremost	hale and hearty	to and fro

1 What is the meaning of each phrase?
2 Did you find the definition under the first word in each pair, or the second?
3 Of the six adjectives or adverbs in the phrases above, two exist only in these phrases. Which ones?
4 What other words are frequently used with the adjectives *foremost* and *hearty*.

Similes

Similes are a way of describing something by comparing it to something else. They have two possible forms:
as + adjective + *as* + noun/noun phrase
verb + *like* + noun/noun phrase

4 Match each object below (1–9) to a sentence (a–i) to form a complete simile.

1 chalk and cheese
2 ditchwater*
3 a fish
4 the hills
5 a lark
6 nails
7 old boots
8 two peas in a pod
9 a picture

a I can't eat this steak. It's *as tough as* ...
b If I were you I wouldn't get on the wrong side of Doug. He's a big fighter and *as hard as* ...
c What's that song you're listening to, Mum? It must be *as old as* ...
d I'm surprised Jane and Sally have stayed friends for so long because their characters are *as different as* ...
e I can't tell which twin is which. They're *as similar as* ...
f Professor Smythe is well-informed about his subject, but his lectures are *as dull as* ...
g In her pink party dress, little Hannah looks *as pretty as* ...
h Catriona's such a happy child. All day long she *sings like* ...
i Since he split up with his girlfriend poor old Harry's been *drinking like* ...

*a ditch is a channel for water by the side of a road or field

5 Read the sentences below then match the similes to the descriptions of when they are used.

1. Margery should really have chosen something a bit more classic. In that outfit she *looked like mutton dressed as lamb.*
2. I put away all my ornaments and vases and things when my grandson comes to visit as he's just *like a bull in a china shop.*
3. That young man who came round selling household goods *looked like butter wouldn't melt in his mouth*, but I've always been the suspicious type so I didn't let him in.
4. I took my niece skiing for the first time last week and she *took to it like a duck to water.* By the end of the holiday she was skiing better than I do!
5. Nick should know by now that any criticism of the government *is like a red rag to a bull* where John is concerned.

Used to describe:

- **a** someone who is very clumsy and always breaking things. ☐
- **b** something which is very likely to make someone angry or upset ☐
- **c** someone who is wearing clothes which are too young in style for them. ☐
- **d** someone who learns something new very quickly and enjoys it from the beginning ☐
- **e** someone who appears to be very nice and sincere, but is not really. ☐

6 Some similes have meanings which are complimentary, some which are derogatory, and some which are neutral or depend on the context. Rewrite the similes in the appropriate column. Three have been done as examples.

Complimentary	Derogatory	Neutral/it depends
sing like a lark, ...	as tough as old boots, ...	as old as the hills, ...
....	....	....
....	....	....
....	....	....
....	....	....

Use your English

The similes above are established collocations. However, new similes are being made up all the time, and many people create their own. Work in teams of three or four people. First write the beginnings of three short sentences, as in the examples below. Then take turns for each team to read out their beginnings. The other teams must suggest endings which are similes. At the end of the activity, vote for which you think are the best similes that your class has created.

Example 1: *Her hair shone like ...*
Answer 1: *silver/newly-polished cutlery/the sun*

Example 2: *He's as clever as ...*
Answer 2: *a fox/Pythagoras/a self-made millionaire*

Word formation: adjectives ending in *-ful* and *-ic*

7 Many adjectives can be formed by adding the suffixes *-ful* or *-ic* to a noun or verb stem. Put the words below in the correct part of the chart, adding the suffix that would be used to change the word into an adjective, and making any necessary spelling changes. The first two have been done as examples.

apathy	**bliss**	**delight**	**ecstasy**	**materialism**	**sarcasm**
art	**chaos**	**disgrace**	**forget**	**play**	**therapy**
artist	**cheer**	**drama**	**idyll**	**rest**	**waste**

- ful	- ic
artful, ...	apathetic, ...
....	....
....	....
....	....
....	....
....	....

8 In most cases, the meaning of adjectives ending in *-ful* is 'full of' or 'displaying the qualities of' the stem noun or verb. In some cases, however, the meaning has changed, for example:

awe (noun) = respect and wonder
awful (adj) = bad or unpleasant

Can you think of another adjective ending in *-ful* which has a similar meaning to *awful*? What is the meaning of the stem of this other adjective?

9 The adjective *artful* can sometimes mean 'displaying the qualities of art' but is more often used with a very different meaning. What is it?

10 There are several words with the ending *-ic* which exist only as adjectives. Some examples are given below. Work with a partner and try to think of at least two more adjectives like this, then share your ideas with the rest of the class.

domestic **exotic** **hectic**

11 Be careful: not all words ending in *-ic* are adjectives! Tick (✓) the words in the list below which are **not** adjectives.

altruistic **critic** **logic** **polemic** **shambolic** **statistic** **topic**

12 What is the adjective form of the words you ticked in exercise 11?

13 Work with a partner. Choose three adjectives ending in *-ful* or *-ic* that you have already studied. Write one or two sentences which illustrate the meaning of each adjective. When all pairs are ready, take turns to read your sentences aloud. The rest of the class must respond with a short phrase including the appropriate adjective.

Example: *They spent their honeymoon in an isolated beach cabin on a tropical island, surrounded by palm trees and the sound of the surf.*

Answer: *That sounds* ***idyllic.***

14 Complete the gaps in the text with a word formed from the word given in the margin. All the words you need to write are adjectives. The first one has been done as an example.

In an effort to escape from their hectic and **(0)** materialistic city lives, more and more Northern Europeans are buying houses in rural areas of France, Spain, Italy and Greece. Some relocate permanently in search of a more **(1)** .... existence. Those who cannot afford to give up their jobs seek a **(2)** .... respite from their **(3)** .... lifestyle by relaxing for a few weeks each year in their second home in the sun.	MATERIALISM MEANING THERAPY STRESS
However, many of those who relocate permanently find that life in the country is not as quiet and **(4)** .... as they had anticipated. Aspects of village life which seemed delightfully **(5)** .... in the context of a two-week holiday can grate on the nerves when you live with them on a daily basis. Recently a group of British residents in an Italian village took local farmers to court because they found the smell of the villagers' pigs **(6)** .... In other cases, foreigners have complained to neighbours about the **(7)** .... early-morning crowing of their cockerels, or to village priests about the regular tolling of church bells.	EVENT ATMOSPHERE DISTASTE ENTHUSIASM
Understandably, the local inhabitants are somewhat **(8)** .... of these attitudes. They argue that the foreigners have an **(9)** .... view of what country life is like and that, since no-one forced them to come and live in a village, they are being **(10)** .... by now complaining about the inconveniences of rural life.	RESENT REALIST HYPOCRITE

Gapped sentences

15 Think of **one** word which can be used to complete all three sentences in each group below. Follow the example.

- The young man devoted his life to the *pursuit* of pleasure.
- I have to admit that hill walking is a *pursuit* which doesn't interest me at all.
- The flustered mother ran out of the supermarket in hot *pursuit* of her absconding toddler.

In each group of words, the missing word is either an adjective or an adverb.

1
- My uncle was a hippie .... in the sixties and he still wears his hair long even now.
- The crowd stood .... to let the bride pass through.
- One of these days I'll pay him .... for treating me so badly.

2
- I've never heard Stella utter even a .... rebuke to any of her children.
- The weather seems unusually .... for the time of year.
- Your daughter is suffering from nothing more than a .... eye infection.

3
- The anthropologist subjected the islanders' rituals and traditions to .... analysis.
- When he first went to work in the Middle East, Bill was highly .... of their methods of doing business.
- The bridegroom's mother fainted from heat at the most .... point of the wedding ceremony.

4
- Although she's far from being poor, Diana is always .... with money.
- Seeing that her boss was in a bad mood, his secretary was especially .... to avoid saying anything that might upset him.
- After .... study of your proposal, we have decided to accept your offer.

5
- I .... remember telling you that I'd be working late at the office today.
- His grammar and vocabulary are impeccable, but he has a .... foreign accent when he speaks.
- The witness says that she saw the defendant's face quite ...., even though it was dark at the time.

16 Using a dictionary, check the exact meaning of any words, collocations or usages that were unfamiliar to you.

Summary

Reading

1 Skim-read these two texts. In terms of subject-matter, what do they have in common?

Text 1

Thirty years ago in Britain it was almost impossible to find a shop open after 6 o'clock in the evening; nowadays supermarkets and convenience stores are frequently open around the clock. Late-night bars, 24-hour fast food outlets and cash machines mean that it is increasingly possible to eat, drink and be merry at all hours of the day and night, and for those of a more stay-at-home inclination, computer games, all-night television and the Internet help to while away the small hours.

This may sound idyllic in comparison to the days of television channels which shut down at midnight and weekends doomed to penny-pinching for those who failed to make it to the bank before closing time on Friday, but there is another side to the coin. Longer opening hours mean increased costs for heating and lighting premises and for footing wage bills. Ultimately, these costs are passed on to the consumer, making prices higher not only for those who benefit from the 24-hour society, but also for customers who favour more traditional shopping patterns.

In addition, there is growing scientific evidence that disrupting natural sleep patterns could trigger numerous maladies, ranging from niggling aches and pains to more sinister problems such as heart disease. Sleep researchers believe that replacing a persistent diet of late nights with a strict daily routine might be as important to our health as giving up smoking or cutting back on saturated fat.

Text 2

Located in the hypothalamus, the biological clock controls every circadian rhythm in the body from when we eat, sleep and play to hormone levels, body temperature and immune functions. The settings of our biological clock determine whether we are by nature early-rising 'larks' or night 'owls'.

The convenience and instant access of today's society make it tempting to regard the biological clock as redundant, but the costs of ignoring our internal timepiece can be great. Despite several scientific studies showing that shift work is unhealthy and disruptive to the biological clock, we are rapidly moving towards a 24-hour society which brings many of the same ills with it.

Studies have shown that although 'owls' prefer late working shifts, their health takes a serious battering. They develop a range of symptoms including indigestion, ulcers, fatigue and heart problems. Nor are the effects only physical: many subjects reported feelings of depression and anxiety. A further hazard of keeping unconventional hours is an increased tendency to accident-proneness. In fact, many of the world's great disasters have taken place in the early hours of the morning because of the body's inability to function efficiently at that time. Sleep researchers believe that the pursuit of a 24-hour society can only lead to more man-made problems, accidents and fatal errors.

Skills development: Explaining the meaning of words or phrases

2 Answer the questions in the tinted boxes, using the clues to help you. They all relate to Text 1.

Question 1: *What is meant by the phrase 'the small hours'? (line 6)*

1 The word 'hours' clearly refers to time. Underline all other references to time which you can find in the first paragraph. Which period of the day or night do most of them refer to?

2 Can you now infer a meaning for 'the small hours' and put it in your own words?

Question 2: *Explain in your own words why the writer has chosen to use the word 'doomed' in line 8.*

1 Read the rest of the sentence following the word 'doomed'. Does it refer to a happy or unhappy situation?

2 Is there anything that could be done to change the situation once it has arisen?

3 Combine your answers to clues 1 and 2 to explain the author's choice of this word.

Question 3: *What does the writer mean by saying 'there is another side to the coin'? (line 9)*

1 Read the sentences following the phrase. Do they refer to positive or negative aspects of the 24-hour society?

2 What about the ideas expressed before the phrase – were they positive or negative?

3 Can you now explain in your own words what the phrase means?

Question 4: *What is meant by the phrase 'trigger numerous maladies'? (line 14)*

1 This has three key aspects: 'trigger', 'numerous' and 'maladies'. The word 'maladies' is followed by 'ranging from', which means that examples are going to be given. What are these examples of?

2 You may not know the word 'trigger' as a verb, but you probably know that it is part of a gun. What is the function of that part of a gun?

3 Now look back at the first part of the sentence. Is there a similar relationship between that part of the sentence and 'numerous maladies' as there is between a trigger and what it does for a gun?

4 'Numerous' is obviously an adjective. What is its stem?

5 Combine your answers into an explanation of the phrase.

Skills review

When answering questions of this type, use these strategies to help you:

- Search for similar or related words in the same paragraph.
- Read the surrounding sentences and see how the ideas relate to each other (e.g. cause and effect, contrasting ideas, additional ideas).
- Refer to other situations in which a word is used and is familiar to you.
- Identify stems of words as clues to their meaning.

3 Now answer these questions on Text 2.

1 What does the word 'owls' mean in this context? (lines 4 and 10)

2 What is mean by the phrase 'takes a serious battering'? (lines 10 to 11)

3 What is meant by the word 'subjects' in line 12?

4 Explain in your own words why the writer has chosen to use the phrase 'keeping unconventional hours' in line 13.

Practice test 1

Part 1

For questions 1 - 15, read the text below and think of the word which best fits each space. Use only **one** word in each space. There is an example at the beginning (0).

Example:

0	T	O														

POLITENESS

The British are widely considered **(0)** ..to.. be a very polite nation, and in **(1)** .... respects this is true. An Italian journalist once commented **(2)** .... the British that they need no fewer than four 'thank yous' **(3)** .... to buy a bus ticket. The first, from the bus conductor means, 'I am here'. The second accompanies the handing **(4)** .... of the money. The third, again from the conductor, means '**(5)** .... is your ticket', and then the passenger utters a final **(6)** .... as he accepts the ticket. **(7)** .... transactions in most other parts of the world are usually conducted in total silence.

In sharp **(8)** .... to this excessive politeness with strangers, the British are strangely lacking **(9)** .... ritual phrases for social interaction. The exhortation 'Good appetite', uttered in **(10)** .... many other languages to fellow-diners before a meal, does not exist in English. The nearest equivalent – Enjoy your dinner! – is said only by people **(11)** .... will not be partaking of the meal in question. What's **(12)** ...., the British wish happiness to their friends or acquaintances **(13)** .... at the start of a new year and at celebrations such as birthdays, **(14)** .... the Greeks routinely wish **(15)** .... and sundry a 'good week' or a 'good month'.

Exam tip

Remember to read the whole passage from start to finish before you complete the gaps. As you read, think about these points:

- Do the ideas expressed in each paragraph complement each other or contradict each other?
- Do the different ideas expressed within the second paragraph complement each other or contradict each other?

Your answers to these questions will help you choose the correct words to complete any phrases which comment on the text as a whole or which link additional or contrasting points. Clue: See gaps 1, 8, 12 and 14.

Part 2

For questions 16 - 25, read the text below. Use the word given in capitals at the end of some of the lines to form a word that fits in the space in the same line. There is an example at the beginning (0).

Example:

0	E	S	S	E	N	T	I	A	L							

CIVILISATION	
Civilisation can be interpreted in many ways and has meant different things to	
different people: to Levi-Strauss its **(0)** ..essential.. feature was boiled food;	**ESSENCE**
Nietzsche wanted to reverse it and Arnold Toynbee called it 'progress towards	
(16) .... '.	**SAINT**
We all use the word loosely to mean culture we approve of. Yet it is not too late to	
rescue civilisation from **(17)** .... An old and disinterested vision of what it means	**REPRESENT**
to be civilised is waiting to be revived.	
At the heart of every civilising project there is a common **(18)** ....: this is the	**IMPEL**
human itch to **(19)** .... nature, to mould earth, cleave waves and warp	**FORM**
environments in **(20)** .... ways. Civilisations are actively engaged in reshaping the	**PROBABLE**
world for human use, stamping landscapes with new patterns of clearings and	
channels, field systems and street grids. In **(21)** .... cases, civilisations try to	**EXCEPT**
secede from nature altogether, to deny the animal side of **(22)** .... and to	**HUMAN**
domesticate the wild man within by elaborate manners.	
Civilisation may be heroic and **(23)** ...., but it is not necessarily good and is	**ADMIRE**
frequently **(24)** .... in the long run. Indeed, if longevity can be taken as a measure	**SUCCEED**
of success, the world's most enduring societies have been the **(25)** .... ones which	**SUBMIT**
abjured the civilising ambition and settled for the food and shelter that nature	
provides.	

Part 3

For questions 26 - 31, think of **one** word only which can be used appropriately in all three sentences. Here is an example (0).

Example:

0 The young man devoted his life to the ...... of pleasure.

I have to admit that hill walking is a ...... which doesn't interest me at all.

The flustered mother ran out of the supermarket in hot ...... of her absconding toddler.

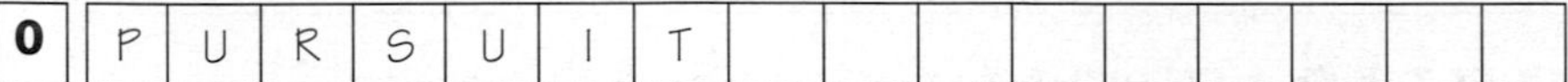

0 P U R S U I T

Exam tip

Remember that the missing word will always be the same part of speech in each sentence. For example, if the missing word was *break*, it could be used as either a noun or a verb, but not a mixture of both.

26

- No sooner does a fashion appear to be ...... and buried than someone decides to revive it.
- Few places are more depressing than a seaside resort in the ...... of winter.
- Every time I pick up the phone, the line goes ....

27

- The worst thing you could have done was to make him lose ...... in front of his colleagues.
- The jury's decision flies in the ...... of all the evidence.
- She laid the tarot cards ...... up on the table in the shape of a cross.

28

- Several newspapers have ...... the government with lying to the public about the true extent of the environmental damage caused by the explosion.
- I didn't have any cash on me, so I just ...... the meal to your account at the hotel.
- As the riot police ......, the demonstrators broke ranks and fled.

29

- Having been ...... to understand that their travel expenses would be paid, the speakers at the conference were annoyed to find that this was not in fact the case.
- I haven't ...... much thought yet to what I'm going to do once I've finished this project.
- Jim was an exceedingly spoilt child as his mother had always ...... way to his every whim.

30

- The annoying thing about Tom is that he always has to have the ...... word in every discussion.
- The ...... person I expected, or wanted to meet at the reception was my former boss.
- He didn't win the competition, but he made it through to the ...... six.

31

- This judge is well-known for taking a hard ...... on petty crimes.
- The lecturer's argument was so complicated that few of his listeners could follow his ...... of thought.
- Whenever you ring that company, they ask you to hold the ...... then play recorded music to you while you wait endlessly to speak to the person you want.

Part 4

For questions 32 - 39, complete the second sentence so that it has a similar meaning to the first sentence, using the word given. **Do not change the word given**. You must use between three and eight words, including the word given. Here is an example (0).

Example:

0 The company's profits appear to be improving significantly this year.
evidence
The company's .... this year.

0	profits show evidence of significant improvement

32 I think it's disgraceful the way they never get round to repairing this pavement.
should
This pavement .... time ago.

33 The team certainly do not intend to give up at this stage.
question
There's .... at this stage.

34 Her son insisted on going with her to the hospital.
accompany
He was adamant .... to the hospital.

35 Nowadays parents and their children seem to have more in common than they used to do.
narrowing
The generation .... days.

36 Mr Brandt says he would much rather go to the opera than be taken out for dinner.
preference
Mr Brandt has .... to the opera, rather than out for dinner.

37 Steve wished he hadn't let his friend persuade him to rob the old man.
talk
Steve regretted .... the old man.

38 Mary became totally engrossed in her novel and forgot to cook the dinner.
absorbing
Mary .... to cook the dinner.

39 Apart from the composition, I thought the test was really easy.
sailing
I .... for the composition.

Part 5

You are going to read two texts on pensions. For questions 40 - 43, answer with a word or short phrase. You do not need to write complete sentences. For question **44** write a summary according to the instructions given.

A

Most adults alive today in Europe take the existence of state healthcare and pension schemes for granted, but they are in fact a relatively new invention, most having been established in the years after the Second World War. On current demographic forecasts, they are also likely to prove a fairly short-lived phenomenon. In many European countries these systems are already groaning at the seams, and the situation is *line 6* bound to get worse.

In 1960 the average life expectancy in Europe was 67.4 years for men and 72.3 years for women. Those figures have risen to 72.8 and 79.4 years respectively. This increased life expectancy strains the budget as older people require more frequent and, thus, more expensive medical attention than younger members of the population. At the same time, the birth rate in Europe has been declining since the 1970s, with the result that there are fewer working people contributing towards the provision of state healthcare and pensions at the same time as costs are rising due to increased use of the services.

The situation is further complicated by the fact that the baby-boom generation will shortly be reaching retirement age. These are the people born during the decade after the Second World War when Europe experienced a small population explosion; as a result of this 37 per cent of the population will be over 60 in 2010, compared to 20 per cent in 1990. Despite having contributed to state health and pension schemes throughout their working lives, they are, alas, unlikely to reap the benefits.

40 Explain in your own words what is meant by the phrase 'groaning at the seams' in line 6.

....

....

41 What image of the future does the writer create in the last paragraph?

....

....

B

If coming to live and work in the United Kingdom on a long-term basis, you are strongly recommended to take out a private pension plan. Although the payment of social security contributions is mandatory and these will automatically be deducted from your salary cheque, along with a contribution from your employer, this can no longer be regarded as adequate provision for your financial needs after retirement.

In the UK, these contributions fund the state healthcare system, the payment of pensions and the provision of financial support to the unemployed. Unlike some other European countries, where payments to the unemployed are linked to the length of time a person has worked and may be suspended after a given period, the UK operates a 'safety net' system. In other words, all jobless people qualify for at least a minimum level of state support and this continues throughout their entire lives, if necessary.

Clearly such a system is costly and, coupled with the growing burden on the healthcare system posed by the ageing population, the state is finding it increasingly difficult to balance the social budget. Pensions are already being squeezed, with many senior citizens existing on less than £70 per week, and the situation is likely to become more critical in the future.

Exam tip

In question 42 the word ***such*** shows you that you have to find a reference earlier in the text.

- First, search in the previous paragraph for the relevant word.
- Read the sentence(s) surrounding the word.
- In this case the description of the system referred to is quite long, so you may summarise it slightly.
- Your do not need to write a full sentence. Start your answer with the words, '*One in which ....*'

42 What exactly does 'such a system' (line 15) describe?

....

....

43 What phrase in the last paragraph echoes the worries expressed about medical help in paragraph 2 of Text A?

....

....

44 In a paragraph of between 50 and 70 words, summarise in your own words as far as possible, the reasons given in the texts why British people who retire in 2010, or later, are unlikely to get a good state pension.

4 Work

Grammar • Modals I: Present and future

Vocabulary • Phrasal verbs and set phrases: work
• Word formation: prefixes *over* and *under*
• Adjectives + *that* clauses

Summary • Answering questions on the content of the text

Grammar: Modals I: Present and future

Grammar overview

Requests ***can, could, may, might, will*** **and** ***would***	**Offers** ***can, could, may, shall, will*** **and** ***would***
***Can** you do some overtime next week as we're going to be very busy?* ***Could** you fill in the application form and return it by Monday?* ***May** I ask who's calling, please?* ***Might** I take a look at your newspaper?* ***Will** you tell the manager that I'm waiting to see him?* ***Would** you please send this letter by express post? It's urgent.* ▶ The use of *might* here is very formal.	*I **can** work your shift for you if you like.* *My father **could** help you with your homework. He's a Maths teacher.* ***May** I take your coat?* ***Shall** I give you a lift to the office as it's raining?* *I'**ll** take the letters. The Post Office is on my way.* ***Would** you like me to do those photocopies for you?*
Suggestions ***can, could, might, shall*** **and** ***should***	**Permission** ***can('t), could*** **and** ***may (not)***
***Can** I make a proposal?* *We **could** commission a report on this subject.* *You **might** try asking John. He knows a lot about computers.* ***Might** I put forward a different idea?* ***Shall** we postpone the meeting until tomorrow?* *We **should** use young people for the modelling campaign.* ▶ The use of *might* here is very formal.	*All staff **can** take the day off on Friday.* *You **can't** go in now. Mr Becket is busy.* ***Could** I take the day off on Friday?* *Only authorised personnel **may** enter the building site.* *You **may not** leave the exam room until told to do so.*
Ability ***can*** **and** ***can't***	**Duty and advice** ***should(n't)*** **and** ***ought (not) to***
*The new secretary **can** take shorthand and type at 45 words per minute.* *It's no use asking me to help you with your Maths homework. I **can't** add up.* *At the end of the course she'**ll be able to** speak fluent French.*	*You look exhausted. You **should** get to bed earlier.* *You **shouldn't** smoke so much.* *You **ought to** buy a new alarm clock. This one doesn't work.* *He **ought not to** treat her like that.*

Obligation and necessity ***have to, must (not)* and *need to***	**Absence of obligation or necessity** ***(don't) have to, (don't) need to* and *needn't***
*She **has to** wear protective clothing and a helmet at all times on the building site. (obligation)* *We'**ll have to** hurry if we don't want to miss the bus. (necessity)* *Visitors **must** report to the managing director as soon as they reach the office. (obligation)* *I **must** do something about the garden – it's in a terrible state! (necessity)* *Both switches **must** be on before the drill will work. (necessity)* *Employees **must not** use the telephone for personal calls. (obligation/prohibition)* *He **needs to** work harder or he'll be made redundant. (necessity)*	*We **don't have to** work overtime but there is a very competitive atmosphere in the office so a lot of us do so anyway. (absence of obligation)* *You **don't need to** pay all the money at once. You can pay in instalments. (absence of obligation)* *The company **doesn't need to** employ any new workers this month. (absence of necessity)* *You **needn't** finish the reports until Friday. (absence of necessity)* ▶ *Needn't* and *don't need to* are interchangeable in the present but see Unit 6, Grammar overview, page 88 for use of these verbs in the past.
Deductions about the present ***can't, must* and *will***	**Speculation (present)** ***could* and *should***
*That **can't** be the new manager. I was told he was bald but this man's got thick black hair.* *It's Monday morning. There **must** be someone at the office.* *Listen, someone's honking a car horn outside. That **will** be the taxi.*	*The letter **could** be from Aunt Martha; open it and see.* *He **should** be home by now; he usually gets home at 6.*
Speculation / prediction (future) ***may (not), might (not), shall (not), should (not)* and *will/won't***	
*Several people **may/might** be made redundant as a result of the economic recession.* *She **may not** have time to finish the report.* *He **might** change his mind.* *Our team **might not** win.* *We **shall** know the results by the end of the week.* *I **shan't** pass the exam; I've done no revision at all.* *She's very ambitious so she **should** do well in her job.* *We **shouldn't be** late; there isn't much traffic.* *The police are letting the traffic through; we **won't** be stuck here much longer.*	*He **will** become Managing Director in the next round of promotions.* *What terrible service! We **won't** come back here in a hurry!* *In a few years from now the 35-hour working week **should have** become common practice.* ▶ For the use of the Future perfect (will have) to make assumptions see Unit 1, Grammar overview, page 21.

Advanced grammar points

Grammar point 1

Two of the sentences below express similar meanings. Which ones?

1 Delia may have lots of money, but she isn't happy.
2 I don't know if Delia has lots of money or not, but I know she isn't happy.
3 Although Delia has lots of money, she isn't happy.

In sentences with a present time reference, the structure *may (not)* + verb ... , *but* ..... is another way to express *although* + present tense verb or *even though* + present tense verb.

Practice A

Complete the second sentence so that it has a similar meaning to the first sentence, using the word given. Do not change the word given. You must use between three and eight words, including the word given.

1 Although Joe is not easy to work with, he's an excellent salesman.
but
Joe .... he's an excellent salesman.

2 I appreciate good food although I'm not much of a cook myself.
may
I .... I appreciate good food.

3 Although this product is expensive, it will last longer than other models on the market.
durable
This product .... than other models on the market.

4 He doesn't have the right to smoke in non-smoking areas even though he's the boss.
that
He .... give him the right to smoke in non-smoking areas.

5 Although she works in the next office to mine, we have very little contact with each other.
adjoining
We .... we have very little contact with each other.

Grammar point 2

1 What time period do the words in italics below refer to – the past, the present or the future?

a Jenny *will sleep* for at least ten hours after she's been on night duty at the hospital.
b My boss *will interrupt* when I'm giving a presentation at a meeting or conference.
c All the computers are down, so we *might as well let* the staff go home early.

2 Which sentence shows that the speaker finds someone else's behaviour annoying?

- *will* + verb can be used with a present meaning to describe a person's typical habits or behaviour.
- *will* + verb can also be used with a present meaning to show that you find another person's habit irritating.
- *might* or *may as well* + verb is used with a present meaning to show that you have a lack of alternative options and are not very enthusiastic about the suggestion you're making.

Grammar point 3

Match the beginnings of sentences below with the ending (a or b) which would logically complete them.

1 Interest rates should rise over the next few months,
2 Interest rates will probably rise over the next few months,

a in which case my loan will be even harder to pay back.
b in which case our savings will grow.

- The structure *should* + verb is used only to predict events which the speaker sees as positive.
- Other structures are chosen to predict events which the speaker sees as neutral or negative, for example:
  *It **will probably** rain tomorrow.*
  *It's **likely to** rain tomorrow.*
  I **expect** it **will** rain tomorrow.

Practice B

Circle the more appropriate verb to fill each gap below. If both are equally suitable, circle **both**.

Don't worry; the taxi (1) .... here any minute now.

1 a should be — b will probably be — c both

No planes (2) .... in this fog, so I think we (3) .... back to the hotel.

2 a should take off — b will take off — c both

3 a should go — b might as well go — c both

Pete (4) .... endless cups of coffee when he's working on a report.

4 a is forever drinking — b will drink — c both

They haven't delivered the materials I need to finish the job, so I (5) .... go home.

5 a may as well — b should — c both

Clare (6) .... late for meetings.

6 a is always showing up — b will show up — c both

My husband (7) .... in a very bad mood when he gets home from work.

7 a might as well be — b will often be — c both

Our transport costs (8) .... substantially this year.

8 a will probably rise — b should rise — c both

You've missed the last bus now, so you (9) .... the night and sleep on the sofa.

9 a will stay — b might as well stay — c both

Practice C

Read the whole text below, then complete it by writing an appropriate modal verb in each gap. In some cases, more than one modal may be suitable. The first one has been done as an example. (0)

The days when employees used their firm's Internet system to send e-mails to friends or book their holidays online **(0)** may/will/might soon be gone. New regulations mean that your employer **(1)** .... now read your e-mail and monitor which websites you have been visiting. They **(2)** .... also monitor and record your telephone calls. The regulations state that, in general, employees **(3)** .... be informed that their e-mails and Internet use **(4)** .... be monitored by their employer. However, employers **(5)** .... tell staff that monitoring is taking place if they suspect that an employee **(6)** .... be using the company's computer systems for unauthorised purposes, such as sending personal e-mails. Understandably, many employees are worried that monitoring **(7)** .... uncover personal information which they would prefer their bosses not to know.

The most useful thing that concerned employees **(8)** .... do is to ask their employers to issue guidelines explaining how and why they **(9)** .... monitor email and Internet use. If they refuse, you **(10)** .... assume that they **(11)** .... be reading everything already. In that case, if you still feel you really **(12)** .... be online for your friends while you are at work, you **(13)** .... think carefully about what you are doing. You **(14)** .... bring a laptop and modem into work and dial up your own Internet Service Provider – although then you **(15)** .... get into trouble for making 'personal' calls. Alternatively, you **(16)** .... as well accept the inevitable and stop using work computers for private email or Web surfing. You **(17)** .... always head for the local cybercafe at lunchtime instead of having a sandwich at your desk.

Vocabulary

Phrasal verbs and set phrases: work

1 The text below contains phrasal verbs or set phrases related in some way to work. Match each phrase or phrasal verb in bold to a definition.

Steve had been working for his company for five years when he (1) **put in for** a promotion and he was delighted when he was offered a managerial post. But not long after he had (2) **taken up** the job, the company (3) **changed over to** a new method of accounting. Steve began suffering from two classic symptoms of stress – headaches and insomnia. 'I'd thought I would enjoy the increased responsibility, but I felt I **was** completely (4) **snowed under**' he says. 'I was (5) **toiling away** until eight o'clock every night just to (6) **keep on top of** the paperwork.'

Steve's experience is far from unique. Many situations at work can cause stress, ranging from (7) **taking on** new duties or responsibilities to poor working conditions, lack of training, fear of being (8) **laid off** and even harassment and bullying. In the current climate of rapid change, many organisations seek flexibility and so expect workers to be able to (9) **turn their hands to** a variety of jobs and this too can be very stressful for employees.

So what can you do about it if you think you're suffering from workplace stress? The good news is that employers are legally obliged to ensure employees' health, safety and welfare at work and this includes (10) **bringing in** measures to reduce stress. However, stress is not a subject an employee can easily (11) **bring up** with an employer; in fact, this in itself can be a very stressful thing to do. So, if you have a problem with stress, let your union know. They have a legal right to (12) **take up** health and safety matters on employees' behalf.

- **a** accept or agree to do additional work ☐
- **b** introduce ☐
- **c** mention ☐
- **d** start ☐
- **e** work extremely hard ☐
- **f** maintain control of ☐
- **g** be able to perform ☐
- **h** adopt a new way of doing something ☐
- **i** make a formal request for something ☐
- **j** ask in an official capacity for a problem to be dealt with ☐
- **k** be overwhelmed by work ☐
- **l** be made redundant ☐

2 The phrasal verb below has the same meaning as a phrasal verb in the text. Find the verb in the text.

slave away = ...

3 One of the phrasal verbs in the text above can be used with another meaning which is the opposite of 'lay off'. Which one is it?

lay off ≠ ....

4 Complete the chart below, ticking each box where a phrasal verb can collocate with a noun.

	grievances	regulations	a pay rise	a salary	a project	new staff	the post of
bring in							
put in for							
take on							
take up							

5 Complete the gaps in these sentences with a suitable set phrase or phrasal verb from this unit.

1 Under the new regulations which were .... last month, all complaints of this type must be .... only by your trade union representative.

2 Jobs boost for North-East: car plant to .... 200 new workers.

3 It's entirely my own fault that I feel like I .... and can't cope with my work; I shouldn't have .... this sales launch alone.

4 Unfortunately, the company is in financial difficulties and consequently has had to .... several workers. Until the situation improves, all remaining staff will be expected to .... any tasks that need to be done, even if these do not fall within their usual area of responsibility.

5 Please don't .... the subject of my monthly report at the meeting. I've been .... on it for the last two days, but I still haven't finished it.

6 He's .... a salary increase, but I don't know if he'll get it, as the company's now .... a performance-based system for reviewing salaries, and he didn't meet all his sales targets last year.

7 Luckily, I've been .... quite a decent salary since I .... this job and that has meant I've been able to .... my financial situation for a change.

Study tip

Phrasal verbs, set phrases and idioms can be quite difficult to remember. One way that may help you to remember them is to associate the verb or phrase with a drawing or mental picture. For example, to help you remember *be snowed under* you could make a picture of a person sitting at a desk working while nearly completely covered by snow. The stranger or funnier the picture is, the more you are likely to remember it and the associated phrasal verb.

Word formation: prefixes *over* and *under*

6 The prefixes *over*- and *under*- can be added to verbs, adjectives or, less frequently, nouns. Put the words below in the correct part of the chart, adding the prefix(es) that can be used. The first three have been done as examples.

active	**developed**	**graduate**	**populated**	**rule**	**take**
age	**draw**	**indulge**	**privileged**	**see**	**time**
charge	**employed**	**nourished**	**qualified**	**sleep**	**tone**
cut	**estimate**	**paid**	**rated**	**staffed**	**view**

over	under	both
overactive, ...	underage, ...	overcharge, undercharge, ...
....	....	....
....	....	....
....	....	....
....	....	....

7 Often the prefix *over* adds the meaning 'too much' or 'to too great an extent', and the prefix *under* adds the meaning 'too little' or 'insufficiently', for example:

*So you mean to tell me you paid only £50 for exactly the same watch as mine? I was obviously **overcharged**.*
*I think they must have **undercharged** me – I paid less today for milk and a loaf of bread in that shop than I did yesterday!*

Underline or highlight all the words in the table where the prefixes carry these meanings.

8 Sometimes the prefix *over* is more closely related to the idea of 'higher' or 'above' and *under* to the idea of 'lower' or 'beneath'.

In the column headed *over* find three examples where the prefix carries this meaning.
In the column headed *under* find two examples where the prefix carries this meaning.

9 In most cases, the pairs of words you have put in the *both* column are direct opposites of each other. However, there is one pair where both words can have the same meaning. Which one is it?

10 There is another pair of words in this column where the meanings are not related at all. Which one is it, and what does each of the words mean?

11 Find words from the chart in exercise 6 to complete the typical collocations below. Follow the example.

0 an .....overpaid..... consultant
1 an .... city/area/region/country
2 .... members of society
3 .... children (from famine-stricken areas)
4 an .... imagination
5 .... drinking
6 (aid for) .... countries

12 Complete the gaps in the text with a word formed from the word given in the margin. All the words you need to write begin with *over* or *under*. The first one has been done as an example.

Britain may be turning into a society of **(0)** ....overtired..... parents and **(1)** .... children who lack the stimulus afforded by social contact with other family members. In the early 1990s, it was widely forecast that, by the turn of the century, large numbers of working people would be involved in family-friendly options such as job-sharing or working from home. As it turned out, the numbers were greatly **(2)** .... A recent survey shows that only one in fifty people is involved in job sharing and less than one in four companies allow employees to work from home. What the pundits did not foresee was the explosion in **(3)** .... working caused by the advent of the 24-hour society. A report out this week **(4)** .... this fact: almost a quarter of British employees now work at some point between 6pm and 6am, and sixty-one percent of working families have one or other parent away from home during early mornings, evenings, nights or weekends. The charity which sponsored the report fears that this situation is **(5)** .... family life in Britain and creating an **(6)** .... of children who are 'passed like batons' in a relay race between shift-working parents, or even left unattended for prolonged periods.	TIRE ACHIEVE ESTIMATE NIGHT SCORE MINE CLASS
In the past, most shift-work was in the manufacturing industry where workers earned **(7)** .... for working unsocial hours. However, the biggest increase in late working in the past five years has come from the retail sector, where staff are rarely paid a premium for night work. As work of this type is typically **(8)** ...., it is difficult for staff to afford the necessary childcare while they work nights.	TIME PAY
Even administrative staff and managerial staff are now frequently expected to **(9)** .... night work. Many would prefer not to, but fear that if they refuse, they will be deliberately **(10)** .... when it comes to time for a promotion or salary review.	TAKE LOOK

Use your English

How prevalent is night working in your country?
Which sectors typically involve night work?
How do people who work nights in your country usually cope with the problem of childcare?
Do you think the 24-hour society is a curse or a blessing? Why?

Adjectives and *that* clauses

Many adjectives can be followed by *that* clauses. They follow two possible patterns:

1 *I am/you/we/they are* + adjective + *that* clause
*I'm **amazed that** he didn't take up that job offer.*

2 *It is/I find it/It seems/I think it's* + adjective + *that* clause
*I **find it amazing that** he didn't take up that job offer.*

13 All the adjectives below can be followed by *that* clauses. Put each adjective in the correct part of the chart. Five have been done as examples. Only two of the adjectives in the list may go in more than one part of the chart.

adamant	**apparent**	**convinced**	**evident**	**obvious**	**positive**
advisable	**certain**	**curious**	**grateful**	**peculiar**	**sad**
anomalous	**concerned**	**essential**	**imperative**	**possible**	**vital**

Adjectives	Pattern 1	Pattern 2
Degrees of certainty	certain, ...	apparent, certain, ...
Personal reactions or evaluating events or situations	adamant, ...	anomalous, ...
Degrees of importance	✗..	advisable, ...

14 Work with a partner and think of at least one more adjective to go in each section of the chart. Share your ideas with the rest of the class, and add their suggestions to your chart.

Note

1 The adjectives describing degrees of importance may be followed by the present subjunctive form in the *that* clause, for example:
It's ***imperative that he report*** *to my office immediately.*
However, this use is very formal. More often the simple present or the modal verb *should* would be used, for example.
It's ***imperative that he reports*** *to my office immediately.* or
It's ***imperative that he should report*** *to my office immediately.*

2 Some adjectives describing degrees of certainty may also be followed by the infinitive – see Unit 1, Advanced grammar point 3, page 23.

15 Complete the second sentence so that it has a similar meaning to the first sentence, using the word given. Do not change the word given. You must use between three and eight words, including the word given.

1 His reaction to the news was most odd.
peculiar
I found .... like that to the news.

2 You must have the monthly sales report ready first thing tomorrow morning.
essential
It .... be ready first thing tomorrow morning.

3 Pat's eagerness to take on this project astonishes me.
so
I'm .... to take on this project.

4 This information must not be leaked to anyone before the press conference.
confidential
It is vital .... until the press conference.

5 I tried to persuade Timothy to accept the promotion but he refuses to change his mind.
adamant
Timothy .... be promoted.

Gapped sentences

16 Think of **one** word which can be used to complete all three sentences in each group below. Follow the example.

- The young man devoted his life to the *pursuit* of pleasure.
- I have to admit that hill walking is a *pursuit* which doesn't interest me at all.
- The flustered mother ran out of the supermarket in hot *pursuit* of her absconding toddler.

All the words in this section have either appeared earlier in this unit, but in a different context, or are related in some way to points you have studied.

1
- A little bit of .... feedback would make a pleasant change from my boss's continual carping.
- Unfortunately, your test result came out .... again, so you'll have to take another course of antibiotics.
- You need to attach that wire to the .... pole of the battery.

2
- General Santiago .... power following a largely bloodless coup-d'etat.
- Since he was wearing a uniform, I .... he was the doorman and gave him a generous tip.
- As she caught sight of her son, her face .... an expression of sheer delight.

3
- I think she's now working in a restaurant in the Chinese .... of the town.
- You're lucky to have such a big office; mine's about a .... the size of yours.
- The company's results are expected to improve in the final .... of this year.

4
- My boss lays particular .... on accurate typing and the correct use of English.
- In some languages getting the .... wrong can completely change the meaning of a word.
- My uncle had a nervous breakdown as a result of .... and overwork.

5
- He's responsible for buying .... and equipment for his company's factories.
- A new hydro-electric power .... is to be built in the next valley.
- A pot .... may not be an original gift, but most people are usually quite pleased to receive one.

6
- Traditionally, this car has been sold on its safety more than its...................., but the new 215 model is as fast as anything else in its class on the road today.
- The company's poor .... this year has been blamed on rising fuel costs.
- I saw an interesting .... of 'Aida' at the Edinburgh Festival last year.

17 Using a dictionary, check the exact meaning of any words, phrases or usages that were unfamiliar to you.

Summary

Reading

1 Skim-read these two texts. In terms of subject-matter, what do they have in common?

Text 1

Each generation of British men has worked for a shorter period than its predecessor. This state of affairs may be considered desirable when it is a matter of choice, but recently many people in their fifties have had their working lives curtailed through redundancy. Nowadays almost a third of British men over 50 but below pension age have no paid work, and most have given up seeking it.

This fast growing trend of early retirement or redundancy risks creating a group of two million men who are doing little with their lives and whose sedentary lifestyle may jeopardise their wellbeing. Men aged 50-64 are between two and three times as likely to die of a heart attack or stroke as are women of the same age. They also consume less fruit and vegetables than women do, while taking sugar in drinks and eating sweets. Those who did not elect to become economically inactive frequently also face the problem of loss of self-respect.

The trend also indicates there will soon be at least as many women past 50 at work as men. A major cause of the differing employment patterns among men and women is structural change: while many manufacturing jobs have disappeared, there has been rapid growth in areas of largely female employment such as hotels, catering and cleaning.

Text 2

In the north-east of England, many men over fifty have already adjusted to a life in which paid work plays no part, and where women have stepped into the breach as breadwinners. Hundreds of men have been made redundant in the region over the past 10 years and, unable to find suitable employment, have given up the search. Instead they top up the income brought in by their wives with state-funded incapacity benefit. Since many of these men had formerly worked on building sites, or in shipyards and coal mines, they didn't have to stretch the truth too much to get a doctor to sign a certificate saying they are too unwell to work. Given the dearth of jobs available in the region, mild deception of this sort is forgivable.

Although many men like these would prefer to find employment, they are unable to reinvent themselves for working life in the twenty-first century. Having been accustomed to a large, unionised workplace, where you had a decent rate of pay and some money to spend, they feel disconcerted by an environment in which you have to be prepared to work unsocial hours for low pay and with little job security, and where young people who can talk on three mobile phones at once are ready to stab you in the back.

Skills development: Answering questions on the content of the text

2 Answer the questions in the tinted boxes, using the clues to help you. They all relate to Text 1.

Question 1: *What situation mentioned in the first paragraph does the writer think is not always a negative one?*

1 The key part of the question is underlined here: 'is not always a negative one'. This implies that the situation can have both positive and negative aspects and so you need to search for a word or phrase which implies contrast (e.g. *while*, *however* etc.).

2 In the sentence you have now identified, there is a reference word. What sentence does this word refer to?

3 Rephrase that sentence briefly in your own words, starting with 'The fact that ...'

Question 2: *What impression does the writer give of men over 50 who have been made redundant?*

1 Identify which paragraph relates to men in this category and read the whole paragraph.

2 Several problems faced both by retired men and those who have been made redundant are described. Underline them. Summarise these problems in a few words.

3 A slightly different category of problem is also mentioned. Is this relevant to men who have been made redundant? If so, rephrase it briefly.

4 Combine your answers to clues 2 and 3 to answer the question.

Question 3: *Why is it easier for women over 50 to get jobs than men in the same age group?*

1 Identify which paragraph relates to this question and read the whole paragraph.

2 Underline the section which contains the answer.

3 Think of synonyms for these words: 'manufacturing', 'disappeared', 'growth'.

4 Can you summarise the phrase 'areas ... such as hotels, catering and cleaning' in two words, the second of which is 'sector'?

5 Combine your answers to clues 3 and 4 to answer the question.

Skills review

Questions of this type may have a variety of forms and focuses. Always:

- Read the question carefully to make sure your answer will be sufficiently specific.
- Rephrase the answer in your own words as succinctly as possible.
- Avoid copying sections of the text word for word.
- Remember that your answer does not need to be a grammatically complete sentence.

3 Now answer these questions on Text 2.

1 What does the writer feel about unemployed men claiming incapacity benefit?

2 What image of current working life does the writer create?

5 Education, study and learning

Grammar • Nouns and articles

Vocabulary • Noun phrases with *of*
• Proverbs
• Word formation: prefix *out*

Summary • Identifying the four content points

Grammar: Nouns and articles

Grammar overview

Uncountable nouns

- Uncountable nouns take a singular verb and cannot be used with the indefinite article (a/an).
  What ~~a~~ terrible weather!
- They are often used with the determiners *some, any, no, (a) little* and *much*. (See Unit 8, Grammar overview, page 120.)
  *Would you like **some** milk?*
- They cannot be made plural but we can add a phrase which specifies an amount. (See this unit page 81.)
  Would you like some spaghetti~~s~~?
  Would you like a plate of spaghetti?

- Some nouns which we normally think of as uncountable can be used as countable nouns in certain contexts. (See this unit, Advanced grammar points, page 78.)
  *The flood **waters** were rising fast.*
  *He doesn't mind the snow. He goes out in all **weathers**.*
  *The spring **rains** were welcomed by farmers and gardeners alike.*
  *The restaurant offers a selection of aromatic **coffees**.*

Collective nouns

- Collective nouns refer to organisations or bodies made up of a number of individuals e.g. *army, audience, cast, clergy, crew, crowd, government, jury, media, press, public, union, youth,* etc.

- They can take either a singular or a plural verb. If a pronoun is used to replace such a noun then it will reflect the verb which has been used.
  *The committee **hasn't** yet reached a decision. **It** needs more time.*
  *The committee **haven't** yet reached a decision. **They** need more time.*

Plural nouns

- Some nouns can only be used in the plural e.g. *cattle, pyjamas, stairs,* etc. and take a plural verb. For more on this group of nouns see this unit, Vocabulary, page 81.

The definite article *(the)*

The definite article can be used with both singular and plural countable nouns and uncountable nouns. It is used:

- to refer to a specific noun we think is known both to ourselves and our listener/reader or to refer to a specific example of something.
  The *college timetable will have to be drawn up again.*
  The *society we have created is based on profit.*
- with objects which we consider to be unique such *the Sun, the Moon, the Sea, the past, the universe, the environment* etc.
  Be careful though – we don't say ~~the~~ *nature* or ~~the~~ *space*
- with certain geographical features such as seas and oceans (*the Channel, the Pacific*), rivers (*the Thames, the Danube*), groups of islands (*the Cyclades*), mountain ranges (*the Himalayas*) and some countries (*the United Kingdom, the USA, the Netherlands, the Lebanon*).
- to describe people of a particular nationality (*the Indians, the French)*.
- with certain adjectives used as nouns (*the young, the disabled*). (See this unit, Advanced grammar points, page 79.)
- with titles (*the Queen, the Chairman, the Headmistress*).
- in the superlative form of adjectives (*the least acceptable, the best*). (See Unit 3, Grammar overview, page 44.)
- with a singular noun to make a generic reference to a group. (See this unit, Advanced grammar points, page 79.)
  The *monk seal is under threat.*
- in the titles of newspapers in which case it is capitalised (*The Independent, The Sunday Telegraph*).
- with musical instruments.
  She plays ***the*** *flute and* ***the*** *saxophone.*

The indefinite article *(a/an)*

The indefinite article is used with singular countable nouns only and we use it:

- to talk about something when we assume our listener/reader does not know which specific thing we are talking about.
  I bought ***a*** *new shirt today.*
- to talk about different kinds of measurements (*2.00* ***an*** *hour, 3 days* ***a*** *week)* although we can also use the word *per (4 hours* ***per*** *day)*.
- to refer to somebody who is unknown to us.
  A *Mrs Spencer phoned while you were out.*
- with a singular noun to make a generic reference to a group. (See this unit, Advanced grammar points, page 79.)
  A *python is not a suitable pet.*

Omission of the article

No article is needed:

- before names (*Jennifer Marshall, Mrs Davies*).
- before names of meals (*lunch, dinner*).
- before most street names (*Princes Street, Oxford Street*).
- when referring to certain public places when we want to talk about their function rather than a specific building.
  He decided not to go to ***university****.*
  Her youngest son is at ***nursery school*** *now.*
  Here are some other examples – *church, court, home, hospital, market, prison, school* and *work*.
- when we use plural nouns or uncountable nouns to talk about somebody or something in general. (See this unit, Advanced grammar points, page 79.)
  Mathematics *is a closed book to me.*
  People *are so strange, aren't they?*
  A lot of abstract uncountable nouns are used in this way.
  Education *is the key to economic prosperity.*
  I never listen to ***advice****.*
- before certain geographical features – lakes (*Lake Windermere*), mountain peaks (*Everest*), continents (*Asia, North America*) and countries (*Tunisia, Greece* – for exceptions see above).

Advanced grammar points

Grammar point 1

Explain why the word in italics in each pair of sentences below is once used as an uncountable noun and once as a countable noun.

1a The floor is made of *stone*.
1b That strangely-shaped object on the floor is *a stone* I found on the beach.

2a The government is worried about falling standards in *education*.
2b Despite being a girl from a poor rural community, Aseye wanted *an education*.

3a I haven't had a lot of *contact* with him recently.
3b It wasn't hard for her to get that job as she had *a contact* on the board of the company.

Many nouns can be used as uncountable or countable nouns, but with a change in emphasis or meaning.

- Many substances, drinks and foodstuffs are uncountable when they are thought of as a mass, but can be countable when they refer to a unit, piece or specimen, for example:

  *We're having **fish** and chips for supper.*
  *In my view, sole is **an** overrated **fish**.*
  *I rarely drink **beer**.*
  *Buy that man **a beer**!*

- Abstract nouns are usually uncountable, but some can also be used countably when they refer to individual instances of a state, quality or concept, for example:

  *I appreciate your endless kindness and **understanding**.*
  *After lengthy discussions, both sides in the negotiation reached **an understanding**.*
  *Swimming is a sport which requires **strength** and endurance.*
  *Your plan has both **strengths** and weaknesses.*

- Some nouns have different meanings when they are used countably and uncountably, for example:

  *Could you open the window, please; I need **some** fresh **air**.*
  *He whistled **a** traditional Irish **air**.*

Practice A

Complete the gaps in each sentence with an appropriate noun in the uncountable form, the singular countable form or the plural countable form. Use each word in the list below twice. Follow the examples.

beauty	coffee	experience	hair	oak	rage	wealth

1 Your daughter looks like she'll grow up to be ...a beauty... .
2 We'll have three ...coffees... and two doughnuts, please.
3 What do you use to make your .... always look so shiny?
4 I can't understand why he can't find a job when he has such .... of talent and creativity.
5 Her face was contorted with ....
6 Driving along winding mountain roads in lashing rain is .... which I'd rather not have to repeat.
7 Our dining table is made of ....
8 She likes to surround herself with objects of ....
9 Applicants for the job should have .... of working with computers.
10 I love .... and bought my house because it had several in the garden.
11 He works for a company which produces ....
12 .... does not necessarily guarantee happiness.
13 I'm fed up with the cat leaving .... all over the sofa.
14 The child flew into .... when his mother told him it was time for bed.

Grammar point 2

Which of the following sentences express a generic reference (that is, a reference to a whole class of things, rather than an individual example of that class)?

1 The panda is threatened with extinction.
2 There's a panda at our local zoo.
3 Pandas eat bamboo.
4 A panda is an animal like a bear with black and white fur and black patches round its eyes.

- With countable nouns, generic reference is usually expressed by plural nouns with no article, for example:
  ***Girls** are often good linguists.* ***Doctors** earn more than **nurses**.*
- However, the definite article may also be used with the noun in the singular form. This is particularly common when talking about animals.
  ***The owl** is a nocturnal creature.*
- When giving an explanation or definition a singular noun is used with a/an, for example:
  ***A modem** is a device used to connect computers via the telephone system.*

Grammar point 3

What part of speech are the words in italics in the sentences below and what does each word in italics refer to?

1 The *good* are not necessarily great and the *great* are but rarely good.

2 The government spokesman said the new measures were designed for the *good* of the population as a whole.

Words which are normally adjectives can be used with *the* to form two types of nouns.

- Nouns referring to types or groups of people. In this case the noun takes a plural verb, for example:
  ***The old** are often neglected in modern society.*
  ***The Greeks** are renowned for their hospitality.*
- Abstract nouns. In this case the noun takes a singular verb, for example:
  *Where advertising is concerned, **the new** is considered superior to the old.*

Practice B

Write complete sentences based on the prompts. Where necessary add articles (*a, an* or *the*) or change nouns into their plural form, and rewrite verbs in the appropriate form. Some of the sentences will have more than one possible form. Follow the example.

(cow) (be) domestic (animal)

The cow is a domestic animal. or Cows are domestic animals.

1 (tapeworm) (be) (parasite) which (live) in (stomach and intestines) of (mammal)

....

2 (pet) often (provide) comfort and company for (elderly)

....

3 (telescope) (be) (instrument) which (allow) you to see long distances

....

4 (orang-utan) (be) native to the forests of Sumatra and Borneo

....

5 I always give money to (charity) which (help) (homeless)

....

6 (hospice) (be) (place) where (terminally ill) (be) looked after

....

7 (teenager) often (go) through a phase of being fascinated by (supernatural)

....

8 (unknown) can be frightening but often (turn) out to be more enjoyable than (familiar)

....

Practice C

Complete the second sentence so that it has a similar meaning to the first sentence, using the word given. Do not change the word given. You must use between three and eight words, including the word given.

1 The only venomous snakes which live in Britain are adders.
native
The .... to Britain.

2 The government is introducing new measures to help people who can't read or write.
illiterate
New measures .... by the government.

3 He's afraid that his company will make him redundant.
ranks
He fears that he will .... unemployed.

4 The subject of her thesis is rats and their social behaviour.
on
She's written .... rat.

5 He frequently criticises rich and famous people for their extravagant habits.
of
He's a frequent .... rich and famous.

Practice D

Complete the gaps in the text with *a, an* or *the* or, if no article is needed, write *0*. The first one has been done as an example.

(0) ...The... figures for GCSE results published yesterday showed that **(1)** .... youngsters took more exams than **(2)** .... previous year – GCSE entries increased by 5.4%, compared with **(3)** .... increase in the number of 15- to 16-year-olds of just 2%. Overall, **(4)** .... percentage of candidates achieving passes in full GCSE courses rose to 56.6% from **(5)** .... last year's figure of 55.7%.

(6) .... girls outperformed **(7)** .... boys both at the top grades and across subjects. Even in Mathematics – **(8)** .... only subject where **(9)** .... boys won more top grades than **(10)** .... girls – achievement by **(11)** .... two sexes was broadly **(12)** .... same. Last week's A-level results also showed girls getting more top grades than boys for **(13)** .... first time, triggering **(14)** .... national debate about boys' so-called under-achievement.

Congratulating candidates on their results, **(15)** .... school standards minister, Estelle Morris, urged young people to consider staying on in **(16)** .... higher education rather than quitting. 'There are plenty of opportunities to progress to higher qualifications and **(17)** .... more secure future,' she said, 'whether at **(18)** .... school or college or in **(19)** .... apprenticeship.'

(20) .... Professional Association of Teachers welcomed **(21)** .... small rise in standards at GCSE but called for **(22)** .... large scale inquiry into **(23)** .... gender differences, pointing out that at university male students still gain more first class degrees, while in **(24)** .... workplace men still dominate **(25)** .... top jobs in academia, politics and business.

Vocabulary

Noun phrases with *of*

1 Put the nouns below in the correct part of the chart. The first three have been done as examples.

animals	**clothing**	**flowers**	**land**	**sand**	**teenagers**
binoculars	**courage**	**friends**	**news**	**scissors**	**trousers**
cheese	**events**	**lies**	**pliers**	**stairs**	**truth**

Countable nouns	Uncountable nouns	Plural nouns
animals, ...	*cheese,*	*binoculars,* ....
....	....	....
....	....	....
....	....	....
....	....	....

2 What kind of nouns appear in the chart below? Complete the chart, ticking each box where a phrase can collocate with a noun.

	animals	events	flowers	friends	lies	teenagers
a bunch of						
a group of						
a pack of						
a series of						

3 Which of the boxes you've ticked above would imply a negative view of the group described, and might be qualified by an adjective such as *rowdy*, *noisy*, *scruffy* etc.?

4 Work with a partner and think of at least two other words that would collocate with the phrases below, then share your ideas with the rest of the class and add their suggestions to your lists.

1 a bunch of ....

2 a group of ....

3 a pack of ....

4 a series of ....

5 What kind of nouns appear in the chart below? Complete the chart, ticking each box where a phrase can collocate with a noun.

	cheese	clothing	courage	land	news	sand	truth
an act of							
a bit of							
a grain of							
an item of							
a piece of							

6 Look back at the third column of nouns in exercise 1. What phrase using *of* do we use before all of these words except *stairs*? What phrase do we use before *stairs*?

7 With what kind of nouns do we use the phrase *a couple of*?

8 The following phrases with *of* may be used with countable or uncountable nouns (but not with plural nouns). Work with a partner and think of at least two nouns that each phrase could collocate with. When you've finished, share your ideas with the rest of the class and add their suggestions to your lists.

1 loads of ....
2 a handful of ....
3 a sack of ....
4 a packet of ....
5 a box of ....
6 a roomful of ....
7 a pile of ....

Proverbs

9 Many English proverbs contain a high proportion of nouns. Work with a partner and reconstruct the proverbs from the prompts below, adding articles where necessary.

1 (beauty) is in (eye) of (beholder)
....
2 (bird) in (hand) is worth two in (bush)
....
3 (apple) (day) keeps (doctor) away
....
4 (pride) comes before (fall)
....
5 (stitch) in (time) is worth nine
....
6 (meek) shall inherit (earth)
....
7 You can't teach (old dog) (new tricks)
....
8 (proof) of (pudding) is in (eating)
....
9 (fools) rush in where (angels) fear to tread
....
10 Neither (borrower) nor (lender) be
....

10 Do you know, or can you guess, what each proverb means?

Use your English

Do any of these proverbs have equivalents in your language?
Do you think proverbs impart useful ideas and wisdom, or are they just boring cliches?
What is your favourite proverb, in English, or translated from your language into English?

Word formation: prefix *out*

11 The prefix *out* can be used to create new nouns, verbs and, less frequently, adjectives. Put the words below in the correct part of the chart. Be careful – one word can be both a noun and a verb.

outbreak outbuilding outburst outdated outdistance outdo outdoor outgrow outlast outlaw outlook outlive outlying outnumber outpatient outperform outset outspoken outstay

Noun	Verb	Adjective
....	....	....
....	....	....
....	....	....
....	....	....
....	....	....

12 The prefix *out* in some nouns and adjectives has the meaning of 'outside' or 'beyond'. Underline three nouns and three adjectives where the prefix has this meaning.

13 In other cases, the noun or adjective has been formed from a phrasal verb with *out*, for example:

break out – *Cholera has **broken out** in the area.*
outbreak – *There has been an **outbreak** of cholera in the area.*

Applying this rule, what phrasal verbs have the remaining three nouns and one adjective been formed from and what do they mean?

14 In most cases, the prefix *out* in a verb has the meaning 'more than', 'better than' or 'longer than'. Only one verb in the chart does not have one of these meanings. Which one is it?

Study tip

When recording vocabulary, you can make a note of the prefixes and suffixes the word may be used with, for example:

Nouns
a bid
a bidd*er*

Verbs
bid, *out*bid, *over*bid, *under*bid

15 Complete the gaps in the text with a word formed from the word given in the margin. Four of the words you need to write begin with *out*. The first one has been done as an example.

Childhood self-esteem can overwhelm academic disadvantage or social
(0) *deprivation* in determining future earnings power, according to major — DEPRIVE
new research.

There is now clear evidence that the earnings of people who had higher
self-esteem at age ten **(1)** .... those of their peers whose academic — STRIP
performance was better at the same age. Bright children often have higher
self-esteem, as do some from more affluent **(2)** .... But the study — GROUND
compared children from similar families and still found that those who
were psychologically well-balanced at ten were now **(3)** .... their — PERFORM
peers.

The research also found, surprisingly, that it is not unusual for children
to have high academic **(4)** .... and low self-esteem, leading to — ACHIEVE
significant later **(5)** .... in the jobs market. A spokesman for the — PERFORM
British Association for Counselling said: '**(6)** .... for children — COURAGE
doesn't come only from crude parental hostility at home; it can just be
(7) .... or the constant feeling that they're making you tired. — RESENT
Children pick that up. Nor is it only **(8)** .... children who suffer. — PRIVILEGE
All too often you can ask affluent parents who the important people in
their child's life are – teachers, friends and so on – and they haven't a
clue.'

Bearing out the findings of this research, many **(9)** .... successful — STAND
entrepreneurs, such as Richard Branson, were **(10)** .... — SHINE
academically when they were at school but had the advantage of
supportive families.

ANITA RODDICK OBE
Business as Unusual
Australian tour speech 2000

Anita Roddick, 'The Body Shop'

Richard Branson , 'Virgin'

Stelios Hatziioannou, 'easyJet'

Gapped sentences

16 Think of **one** word which can be used to complete all three sentences in each group below. Follow the example.

- The young man devoted his life to the *pursuit* of pleasure.
- I have to admit that hill walking is a *pursuit* which doesn't interest me at all.
- The flustered mother ran out of the supermarket in hot *pursuit* of her absconding toddler.

All the words in this section form part of a phrasal verb.

1
- That student is exceedingly good at .... up ingenious excuses for not having done her homework.
- I'm still .... over their offer of a place at university as I'm not sure if it's what I really want to do next.
- Don't talk to me at the moment; I'm .... out the best way to get to my classes tomorrow with all the trains on strike.

2
- Our previous teacher .... across as being less confident than the new one.
- The truth about why Phil was expelled from school only .... out a few days ago.
- An interesting point .... up when we were discussing the environment in class yesterday.

3
- I only just scraped .... my final exams, but I was quite pleased anyway.
- It's very hard for teachers to get .... to students who would rather not be in the classroom at all.
- Remember that you should always look .... your completed exam paper before you hand it in.

4
- No matter how hard I try I can't seem to get the idea of uncountable and countable nouns .... to my students.
- I came .... a really strange web site when I was looking for some information on the Internet last night.
- The shrill sound of the school bell cut .... the shouts and laughter in the playground.

5
- Looking .... to the future, what are you planning to do after you leave school?
- My oral exam is looming ...., and I'm really nervous about it.
- If you want to get .... in life, you really need good qualifications.

17 Using a dictionary, check the exact meaning of any of the phrasal verbs that were unfamiliar to you.

18 The phrasal verbs below could be used with the same meaning as the existing phrasal verb in five of the above sentences. Which ones?

come upon	**get on**	**make up**	**put across**	**work out**

Summary

Reading

1 Skim-read these two texts. In terms of subject-matter, what do they have in common?

Text 1

The most striking feature of the Dutch education system is that educators have worked assiduously to develop a structure that could be considered elitist – precisely in order to avoid elitism. It is not perfect, but in principle they have thought their way through the paradox of equal educational opportunity.

All Dutch children go through the same non-selective primary schools. They then go through a sophisticated assessment process, based on which the head-teacher produces a recommendation to the secondary school. As they enter secondary school, pupils are divided into four pathways within the same school, each studying the same 15 subjects from the same books but at four different levels and speeds. After two years, these four pathways take radically different routes. About 15% of the children take the most demanding academic route, which lasts a further four years; 25% take the slightly less demanding academic route, which takes three years; 45% take a two-year academic route that includes some practical vocational work; and the remaining 15% take an essentially vocational pathway with some academic extras for two years.

As a key element of flexibility, students can finish one pathway, take a diploma and then continue their secondary schooling by moving across to a more academic one. Some 5% do so. Supported by vocational lessons, Dutch schools invite the failing child, first to succeed at its own level; and then, where appropriate, to move on to a higher level. And here is the key statistic: at the end of their vocational pathway, 94% of these least academically able students pass exams for a diploma in six subjects, some of them academic.

Text 2

Dutch children in vocational streams spend up to 18 of their 32 weekly lessons in activities like running catering outfits that serve meals in real restaurants, building mock houses, plumbing bathrooms, running shops with goods and tills or repairing cars. This is a form of secondary education that scarcely exists in Britain – practical, vocational learning – but in the Netherlands is part of the mainstream of school life, with 60% of pupils on some form of vocational pathway.

The key point here is not the obvious one. This is not about training pupils for vocational careers – although that may be a helpful side-effect. This is about motivating pupils who fail to engage with conventional academic schooling. Dutch teachers say that as a result of lifting their students' motivation and building their self-confidence in the practical classes, they get much better results in the academic ones.

The Dutch also reject the idea that all children should move up a year or sit their exams at the same age. They recognise that some children will take longer to reach agreed goals and so they allow repetition to ensure that as many as possible reach the same minimum standards sooner or later. Nationally up to 15% of primary pupils and 30% of secondary pupils repeat a year. Although a child who is held back for a year may feel like a failure, Dutch educators argue that this is a lesser evil than processing an unprepared child through a more demanding syllabus that will condemn it to accumulating failure, ending in an early departure from education.

Skills development: Identifying the four content points

2 Read the rubric below, but do not write a summary.

Summarise, in your own words as far as possible, the ways in which the Dutch education system helps pupils who are not academically gifted.

3 Four of the points listed (1 to 10) below should **not** be included in the summary. Find these four points and the reasons why they should not be included. The reasons are listed (a to d) below.

1. All Dutch children go through the same non-selective primary schools.
2. Pupils are divided into four pathways, each studying the same 15 subjects from the same books but at four different levels and speeds.
3. After two years, these four pathways take radically different routes, ranging from the most demanding academic one to an essentially vocational pathway with some academic extras.
4. Students can finish one pathway, take a diploma and then continue their secondary schooling by moving across to a more academic one.
5. Supported by vocational lessons, Dutch schools invite the failing child, first to succeed at its own level, and then, where appropriate, to move on to a higher level.
6. 94% of these least academically able students pass exams for a diploma in six subjects, some of them academic.
7. Dutch children in vocational streams spend up to 18 of their 32 weekly lessons in activities like running catering outfits that serve meals in real restaurants, building mock houses etc.
8. Dutch teachers say that as a result of lifting their students' motivation and building their self-confidence in the practical classes, they get much better results in the academic ones.
9. The Dutch allow repetition to ensure that as many (children) as possible reach the same minimum standards sooner or later.
10. A child who is held back for a year may feel like a failure.

Reasons

a It is an example proving that the system works, not an example of a way in which it helps pupils.

b It is an example of how one of the methods works in practice, but not of a way in which it helps pupils.

c It is an exception to the theme, which is explained and qualified later in the text.

d It is not relevant to the topic.

4 You now have six points left. Some of these can be grouped together, thus making a total of four content points. Complete the sentences below, which summarise the four content points. You may refer to the appropriate sentences from exercise 3, and to the original texts, if necessary.

- Learners can study at their .... and follow .... with varying .... content.
- Students can .... after completing ....
- .... builds their .... and leads to ....
- They may .... until they ....

6 Archaeology and history

Grammar
- Modals II: Past

Vocabulary
- Phrasal verbs: historical research
- Set phrases including modal verbs
- Word formation: adjectives ending in *-ial* and *-ical*

Summary
- Identifying the four content points

Grammar: Modals II: Past

Grammar overview

Giving or refusing permission in the past ***could(n't), was/were(n't) allowed to* and *wouldn't***	
*The researchers **could** examine the artefacts as long as they put each one back in place.* *When he worked for CompuInk he **couldn't** send personal e-mails in work time.* *She **was allowed to** enter the archaeological site because she had a special permit.*	*We **weren't allowed to** touch any of the exhibits in the museum.* *The manager **wouldn't** let the teenagers into the cinema because they were underage.*
General ability to do something in the past ***could(n't)* and *was(n't)/were(n't) able to***	
*She **could** see the mountains in the distance from her grandmother's house.* *He **couldn't** read and write until he was six years old.*	*James **wasn't able to** walk properly after the accident.* *After a week's training the staff **were able to** use the new computer system.*
Ability to do something in a specific situation in the past ***was(n't)/were(n't) able to* and *managed to / didn't manage to***	
*There were two questions on ancient history and he **wasn't able to** answer either of them.* *The climbers **were able to** find their way out of the cave through a tunnel in the rock face.*	*She **managed to** free her foot from under the rock and swim to the surface.* *I **didn't manage to** finish my essay in time for the deadline.*
Necessity and obligation in the past ***had to/didn't have to* and *needed to/didn't need to***	
*We **had to** walk home because we missed the bus.* *They **didn't have to** show their passports again after they crossed the border.*	*He **needed to** rest after his long and tiring journey.* *She **didn't need to** sit the exam again because she passed first time.*

didn't need to* v. *needn't have	
When you do something in the past which you later discover was not necessary, you use ***needn't have***. *We **needn't have** rushed to get to the cinema. We arrived far too early and had to stand outside in the cold for half an hour.*	If you don't perform a certain action in the past because you knew beforehand that it was not necessary you use ***didn't need to***. *The second showing of the film wasn't until 11pm so we **didn't need to** rush to get to the cinema. We finished out supper and strolled to the cinema.*
Expressing criticism of somebody's past actions *should(n't) have* or *ought (not) to have*	
*You **should have** asked me before you borrowed the car.* *We **shouldn't have** left so abruptly; they'll think we're terribly rude.*	*He **ought to have** consulted me before he told the boss.* *They **ought not to have** spoken to the headmistress like that.*
Deductions, assumptions and speculation about the past *must have, may (not) have, might (not) have, could(n't) have* and *can't have*	
*He **must have** worked very hard to get to the position he is in today.* *She **may not have** heard you. Ring the bell again.* *They **may have** changed their minds about coming today.* *You **might have** left your keys in the lock; go and have a look.*	*Thomas **might not have** heard the news yet.* *Helen **could have** meant Tuesday, not Thursday.* *That boy **couldn't have** stolen the money; he wasn't even here that day.* *They **can't have** forgotten! I reminded them this morning.*

Advanced grammar points

Grammar point 1

1 All the sentences below contain *could/couldn't have* + past participle. Match each sentence to one function.

1 My grandmother could have become an opera singer, but she got married and raised a family instead.
2 She could have said she'd be working from home today – I don't really remember.
3 She could have said she'd be working from home today – I went to the office to meet her.
4 He couldn't have joined the police force anyway – he's too short.
5 You couldn't have come at a better time.

a Describing a perfect situation.
b Describing a possibility in the past.
c Describing an impossibility in the past.
d Describing an unfulfilled possibility in the past.
e Expressing annoyance.

2 In two of the sentences above, *could have* or *couldn't have* can be replaced with *might have* or *might not have* without changing the meaning in any way. In which sentences?

- *could have* + past participle is used to describe unfulfilled possibilities in the past.
  *I **could have** gone on to university after school but I wanted to start earning money, so I decided to get a job.*

- *could have* + past participle or *might have* + past participle are used to describe possibilities in the past.
  *She **could/might have** phoned to say she wasn't coming [but I wasn't here to take a call].*

  or to express annoyance.
  *She **could/might have** phoned to say she wasn't coming [but she hasn't/didn't].*

The difference between the two uses depends on the context in which they are uttered, and the intonation used. Sometimes the words *at least* are said immediately after *might* or *could* when annoyance is being expressed.

- *couldn't have* + past participle is used to describe impossibilities in the past.
  *My mother always said her uncle had fought in the Battle of Crete, but he **couldn't have** done because his army records show he didn't join up until 1942.*

- It is also used with comparative adjectives to describe an extremely good or bad situation.
  *You **couldn't have** picked a worse moment to bring that subject up. (= That was the worst possible moment to bring that subject up.)*
  *The food **couldn't have** been more delicious. (= The food was absolutely delicious)*

Grammar point 2

Match the beginnings of sentences (1 – 3) to the endings (a – c) which would logically complete them.

1 My parents didn't let me, but otherwise I
2 For all the fun we had we
3 They were getting the six o'clock train so they

a should have arrived at least an hour ago.
b would have gone to the party.
c might as well have stayed at home.

- *would have* + past participle is used to express unfulfilled intentions in the past.
  *I **would have** met you at the station, but my car broke down at the last minute.*

- *might as well + (not) have* + past participle is used to describe something that you didn't do but which would have been better than what you did do.
  *I'd hoped to save time by driving there, but I got stuck in a huge traffic jam so **I might as well have** taken the train after all.*

  *She was so ungrateful for my help that I **might as well not have** bothered doing her shopping for her.*

- *should have* + past participle or *ought to have* + past participle is used to describe something that was supposed to happen but didn't or hasn't.
  *I sent the parcel on Monday so you **ought to/should have** got it by Thursday at the very latest.*

Practice A

Circle the more appropriate verb to fill each gap below. If both are equally suitable, circle both.

1 Archaeologists believe that the destruction of the Minoan palaces .... by severe earthquakes and subsequent fires.
a might have been caused **b** could have been caused **c** both

2 The evening .... more perfect.
a wouldn't have been **b** couldn't have been **c** both

3 With a brain like that, he .... a lawyer.
a should have become **b** could have become **c** both

4 Since it was your friends who made the mess, you .... after them.
a might have tidied up **b** could have tidied up **c** both

5 Your story is interesting and lively, but it contains several historical inaccuracies. For example, your hero .... Miss Swinton shelter under his umbrella, as they weren't invented until a hundred years later.
a might not have offered **b** couldn't have offered **c** both

6 The lecture started half an hour late so I .... money on a taxi to get to it.
a might as well have spent **b** might as well not have spent **c** both

7 I .... a year off between school and university and gone travelling, but my father advised me against it.
a would have taken **b** could have taken **c** both

Look back at the sentences in Practice A where you chose the answer *both*. Is there any difference in the meaning expressed by the two possible verbs? If so, what is it?

Practice B

Complete the second sentence so that it has a similar meaning to the first sentence, using the word given. Do not change the word given. You must use between three and eight words, including the word given.

1 This is the best present I've ever been given.
chosen
You .... for me.

2 He was offered a job as a lecturer in Aberdeen but he didn't want to be so far away from his family.
gone
He .... at Aberdeen University but he didn't want to be so far away from his family.

3 I don't recall being given that message, but it's possible that my secretary did so.
have
Well, I suppose my secretary .... message.

4 You were supposed to hand this essay in three days ago.
have
This essay .... three days ago.

5 I fully intended to finish my essay on time, but my mother fell ill.
would
But for my mother's .... my essay on time.

6 He paid me no attention at all, which made me feel I'd wasted my time by going to see him.
well
For all the attention he paid me. I .... to see him.

7 I have no idea who drank your bottle of vintage port, but it certainly wasn't Auntie Maude as I bought it after her visit.
been
I bought that bottle of vintage port after her visit, so it .... drank it.

Practice C

Read the whole text below, then complete the gaps by writing an appropriate modal form of the verb in the margin, or an appropriate tense of the modal verb given. In some cases, more than one modal may be suitable. The first one has been done as an example.

During the 10 years it took him to clear Tutankhamun's tomb, archaeologist Howard Carter discovered great quantities of textiles and clothes. These **(0)** must/would originally have been.. carefully folded and stored, but were now stuffed	(ORIGINALLY) BE
randomly into storage chests, suggesting that thieves **(1)** .... not long	STRIKE
after the burial and pulled many of the garments out in their search for gold. The officials sent in to restore the tomb **(2)** .... something resembling a	FIND
closing-down sale, and, in their attempts to tidy up quickly, stuffed the clothes back into the nearest box. A find of this fragile nature **(3)** .... carefully, yet the	PRESERVE
young king's wardrobe lay neglected for a full 70 years before a team of textile historians began to study it. By then the original garments had deteriorated so much they decided to save them from further damage by making exact copies. As the recreated garments **(4)** .... be made of gossamer-like linen finer than any	HAVE TO
modern machinery **(5)** .... produce, specialists in ancient methods of textile production were called in.	BE ABLE TO
The replicas also served to show how some of the more curious-looking garments **(6)** .... For example, by trying them on, the team discovered that two	WEAR
strange objects **(7)** .... headdresses as they had originally thought, but were actually meant to be worn on the arms to form the wings of the falcon, emblem of the Egyptian king. In fact, many of the clothes enhanced the king's status by using regal motifs and symbols of power as decoration. Even as he walked along,	(NOT) BE
Tutankhamun **(8)** .... his enemies with every step, since their images were painted on the soles of his gilded sandals. As 'son of the Sun god', he	CRUSH
(9) .... his subjects in his glittering robes. With each outfit completed by a selection of golden collars, earrings, bracelets and one of the many royal crowns,	DAZZLE
the pharaoh **(10)** .... an awe-inspiring sight, a living god who	BE
(11) .... look the part at all times.	HAVE TO

Vocabulary

Phrasal verbs: historical research

1 The text below contains phrasal verbs related in some way to historical research. Match each phrase or phrasal verb in bold to a definition.

> Family history is one of Britain's fastest growing passions. Genealogy used to be considered the preserve of bearded boffins or snobbish eccentrics, but now thousands of people who would scorn the idea of (1) **ploughing through** academic tomes of historical information are now eagerly (2) **delving into** official archives and public records in an effort to (3) **hunt down** their ancestors. Some are motivated by curiosity and the desire to (4) **piece together** a family tree; others hope to add excitement to their lives by (5) **digging up** a colourful or illustrious forebear. As a hobby, it's slow and time-consuming; some enthusiasts have spent years (6) **poring over** records of births, marriages and deaths in search of an elusive ancestor. However, the advent of the Internet has made things much easier and may partly explain the explosion of interest in tracing one's roots. A host of online databases allow you to (7) **look up** a specific surname quickly and instead of visiting your local public records office to examine the official files, it is now possible to (8) **carry out** much of your research online. Even so, the results may not be what you hoped for. A friend of mine spent two years trying in vain to (9) **trace** her family **back** to a famous eighteenth century novelist; what she (10) **turned up** instead was a forefather of the same name who had been the local hangman!

a discover by chance
b search for someone or something until you find it ☐
c find hidden or forgotten information by careful searching ☐
d read all of something, even though it is boring and takes a long time ☐
e try to find a particular bit of information in a book or on a computer ☐
f search in a collection of information sources ☐
g read or look at something very carefully for a long time ☐
h follow the development of something from now to its original source ☐
i do or perform (an activity) ☐
j add various bits of information to create a complete picture of something ☐

2 The phrasal verbs below have the same meaning as phrasal verbs in the text. Find the verbs in the text.

happen on = ...
wade through = ...

3 One of the verbs in exercise 1 may also be used literally, and could collocate with the phrase 'some ancient silver coins'. Which one?

4 One of the verbs in exercise 1 also has an intransitive use (i.e. the verb has no object), in which case it means 'appear unexpectedly after having been lost'. Which one?

5 Complete the chart below, ticking each box where a phrasal verb can collocate with a noun.

	an ancient manuscript	an archive	an artefact	a dig/ an excavation	fragments of pottery
carry out					
delve into					
dig up					
piece together					
pore over					

6 Complete each gap in the text below with a suitable verb, adverb or preposition.

Archaeologists always prefer to see artefacts in their original setting, for it is by **(1)** .... over objects in context that they can piece **(2)** .... an idea of how life was lived during a particular historical period. However, many of their best efforts are being foiled by the international trade in stolen antiquities, which is now estimated to be the world's fourth largest criminal enterprise after drugs, arms and money laundering.

The supply of looted antiquities ultimately depends on grave robbers, few of whom are ever caught. Most grave robberies are carried **(3)** .... at night and many of the robbers have become as expert at identifying tombs and **(4)** .... up relics as any professional archaeologist. As the artefacts they steal are passed along a chain of dealers before finally **(5)** .... up on the legitimate art market, it is hard to **(6)** .... them back to the original thief. On the rare occasions that grave robbers are caught in the act, it is usually because the police have happened **(7)** .... them by luck.

At the opposite end of the supply chain, police regularly **(8)** .... into the catalogues of auction houses like Sotheby's and Christie's, looking **(9)** .... suspicious items on a database of stolen artworks. As a result of such searches, some major pieces have been extricated from auction houses and museums.

Set phrases including modal verbs

7 A number of set phrases which include modal verbs exist in spoken English. Some of these are listed below. Work with a partner and try to work out where each phrase would be used in the dialogues and sentences below. Use each phrase only once.

a I could have kicked myself!
b I could have murdered him!
c I couldn't agree more.
d I might have known/guessed
e I must say
f I should have thought
g pigs might fly
h you could/might have told me
i you should have seen/heard
j you shouldn't have

1 ' .... Paul's jokes in the pub last night. I haven't laughed so much for years.'

2 A: .... today was a public holiday. I went all the way to the shops for nothing.
B: Oh, I'm sorry. I completely forgot. .... I think public holidays are a terrible waste of time.
A: .... In this case, my time especially.

3 '.......................... . It was the first time in two years that I didn't buy a lottery ticket, and four of my usual numbers came up – I would have won a thousand pounds or more!'

4 A: Mum, I've got a history quiz for homework and I can't answer one question. Do you know if Julius Caesar was born in the year 120BC, 100BC, or 80BC?
B: Well, I'm not certain but .... it was 100BC, as his first attack on Britain was in 55BC and he was a middle-aged man by then

5 A: And these are for you. I know you like carnations.
B: That's ever so kind of you, but really ....

6 'I let him borrow the car for just half an hour, and when he brought it back there was a huge scratch down one side of it and one headlight was smashed. ....'

7 A: The film starts in five minutes and Lisa's not here. .... she'd be late as usual.
B: Well, she promised she wouldn't be late this time. I expect she'll be here in a moment.
A: Sure, and ....

8 Now match each phrase in exercise 7 to a definition in the list below.

You use this phrase:

1 to show you are not surprised about a disappointing fact or event. ....
2 when you think something is true, but you are not sure. ....
3 to show you were very angry with yourself. ....
4 to show complete agreement with another person's opinion. ....
5 when you are annoyed someone didn't give you information you needed. ....
6 to show you were exceedingly angry with someone else. ....
7 when thanking someone for a gift or a favour. ....
8 to show that you think something is very unlikely. ....
9 to emphasise how funny or shocking something was. ....
10 to emphasise a point you're making. ....

Word formation: adjectives ending in *-ial* and *-ical*

9 Many adjectives can be formed by adding the suffixes *-ial* or *-ical* to a noun stem. Put the words below in the correct part of the chart, adding the suffix that would be used to change the word into an adjective, and making any necessary spelling changes. The first two have been done as examples.

adversary	**conspirator**	**picture**
alphabet	**experience**	**preference**
benefit	**farce**	**substance**
biology	**method**	**type**
colony	**nonsense**	**vestige**
commerce	**philosophy**	**whimsy**

-ial	-ical
adversarial, ...	alphabetical, ...
....	....
....	....
....	....
....	....

10 Not all words ending in *-ial* are adjectives. Which two of the words below cannot function as adjectives? What part of speech are they?

aerial denial immaterial memorial official palatial sundial

11 Of the five remaining words in the list above, which three can act both as adjectives and as nouns?

12 Work with a partner and think of three other words ending in *-ial* which can be nouns or adjectives. Share your ideas with the rest of the class, and add their words to your list.

13 There are a number of adjectives ending in *-ical* which also have another form, ending in *-ic*, which has a slightly different meaning. Use a dictionary to help you check the meanings of the pairs of adjectives below.

classic – classical	**comic – comical**	**economic – economical**
historic – historical	**politic – political**	

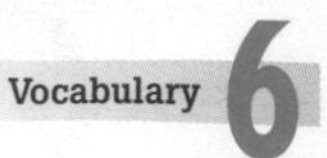

14 Work with a partner. Choose three adjectives from exercises 9 and/or 13 above. Write three sentences, each including one of the words you have chosen. The sentences should not be definitions, but should illustrate the meaning of the word. When all pairs are ready, take turns to read your sentences aloud, saying 'beep' instead of the word. The rest of the class must guess what the missing word is.

Example: *I feel ashamed of my ignorance of 'beep' music.*
Answer: ***classical***

Study tip

When you record new vocabulary it is a good idea to write down the different forms of the word. This is particularly helpful for building your vocabulary for Part 2 of the Use of English paper. For example:

Noun	Verb	Adjective	Adverb
benefit	benefit	beneficial	beneficially
office, official	officiate	official	officially

15 Complete the gaps in the text with a word formed from the word given in the margin. All the words you need to write are either adjectives or adverbs. The first one has been done as an example.

In 1887 the German archaeologist Heinrich Schliemann visited the site of Knossos in Crete and became convinced that a **(0)** substantial palace lay waiting to be unearthed. However, his attempts to purchase land at the site were frustrated by its Turkish owners and the general **(1)** .... turmoil leading up to the end of Turkish rule in Crete. Five years earlier Schliemann had entertained a young English scholar, Arthur Evans, at his home in Athens and had spoken **(2)** .... of his desire to dig at the site from whence, according to Homer 'came forth the men of Knossos'. Ironically, it was to be the Englishman who unearthed this great **(3)** .... prize.	SUBSTANCE POLITICS LYRE ARCHAEOLOGY
Evans arrived in Crete in March 1894 and immediately ran into **(4)** .... the same problems that had beset Schliemann in his efforts to purchase the land at Knossos. However, Evans persevered and, **(5)** ...., the expulsion of the Turks in 1898 removed the major obstacle to his work. By March 1900 Evans had bought the land and excavations began. He soon realised he was dealing with a **(6)** pre-.................... site far older even than the Mycenaean period, and named the newly-discovered civilisation 'Minoan' after the **(7)** .... Cretan king.	ESSENCE PROVIDENCE CLASS MYTH
The fact that Evans was **(8)** .... independent and owned the site personally allowed him to act somewhat **(9)** .... and enabled him to make the still highly **(10)** .... decision to reconstruct parts of the palace, rather than just uncover it. No professional archaeologist would be allowed, or would indeed expect, to carry out such a work again.	FINANCE DICTATOR CONTROVERSY

Use your English

Do you think a private individual should have been allowed to purchase a site of major archaeological importance for Greece? If not, how should the excavation have been carried out? What do you think about the fact that Evans reconstructed part of the palace at Knossos?

Gapped sentences

16 Think of **one** word which can be used to complete all three sentences in each group below. Follow the example.

- The young man devoted his life to the *pursuit* of pleasure.
- I have to admit that hill walking is a *pursuit* which doesn't interest me at all.
- The flustered mother ran out of the supermarket in hot *pursuit* of her absconding toddler.

All the words in this section have appeared earlier in this unit, but not necessarily in the same context or in the same grammatical form.

1

- If she continues talking to the boss like that she'll end up .... her own grave.
- Since John lost his job we've been .... into our savings just to pay the monthly bills.
- You don't need to keep .... me in the ribs every time you make a joke; if it's funny enough, I'll know when to laugh on my own.

2

- That big field near the woods has just been .... up, so if you're planning to take the dog for a walk today you'd better go to the park instead.
- I turned to speak to my passenger for a second, and the next thing I knew I'd .... into the car in front.
- Despite her fatigue, the teacher .... on until she'd marked every child's composition.

3

- The house itself is nothing special, but it has a wonderful .... on a hill overlooking a river.
- The .... of the film is Germany in the years immediately after the Second World War.
- For their anniversary he gave her a large diamond brooch in a gold ....

4

- Mary Queen of Scots was nine months old when she was ...., but she did not rule Scotland until she was eighteen years old.
- The dentist says I need to have that broken tooth ...., which is going to be expensive.
- In late spring the sea is warm enough to swim in and, floating in the water, you can look up and see the mountains still .... with snow.

5

- Her cooking is good, but it's not in the same .... as her husband's.
- He graduated from Oxford with a first .... degree in English literature.
- She's attending an extra-mural .... in medieval history at the university.

17 Using a dictionary, check the exact meaning of any words, set phrases or usages that were unfamiliar to you. With a partner, write your own sentences to illustrate the usage and meaning of the new items.

Summary

Reading

1 Skim-read these two texts. In terms of subject-matter, what do they have in common?

Text 1

When modern humans moved into Europe from Africa about 40,000 years ago, we had to share it with the Neanderthals, who had been doing quite nicely there for at least 200,000 years. Yet within 10,000 years of our arrival, we had rendered them extinct. So did these sibling people disappear because of species-cleansing by Rambo-like thugs wielding the latest in rock weapons, or was it more gradual? Many anthropologists take the latter view. They believe that *homo sapiens* strangled the opposition, slowly but effectively, by monopolising resources. Neanderthals liked to move around but returned to favourite caves when times got hard. Slowly groups would find that when they went back to those caves they had been taken over by spreading tribes of *homo sapiens*. They ran out of places to hide.

The other scenario, that of a Stone Age holocaust, is less easy to support – for no Neanderthal skeletons peppered with arrow heads have been dug up by palaeontologists. Nevertheless, it is hard to avoid the notion that our meetings with Neanderthals were often violent and fatal. Backed by improved linguistic abilities and a capacity to use mental symbols when working out problems, *homo sapiens* would have been a deadly foe. Neanderthals had little to offer modern humans – except competition. For too long we have regarded the extinction of Neanderthals as a chance historical accident. Rather, where Neanderthals and modern humans could not coexist, their disappearance may have been the result of the modern human race's first and most successful deliberate campaign of genocide.

Text 2

Many theories have been put forward to explain what happened to the Neanderthals. One of these suggests that they were simply outperformed and replaced, within a relatively short time, by the more flexible and technologically advanced *homo sapiens*. Certainly, modern humans had more complex and specialised tools and their superior language skills would have allowed them to plan and adapt their methods of hunting to the circumstances. As the Neanderthals had to compete with the shrewder *homo sapiens* for their meals, they would have suffered bouts of starvation and a consequent decrease in the overall Neanderthal population, which could have been the cause of extinction.

It is also possible that when *homo sapiens* first encountered Neanderthal man, he could have introduced devastating new diseases, much as the conquistadors did when they arrived in Latin America. Not having developed immunity to these illnesses, Neanderthals would have quickly perished.

Another theory postulates that Neanderthals interbred to a greater or lesser extent with the incoming *homo sapiens*, whose genes eventually became dominant at the expense of the genes delivering Neanderthal characteristics. This hypothesis comes from the fact that Neanderthals and *homo sapiens* inhabited the same regions of Europe for thousands of years, and archaeological evidence from the site of Auxerre in France suggests that Neanderthals not only came into contact with, but may have been actively trading with their successors. With the idea of interbreeding in mind, many scientists see a more gradual replacement, not by people, but by modern genes that spread virus-like around the world, slowly transforming populations.

Skills development: Identifying the four content points

2 Read the rubric below, but do not write a summary.

> *Summarise, in your own words as far as possible, the possible reasons for the disappearance of Neanderthal man.*

3 Which of the points below would be appropriate to include in the summary? (Remember that the final summary should be between 50 and 70 words long.)

		Yes	No	Possibly
1	Dates when the Neanderthals existed?	☐	☐	☐
2	The date of the arrival of *homo sapiens* (i.e. modern humans) in Europe?	☐	☐	☐
3	Scientists' theories about the extinction of the Neanderthals?	☐	☐	☐
4	Examples of Neanderthals' behaviour and customs?	☐	☐	☐
5	Examples of *homo sapiens*' behaviour and customs?	☐	☐	☐
6	Examples of archaeological evidence found to support scientists' theories?	☐	☐	☐

4 For what reasons did you reject some of the points in 3 above?

5 Now re-read Text 1 in detail. You should find two possible reasons. Underline or highlight them.

6 Now re-read Text 2 in detail. You should find three possible reasons. Underline or highlight them.

7 You should now have a total of five possible reasons in answer to questions 5 and 6 above. Remember that the summary has only four content points in it. Combine the first point from Text 1 and the first point from Text 2 into one sentence.

8 Work with a partner and write three more sentences. Each sentence should summarise one of the three remaining content points. (Remember to use appropriate past modal forms.)

9 Compare your answers to questions 7 and 8 with the rest of the class. Make a note of the answers which you think are the best, i.e. the most succinct but complete.

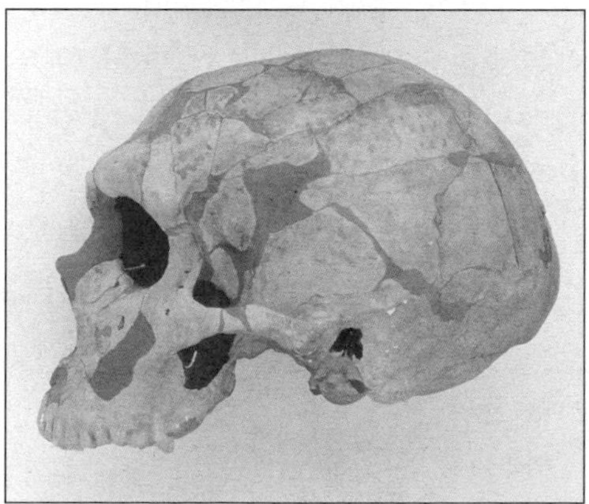

Practice test 2

Part 1

For questions 1 – 15, read the text below and think of the word which best fits each space. Use only **one** word in each space. There is an example at the beginning (0).

Example:

0	A	S													

Homework

The homework question is **(0)** ..as... old as it is difficult to answer. Educators in Britain have been arguing about it **(1)** .... homework became commonplace in the mid-19th century. Any **(2)** .... the public has voiced concern about falling educational standards, schools have responded by assigning more homework. Eventually they give **(3)** .... assignment too many, then there is an outcry about the cruelty of it all. Schools respond by assigning **(4)** .... homework until one day **(5)** .... asks why standards are dropping, draws the **(6)** .... that more homework is needed and the pendulum swings **(7)** .... again.

Although primary schools are **(8)** .... no obligation to assign homework, the current government guidelines **(9)** .... that children in the first three years of primary school do one hour of homework a week, while children in years five and six **(10)** .... be assigned half an hour daily. However, a 1999 study carried **(11)** .... at Durham University found there was no evidence that homework in primary schools boosted academic performance, and **(12)** .... evidence that it might even cause harm. There is also widespread concern in the profession that badly-constructed homework policies could **(13)** .... to a widening of the **(14)** .... between children with educated parents and children **(15)** .... parents left school early.

Part 2

For questions 16 – 25, read the text below. Use the word given in capitals at the end of some of the lines to form a word that fits in the space in the same line. There is an example at the beginning (0).

Example:

0	M	O	V	E	M	E	N	T	S							

Mayan throne	
The Mayas developed the only pre-Columbian writing in the Americas and devised	
an intricate astronomy to chart the **(0)** movements of the heavens. Archaeologists	**MOVE**
have long been **(16)** .... as to why their civilisation seems to have collapsed	**MYSTERY**
abruptly in the ninth century, resulting in the **(17)** .... of formerly flourishing	**ABANDON**
cities. However, a team of Mexican and American archaeologists have recently	
(18) .... a monumental art work that may give some clues to their sudden	**EARTH**
(19) .... While digging at Palenque, in the Yucatan peninsula, the researchers	**APPEAR**
(20) .... a bench-like throne more than 2.8m wide and 1.7m deep in vermilion-	**COVER**
painted limestone. The archaeologists say the grandeur of the throne and the	
(21) .... of the palace that houses it indicate that the last rulers of Palenque were	**SPACE**
more ambitious and **(22)** .... than had once been thought. The throne itself was	**POWER**
built in about AD 760 by one of the last Mayan rulers and is adorned with at least	
200 hieroglyphs and six sculptured portraits. The experts hope that once the	
(23) .... have been deciphered, something which could take some time, they may	**SCRIBE**
disclose the **(24)** .... and aspirations of the Mayas in the decades before their	**ACHIEVE**
demise and lead to a better **(25)** .... of the reasons for their decline.	**STAND**

Exam tip

Remember that more than one transformation to the stem may be needed. This could involve adding a prefix and a suffix, or more than one prefix or suffix at a time.

Part 3

For questions 26 – 31, think of **one** word only which can be used appropriately in all three sentences. Here is an example (0).

Example:

0 The young man devoted his life to the ...... of pleasure.

I have to admit that hill walking is a ...... which doesn't interest me at all.

The flustered mother ran out of the supermarket in hot ...... of her absconding toddler.

0	P	U	R	S	U	I	T								

26

- As soon as the policeman had turned his back, the prisoner made a ...... for freedom.
- We'll be back with you for round three of the competition after a short ...... for the commercials.
- Gail and I have decided to make a clean ...... and no longer see each other at all.

27

- He won his first ...... in 2000, at the Sydney Olympics.
- The three wise men bore gifts of ......, frankincense and myrrh.
- The puppy was as good as ...... while I was looking after him.

28

- The museum has ...... an important collection of late Roman coins.
- When her children had grown up and left home, Sandra went to secretarial school and ...... new skills.
- She ...... a taste for olives during her holiday in Greece.

29

- When our neighbours started having noisy parties every night, my husband ...... by getting up at seven every day and playing the radio at full volume.
- Unfortunately, the patient has not ...... to the treatment given
- I'm surprised that no-one has ...... to the advertisement you placed in the local paper.

30

- The team has been working against the ...... to get the project finished on time.
- A group of idealists are trying to turn the ...... back by living in a remote village without electricity or running water.
- Could you set the ...... for six, as I have to catch an early train tomorrow?

31

- Her expression was a ...... in grief as she surveyed the damage caused by the fire.
- My niece is carrying out a ...... into the learning styles of primary school children.
- You'll find Professor Roberts in the ...... at the end of the corridor.

Part 4

For questions 32 – 39, complete the second sentence so that it has a similar meaning to the first sentence, using the word given. **Do not change the word given**. You must use between three and eight words, including the word given. Here is an example (0).

Example:

0 The company's profits appear to be improving significantly this year.

evidence

The company's .... this year.

0	profits show evidence of significant improvement

32 The closing date for the competition is next Tuesday.

entry

You .... next Tuesday.

33 Pat is forever forgetting her key, even though I keep reminding her to take it with her.

often

No .... her key, Pat still forgets it.

34 Lives could be endangered if the safety procedures are not followed strictly.

risk

To ensure that no-one .... to the safety procedures.

35 The only person that can explain this situation to us is Paul.
light
No-one .... the situation.

36 As the merry-go-round picked up speed, the children's shrieks grew ever more piercing.
span
The faster .... the children shrieked.

37 If it hadn't rained so heavily, the garden party would have been a success.
downpour
Had ...., the garden party would have been a success.

38 Another five years were to pass before she saw her brother again.
gone
Not .... she see her brother again.

39 Several students said they didn't learn anything because they found their lessons boring.
failure
Several students blamed .... that their lessons were boring.

Exam tip

When you check your answers to this part, make sure that:

- You have remembered to include the key word.
- You haven't altered the key word in any way.
- You have written no more than eight words, including the key word (contracted forms e.g. *they've*, *he's* count as two words).

Part 5

You are going to read two texts on work. For questions 40 – 43, answer with a word or short phrase. You do not need to write complete sentences. For question **44** write a summary according to the instructions given.

A

Whether we are damning the impact of work on our health, our families, our time, or celebrating its new-found flexibility, rewards and opportunities, people are talking, writing and thinking about work like never before. This work fixation springs from a series of profound changes in the nature of employment, all of which push work more deeply into our individual lives, our families and our communities. Work has become an important personal identity tag, supplanting the three traditional indicators of our uniqueness – place, faith and blood. *line 8*
As geographical roots have weakened, religious affiliations have diminished and the extended family has dispersed, how we spend our labouring hours has become a window into our souls. This trend reflects and reinforces a desire for work which brings personal fulfilment, for work we are proud of. We want our work to demonstrate our individuality, not box us into a stereotype.

The ability – or requirement – to create our own working life, rather than having it laid out for us by a corporate parent-replacement is another reason for our renewed interest in work. While job security was once based on one employer, or at least one set of skills, security now comes from an ability to move with the times. The young are in the *line 19*
vanguard of the do-it-yourself career-makers. In the US, the average 32- *line 20*
year-old has had nine jobs. In the UK, one in four youngsters want to work for themselves. This generation have seen for themselves that a clever and skilful employee can call the shots. It is exhausting – but it can be liberating, too.

40 What importance does the author attach to 'the three traditional indicators of our uniqueness' (line 8)?

....

....

41 Explain in your own words what is meant by the phrase 'are in the vanguard of the do-it-yourself career-makers' (lines 19 – 20).

....

....

B

Women will shortly outnumber men in the UK labour force, and have been flooding into work for the past few decades. The real impact of this seismic social and economic shift has been to increase the importance of work in all our lives. When the roles of breadwinner or homemaker were segregated by gender, the female half of the population was, by and large, excluded from conversations about work – that was 'men's talk'. Now women talk and care about work as much as men. The nature of the jobs now done by women has also pushed work up the agenda. In 1911, 39 per cent of Britain's working women were domestic servants, now they are knocking at the boardroom door. There are currently more women than men studying to be doctors and lawyers.

The increase in the numbers of women at work has also changed the atmosphere of the workplace and helped to create a more natural and sociable environment than the offices and factories of the past. The arrival of women has coincided with an increase in the levels of personal interaction at work. This reflects not only the influence of women, but also a shift in the nature of work, away from manufacturing and towards services that need a human touch and where communication skills are far more highly valued than they were in previous generations. So, while the working day is not filled with enjoyable interaction for everyone, there is no questioning the fact that for most people, most of the time, work is better now – which inevitably makes it more valuable.

42 What phrase later in paragraph 1 echoes the mention in lines 3 to 4 of this text of the increasing importance of work?

....

....

43 What reflects 'the influence of women' (lines 16 – 17)?

....

....

44 In a paragraph of between 50 and 70 words, summarise in your own words as far as possible, the ways in which the role and nature of work has changed.

7 The media and entertainment

Grammar
- Reported speech

Vocabulary
- Phrasal verbs and set phrases: leisure
- Reporting verbs
- Word formation: revision

Summary
- Rephrasing the four content points

Grammar: Reported speech

Grammar overview

Tense changes	
'I'll buy a Playstation.'	*He said he **would** buy a Playstation.*
*'I **must** hurry up.'*	*He said he **had to** hurry up.*
*'I **may** change my mind.'*	*He said he **might** change his mind.*
*'I **can't** tell the difference.'*	*He said he **couldn't** tell the difference.*
*'You **needn't** dress up for dinner.'*	*He said I **didn't have to** dress up for dinner.*

Modal verbs		
Present simple ➠ past simple	*'Sports programmes **are popular** with most teenagers.'*	*He said sports programmes **were popular** with most teenagers.*
Present continuous ➠ past continuous	*'Jenny Fernandez **is starring** in the new film.'*	*He said Jenny Fernandez **was starring** in the new film.*
Past simple ➠ past perfect	*'The audience **walked** out.'*	*He said the audience **had walked** out.*
Past continuous ➠ past perfect continuous	*'They **were playing** Super Mario.'*	*He said they **had been playing** Super Mario.*
Present perfect simple ➠ past perfect simple	*'She **has been playing** basketball for years.'*	*He said she **had been playing** basketball for years.*

Other changes	
today	*that day*
tomorrow	*the next/the following day/the day after*
yesterday	*the previous day/the day before*
this evening/this week/etc.	*that evening/that week/etc.*
here	*there*
now	*then*
this	*that*
I – You – We	*he/she – I – they*
me – us – my	*him/her – them – his/her*
your – our – mine – yours – ours	*my – their – his/hers – mine – theirs*

When does the verb not change in reported speech?

- When the situation in question has not changed and is known to the reporter to still be true we don't need to change the tense of the original statement.
  *'The Sun **rises** in the East'*
  *He said the Sun **rises** in the East.*

- When the reporting verb is in the present tense this also shows that the original statement is still true as we report it.
  *'My head **is killing** me. I'm going to lie down.'*
  'Where's Linda?'
  *'She's lying down. She says her head **is killing** her.'*
- With the Past perfect tense and some modal verbs there are no further changes which can be made to the verb. (See Advanced grammar points page 110.)

Questions in reported speech

The changes to tenses and time references etc. for reporting questions are the same as for reporting statements.

- *Wh-* questions
  To report questions which begin with *wh-* words (*where*, *who* etc.), we always use the pattern subject-verb, not verb-subject.

*'Where **are you going**?'*	*He asked me **where I was going**.* ~~*He asked me where was I going.*~~
*'What **have you done**?'*	*He asked me **what I had done**.* ~~*He asked me what had I done.*~~

- *Yes / No* questions
  If the answer to a question is *yes / no* we use *if* or *whether* to report the question.

***'Have you seen** that new advert?'*	*He asked me **if I had seen** that new advert.* ~~*He asked me had I seen that new advert.*~~

Commands in reported speech

***'Leave** the room immediately!'*	*He ordered me **to leave** the room immediately.*
***'Don't take** the red file.'*	*He told me **not to take** the red file.*

Reporting alternative suggestions with *if/whether*

'Would you like to go to the cinema or the theatre?'
*He asked me **if** I would like to go to the cinema or the theatre.*
'Shall we stay in or eat out?'
*She asked me **whether** we should stay in or eat out.*

Advanced grammar points

Grammar point 1

Read the monologue below, then match each verb in bold to the form you would use when reporting what was said. Some verbs can be matched with more than one form.

'You (1) **can** borrow the car for the whole weekend, but you (2) **mustn't** drive it if you've had a drink. Well, of course, you're a sensible person, so you (3) **must** know that anyway. You (4) **needn't** put any petrol in now, as I've just filled it up, but I hope you (5) **will** replace what you've used. Oh, and perhaps you (6) **should** check the tyres, as I haven't done it for a while – they (7) **may** need some air in them. It (8) **might** be a little bit hard to start in the morning if the weather's cold, but it usually isn't a problem.'

a could	**b** didn't have to	**c** didn't need to	**d** might	**e** was not to
f would	**g** would be able to	**h** wouldn't have to	**i** no change	

Many modal verbs do not change when they are reported. Those that can change are:

- *can* changes to *could* or *would be able to.*
- *will* changes to *would.*
- *needn't* changes to *didn't need to* or *didn't have to* or *wouldn't have to.*
- *must* changes to *had to* or *was/were to* when it is used to express an obligation placed on someone by another person, to *had to* when it is used to express an obligation placed on oneself, but does not change when it is used to make assumptions. e.g.
  'You must go now.' ➠ *She said I **had to/was to** leave immediately.*
  'I must go and see my mother.' ➠ *He told me he **had to** go and see his mother.*
  'She must be rich.' ➠ *He assumed she **must** be rich.*
- *mustn't* changes to *was/were not to.*
- *may* changes to *might* (or *could* if it is used to express permission). e.g.
  'I may come to the party.' ➠ *He said he **might** come to the party.*
  'You may smoke here.' ➠ *They told us we **could** smoke here.*

Practice A

Complete the reporting sentences below, making any necessary grammatical changes.

1 'You may go home early since you're not feeling well.'
Her boss said she ....

2 'I'll be there by six thirty.'
He said he ....

3 'You needn't help with my homework today, Mum. I can manage it on my own.'
The child told his mother ....

4 'You should have taken the second turning on the right, not the first.'
He explained to us that ....

5 'And you must be Daphne's daughter – you look just like she did at the same age.'
I assumed that the girl in the white dress ....

6 'I may join you for a drink after dinner but I must go and visit my sister in hospital first.'
He said he ....

7 'You mustn't write on the question sheet.'
The examiner told them they ....

Practice B

Read the whole text below then rewrite the sections in bold in direct speech.

Tonight Fox television network is screening just the kind of exploitative and voyeuristic reality show that Fox personnel (1) **vowed would never happen again** after last year's controversial *Who Wants to Marry A Millionaire. Temptation Island* takes reality television to a new level. Four couples have been flown to an island where they will be confronted by a team of 26 attractive creatures of both sexes who attempt to test their commitment to each other. A Fox executive (2) **explained that viewers could vote people off the programme, if they thought they constituted temptations.**

Already church and family groups have attacked the programme. A Texas rabbi (3) **has asked his local affiliate station not to show it** and a spokesman for the Parents' Television Council (4) **said the producers of Temptation Island should be ashamed of themselves for trying to force the destruction of four relationships for entertainment purposes.** However, the chairman of Fox Television Entertainment Group (5) **countered that viewers would see that the show was not immoral but was exploring the dynamics of serious relationships.**

1 Fox personnel: '..'
2 Fox executive: '..'
3 Texas rabbi: '..'
4 Spokesman: '..'
5 Fox chairman: '..'

Use your English

1 Work with a partner. Take turns to tell your partner your answers to these questions.
Have you watched any TV reality shows?
Did you enjoy them? If so, why? If not, why not?
What do you think about the show *Temptation Island* described in the text above?

2 Report what your partner said to the rest of the class, making appropriate tense changes when necessary.

Model

Maria told me that she doesn't usually watch reality shows, but she has seen a couple of episodes of *Big Brother.* She found them fascinating in a way, but she wouldn't like to be involved in it herself. She said she thought *Temptation Island* sounded rather silly but that she didn't think the couples were being exploited as presumably they had chosen to take part in the programme.

Grammar point 2

Focus

The two statements below are reported in four different ways. One of these reports is grammatically incorrect. Which one?

> 'Everyone agrees that a new leisure centre will benefit the people of the town and create an important source of income for the city', a spokesman for the Town Council said.

> 'Mandy is upset about the negative publicity around her divorce and is taking a holiday. People are saying she is staying with Frank Jordan on his Caribbean island, but I cannot confirm this', her press agent said today.

1 It is accepted that a new leisure centre will benefit the residents and create income for the city.

2 A new leisure centre is accepted to benefit the residents and create income for the city.

3 Recently-divorced pop star Mandy Bloom is rumoured to be holidaying with millionaire Frank Jordan on his Caribbean island.

4 It is rumoured that recently-divorced pop star Mandy Bloom is holidaying with millionaire Frank Jordan on his Caribbean island.

A number of verbs can be used to make impersonal reports or to report the views of a number of people. They can follow two grammatical patterns:

- *It* + verb in the passive + *that* clause
  ***It is** widely **believed that** watching too much TV is bad for the eyes.*
  ***It has been announced that** a new leisure centre will be built in the town.*

- subject + verb in the passive + infinitive clause
  ***Watching too much TV is believed to be** bad for the eyes.*

Some verbs may be used in both grammatical patterns. These include – *agree, be reputed, believe, claim, estimate, feel, know, predict, report, rumour, say, think, understand.*

Others may be used only with *that* clauses. These include – *accept, announce, argue, decide, hope, learn, recommend, suggest.*

Practice C

1 Each of the sentences below could be reported in a variety of ways. Work with a partner. Choose an appropriate reporting verb from the lists in Grammar point 2 and rewrite each sentence below once only, making any necessary grammatical changes. Follow the example.

Example: Medical personnel say that is unwise to drive after taking this medicine.
You write: *It is recommended/suggested that you do not drive after taking this medicine.*

a Before Columbus' historic voyage, many people said the Earth was flat.
b An international group of scientists say that sea levels could rise by 88cm by 2100.
c Apparently he's very rich and owns a yacht; at least that's what I've heard.
d No-one's sure, but a lot of people seem to think that her next album will be a solo one.
e You're not the only one who thinks Internet charges are too high – we all hope they'll come down.
f The exact figures for the film's production costs are not out yet, but it is said they are in the region of £5 million.

2 Now compare your ideas with those of other pairs in the class. Whose versions of the rewritten sentences do you like best, and why?

Practice D

Complete the second sentence so that it has a similar meaning to the first sentence, using the word given. Do not change the word given. You must use between three and eight words, including the word given.

1 From what we've been told, the victim has left hospital and is recovering rapidly.
understood
The victim .... recovering rapidly.

2 Several people say she's not going to make any more films
rumoured.
The star .... any more films.

3 Sources within the company say that the chairman will resign.
believed
It .... resignation.

4 Many teachers say you should spend at least two years preparing for the Proficiency exam.
recommended
It .... less than two years preparing for the Proficiency exam.

5 The latest reports indicate that about 100 people have survived the fire and have been treated for shock.
reported
The 100 or so .... been treated for shock.

Practice E

Complete each gap in the text below with one word only. Follow the example.

If intelligent life forms from another galaxy were shown samples of the world's media in preparation **(0)** ..*for*.. a visit to our planet they might **(1)** .... assume that the male of our species usually outlives the female or that **(2)** .... majority of women are put down **(3)** .... they reach the age of forty. This conclusion, **(4)** .... erroneous, would not be surprising, for photographs of women over forty rarely appear in newspapers, very **(5)** .... television presenters over forty are female, and parts for mature actresses are few and far **(6)** .... Actresses and entertainers **(7)** .... have survived the watershed age of forty, such **(8)** .... Madonna or Michelle Pfeiffer, are said to **(9)** .... 'inspirational', yet the fact **(10)** .... that they look a **(11)** .... ten years younger than they really are. What would really inspire most 40-plus women would be images in **(12)** .... media of 'normal' older women, wrinkles and **(13)** ...., just as TV, magazines, films and newspapers have no **(14)** .... about showing us older men **(15)** .... their grey hairs and expanding waistlines.

Vocabulary

Phrasal verbs and set phrases: leisure

1 The text below contains phrasal verbs or set phrases related in some way to leisure, or which include words related to the topic of leisure. Match each phrase or phrasal verb in bold to a definition.

I (1) **took up** amateur dramatics by chance really. After my divorce I no longer (2) **kept up with** my old friends and my mother, worried perhaps that I might (3) **take to** drink or gambling for solace, suggested that I join the local drama group as a way of (4) **taking my mind off** my problems. I've never really enjoyed organised group activities – as a child the only reason I (5) **took part in** team sports was that we were obliged to do so by the school – so her idea didn't really appeal to me, but I (6) **played along** for a while, promising to go to their weekly meetings, but not actually doing so. Then she discovered that a professional theatre company was going to (7) **team up with** the local group to (8) **put on** an outdoor performance of Shakespeare's *Richard III* in the summer. She (9) **played on** my interest in the history of that time and (10) **played up** the fact that I'd enjoyed studying Shakespeare at school and suggested that I audition for a part. When I objected that I had no acting experience, she reminded me how I used to make her laugh by (11) **sending up** the advertisements on TV and insisted that all I had to do was go along to the audition and (12) **play it by ear**. Finally, I was persuaded and, in fact, I (13) **sailed through** the audition and landed a small speaking role. I thoroughly enjoyed everything to do with that performance and since then my career as an amateur actor has really (14) **taken off** – next week I'm playing the male lead in a romantic comedy we're doing at the local theatre.

a begin an activity or habit (often, but not always, a bad, self-destructive or annoying one) ☐
b begin to succeed ☐
c copy in a humorous manner; make fun of by copying ☐
d deal with something as it happens, without any advance plans ☐
e deal with a situation successfully and easily ☐
f exaggerate or make something seem more important than it really is ☐
g make use of someone's feelings for a specific purpose ☐
h participate in ☐
i organise, perform or produce ☐
j pretend to agree ☐
k start a new hobby ☐
l stay in contact with ☐
m stop worrying about ☐
n work together with ☐

2 Which phrasal verb in the text:

1 can also be used to mean 'make sure you are informed about' and could collocate with the phrases 'the news' or 'current events'?

2 can also be used with a pronoun between the verb and adverb, in which case it means 'keep someone waiting for an answer or decision'?

3 can also be used intransitively to mean 'misbehave'?

3 The phrasal verb below has the opposite meaning to a phrasal verb in the text. Find the verb in the text.

play down ≠ ....

4 Rephrase the parts of these sentences in bold by using phrasal verbs from this unit. Add appropriate nouns, noun phrases or pronouns if necessary.

1 A: How's work going?
B: Well, it's not great at the moment. When I started my boss was really nice, but recently he's **started** doing something I don't like much.
A: What's that?
B: Well, there have been quite a few redundancies in our department and now he's **using** people's fear of being laid off in order to make us work longer hours.

2 I was dreading my Proficiency interview, but the examiners were so friendly that **the time passed quickly and I think I did quite well**.

3 Sam has **started** playing squash after work as he says it helps him to relax and **forget about** office politics.

4 Sylvia's still not heard whether she's got the job yet – they've been **keeping her waiting** for six weeks now.

5 It has been suggested that game shows with big money prizes **become successful** when the economy is doing badly.

6 I don't want to **make my grandmother's senility seem worse than it really is**, but she does live in the past a lot of the time. So if she tells you she was out dancing last night, or that Winston Churchill is the Prime Minister, could you just **pretend to believe her**?

7 A local charity is **getting together with** students from the drama college to **organise** an unusual fund-raising cabaret. The students who **participate in** the cabaret will be given a topic drawn at random from a hat, for example to **copy and make fun of** a famous politician. As they won't know the topics in advance, the students will have to **make up what they say as they go along**. It remains to be seen if the results will be humorous or disastrous.

Reporting verbs

Reporting verbs may be followed by a variety of grammatical structures. The four basic types are listed below. Several verbs may take more than one form of complementation, with slight changes in meaning or emphasis. Some may take all four, as below:

Don't drink and drive — it's really dangerous.

- *I warned him about/against drinking and driving.* [+ preposition + -ing form]
- *I warned him not to drink and drive.* [someone + infinitive]
- *I warned him that it was dangerous to drink and drive.* [+ that clause]
- *I warned him that he shouldn't drink and drive.* [+ that + should]

5 Put each verb in the correct part of the chart below. Follow the examples.

acknowledge advise (against) agree beg boast (of/about) complain (of/about) confirm demand emphasise forbid imply insist (on) instruct invite offer persuade propose promise remind reply respond suggest talk about vow

(+ preposition) + -ing	(someone) + infinitive	+ that clause	+ that + should
acknowledge, ...	advise, ...	acknowledge, advise, ...	advise, ...
advise against, ...	....	....	....
....	....	....	....
....	....	....	....
....	....	....	....

6 Circle the more appropriate verb form to fill each gap below. If both are equally suitable, circle both.

1 He boasted .... the most expensive car in town.
a to have **b** of having **c** both

2 Her mother forbade .... out with such a scruffy-looking boy.
a her to go **b** that she should **c** both

3 He promised .... so selfish again.
a that he wouldn't be **b** not to be **c** both

4 I thought she was implying .... incompetent when she said that to me.
a me to be **b** that I was **c** both

5 Her boss insisted .... on that new project though she was reluctant to do so in the beginning.
a on her taking **b** that she take **c** both

6 We were talking about .... to France on holiday but in the end we never did.
a that we should go **b** going **c** both

7 My bank manager advised me .... involved in such a financially risky venture.
a against getting **b** not to get **c** both

8 The staff are demanding .... for working extra hours.
a to be compensated **b** being compensated **c** both

Study tip

There is a great variety of reporting verbs in English and it is not possible to list them all here. When you come across a new reporting verb, it is a good idea to look it up at home in a good English-English dictionary. This will not only explain the meaning of the word but will also show you the grammatical structures it can be used with and give examples of its use, for example:

swear
SERIOUS PROMISE [transitive] to make a very serious promise: **swear to do sth**: Mona swore never to return home. | **swear (that)**: Victor swore he would get his revenge.

7 Work with a partner. Together, write three sentences in direct speech on a piece of paper. Each sentence should be able to be reported using one of the verbs in exercise 5 and/or verbs in the Vocabulary section of Unit 2 (verbs followed by *-ing* clauses, page 38). When you are ready, exchange your paper with that of another pair. Rewrite the sentences from the other pair in reported speech, then return the papers for comments and correction.

Word formation: revision

8 Complete the gaps in the text with a word formed from the word given in the margin. The first one has been done as an example. All the words you need to write are formed in ways you have studied already in Units 1 to 6. They could include:

- noun suffixes: *-ance/-ence, -cy, -dom, -hood, -ity, -ment, -ness, -tion, -ure*
- negative prefixes: *anti-, dis-, im-, in-, un-, mal-, mis-*
- adjectives ending in *-ful, -ic, -ial* and *-ical* and their related adverbial forms
- prefixes *over-*, *under-* and *out-*

The belief that play has a serious purpose – that of acquiring skills and experience needed in **(0)** ...adulthood... – is an old one. Modern	ADULT
science supports this belief. One of the most important messages to emerge from **(1)** .... research is that individuals are active agents	BIOLOGY
in their own development – seeking out and acquiring experiences, sensations and skills that they will need later in life.	
However, studies show that nowadays many British parents **(2)**	PROTECT
their offspring and opportunities for **(3)** .... play have been	STRUCTURE
replaced by television, computer games or organised physical activities such as swimming or ballet classes. Once-normal activities such as roaming	
about **(4)** .... with friends, or even simply walking alone to and	DOOR
from school, are becoming increasingly rare. In addition, many parents put too much emphasis on **(5)** .... achievement, pressuring their	ACADEMY
children to become literate and numerate at the earliest possible age. In their ambition or anxiety, parents **(6)** .... the importance of the	ESTIMATE
seemingly pointless activities of childhood and thus risk damaging their children **(7)** .... Without the right formative experiences, some	PSYCHOLOGY
may find it hard to cope with conflict or may become **(8)** .... In	SOCIETY
the long term this could result in poorer **(9)** .... later in life, as well	ATTAIN
as personal unhappiness and **(10)**	SATISFY

Gapped sentences

9 Think of **one** word which can be used to complete all three sentences in each group below. Follow the example.

- The young man devoted his life to the *pursuit* of pleasure.
- I have to admit that hill walking is a *pursuit* which doesn't interest me at all.
- The flustered mother ran out of the supermarket in hot *pursuit* of her absconding toddler.

All the words in this section form part of an idiom or set phrase which is based on leisure activities.

1
- I've made my final offer, so the .... is in their court now – we'll see if they accept it or not.
- Sally suggested that they get together and discuss the problem face-to-face, but Rupert won't play .... and apparently wants to bring in a lawyer instead.
- If everyone's here and ready now, then I think we should get the .... rolling.

2
- I thought she was a friend, but later I discovered she was .... under false colours and was just using me to enlarge her social circle.
- I think you're .... a bit close to the wind by spending so much time online at work.
- Mary was terribly anxious about her driving test but in fact she found it plain .... and passed at the first attempt.

3
- The management are playing their .... close to their chest when it comes to informing us about what will happen after the takeover.
- Judging from the political turmoil in the country, an election could be on the .... soon.
- Tony finally laid his .... on the table and told his parents that he'd dropped out of university.

4
- The situation is complicated as several different factors come into ....
- Much of his humour involves a .... on words.
- Apparently the police do not believe that foul .... was involved in the death of pop star Jason Gordon last week.

5
- He's alleged to have made his fortune by .... in troubled waters after the collapse of communism in Russia.
- Penny's so lacking in confidence that she's forever .... for compliments.
- As usual several reporters were hanging around the bar .... for titbits of gossip.

10 Using a dictionary, check the exact meaning of any of the phrases or idioms that were unfamiliar to you. With a partner, write your own sentences to illustrate the usage and meaning of the new items.

Summary

Reading

1 Skim-read these two texts. In terms of subject-matter, what do they have in common?

Text 1

In April 1999, Americans began queueing outside a Los Angeles cinema for the opening of a new film that would not be premiered for another six weeks. Because of fears about the illicit fortunes to be made from the resale of tickets, the studio had refused to allow advance booking. The early arrivals outside the LA movie theatre hoped to be able to boast that they were present at the first ever screening of *The Phantom Menace*, the fourth of George Lucas' *Star Wars* films. It was clear that a science-fiction film that was originally almost laughed out of Hollywood had moved beyond entertainment and taken on the shape of a faith.

Part of the legend of the film is that the only early viewer to appreciate it was Steven Spielberg. But then, modern cinema's two great money-spinners – Lucas and Spielberg – are both regressives, producing what in effect are big-budget children's movies with enough visual panache and sub-spiritual mumbo-jumbo that adults find them entertaining as well. The plot of *Star Wars* draws heavily from fairytale and nods to Tolkien in the large quantities of furry creatures featured. In addition, examination of box-office history reveals that a high percentage of the most famous movies of all time share one element: their central characters are either wholly or partially removed from the soil on which the cinemas stand. If Hollywood is indeed a dream factory, then the most popular reverie it sells seems to be the one about in some way leaving Earth.

Text 2

It is, perhaps, no surprise that the most successful cinematic franchise of all time originated in the Seventies. For there is increasing evidence in our current culture that the generation that grew up in that decade is becoming tyrannically nostalgic, engineering the return of their formative obsessions to stage, screen and record store, and imposing their infatuations on a new generation.

However, parental nostalgia alone cannot explain the continuing popularity of the *Star Wars* series of films. Perhaps it seemed much more obvious in the Nineties than it did in the Seventies that at the heart of the *Star Wars* films is the story of a boy whose father has left him. Luke Skywalker has an absentee dad who is eventually shown to have betrayed the family in a terrible way by defecting to the enemy and becoming the evil Darth Vader. Luke's journey is to redeem his relationship with his father, and he is helped in this by a series of father-figures. By coincidence, a novel published soon after the appearance of *The Phantom Menace* explored the possibility that the films are marital parables. In the novel, children of the current pre-teen generation obsessively watch *Star Wars* videos as they are shunted between the separate homes of their mummies and daddies, clutching plastic Jedi light-sabres and other tie-in merchandise. Crucially, not only do they identify with Luke, but a love of these celluloid fantasies gives them a bond with their parents, who share this language with them.

Skills development: Rephrasing the four content points

2 Read the rubric below, but do not write a summary.

Summarise, in your own words as far as possible, the reasons for the enduring popularity and success of the Star Wars series of films.

3 Work with a partner and decide what the four content points are. Then check your ideas with the rest of the class and your teacher.

4 The key sentence for Point 1 is written out below in sections. Two of these sections are redundant, that is they include information which is not essential. Which ones?

1 big-budget
2 children's movies
3 with enough visual panache and sub-spiritual mumbo-jumbo
4 that adults find them entertaining as well

5 Rephrase point 4, then complete the two possible versions of the summary sentence below.

They are .... which adults .... as well. (9 words in total)
The films .... both adults and children. (8 words in total)

6 The key sentence for Point 2 is written out below in sections. Again two of these sections are redundant. Which ones?

1 Examination of box-office history reveals that
2 a high percentage of
3 the most famous movies
4 of all time
5 share one element
6 their central characters are
7 either wholly or partially
8 removed from the soil on which the cinemas stand.

7 Substitute the words below for all or part of the remaining sections in exercise 6 and rewrite the resulting summary sentence.

best-known	ever	extraterrestrials	Like	main	many

Like ...., ... (12 words in total)

8 In the case of Points 3 and 4, the main ideas are already succinctly presented, so you will need to rephrase them with reference to other parts of Text 2.

... not only do they identify with Luke, but a love of these celluloid fantasies gives them a bond with their parents, who share this language with them.

1 Who are 'they'? Look earlier in paragraph 2 for whom this refers to, then rephrase the information in your own words.
2 Why do they identify with Luke? Look earlier in paragraph 2 for the reasons. Can you think of any short synonyms for children whose fathers who have left them, or whose parents live in separate homes? Can you think of a synonym for 'identify with'?
3 Rephrase 'celluloid fantasies'.
4 Remember that the summary rubric states 'in your own words, as far as possible'. Some words, like 'bond' do not have synonyms that keep the full meaning of the word. If it is not possible to find a good synonym, leave the word as it is!
5 'share this language' is used in a metaphorical sense. Look at paragraph 1 for what this means, and rephrase the idea in your own words.

9 Combine your answers to questions 1 – 5 in exercise 8 above into one or two sentences, totalling not more than 40 words.

8 The Arts and architecture

Grammar • Determiners and pronouns

Vocabulary • Verbs used with reflexive pronouns
• Set phrases including determiners
• Word formation: more noun suffixes

Summary • Practice

Grammar: Determiners and pronouns

Grammar overview

this, that, these* and *those	
• We use *this* and *these* to refer to things which are close to us in time or distance and *that* and *those* for things which are further away. • We use *these* and *those* as determiners. ***Those** faults are soon to be remedied.*	• We use *this* and *that* as pronouns to refer back to an idea or ideas which have already been mentioned. *He grew up in a household of artists. **That** is why he is so creative.* *Museums have had their funding slashed, curators are underpaid and new exhibitions are rarely mounted. **This** is the sorry state many institutes are in today.*
***It* for reference**	
• We can use *it* to refer back to a previously mentioned idea. *The thieves' plan was to hide the diamonds in their shoes but **it** didn't work.*	• Or to refer forward in the sentence. ***It** is not unusual **to see famous painters and writers in this café**.* ***It**'s not often **that we have good weather in the summer**.*
***It* as a 'dummy' subject**	
Sometimes *it* doesn't refer back to a previous idea but is used as what is called a 'dummy subject'. This structure is often used to describe things.	***It**'s very hot today.* ***It**'s raining again.* ***It**'s almost midnight.* ***It** smells funny in here.*
much, many, a lot of, a few* and *a little	
We use *much, a lot of* and *a little* with uncountable nouns. We use *many, a lot of* and *a few* with countable nouns. We usually use *much* and *many* in negative statements and questions.	*We don't have **much** time.* *Are there **many** paintings by Klee in the exhibition?* ▶ *A lot of* is more common in informal English. *We haven't got **a lot of** time.*
each* and *every	
• *Each* and *every* are used with a verb in the singular and a noun in the singular and are usually interchangeable. ***Each** / **Every** child was given a present.* • *Each* as a pronoun. *The students were discussing the same subject but **each** had a different point of view.* • *Each* with *of*. ***Each of** the drawings is unique.*	• *Each* for emphasis. *Peter and Kate **each** carried their money separately for fear of being robbed.* • *Every* for emphasis. *You had **every** right to speak your mind.* *I had **every** reason to believe he was lying.* • *Every* after possessives for emphasis. *The secret police were watching the spy's **every** move.*

one(s), another, other(s)	
• *One* and *ones* can replace countable nouns. *Which* ***one*** *do you like?* *Could I have the red* ***ones****, please?* • *One* + *of* (with a singular verb). ***One of*** *the first people I met there was Michael.* ***One of us*** *is going to have to leave.* • *Another* can mean 'a different one' or 'the same again'. *I don't like this book – will you give me* ***another****?* *Shall we have* ***another*** *drink?* *Give me* ***another*** *of those paper clips.*	• *Other* can be used as a determiner or a pronoun. *Where's my* ***other*** *sock?* *Here's one of the books; have you got the* ***other****?* • *Others* can only be used as a pronoun. *I've only seen the first episode. I can't wait to see the* ***others****.* • Sometimes *the others* means 'people'. *Did you come alone? Where are* ***the others****?*
all **and** ***both***	
• *All* and *both* can be used as determiners or pronouns. ***All*** *the spectators cheered wildly.* *She talks* ***all*** *the time.* *Where are the chocolates? Have you finished them* ***all****?*	***All*** *of them came.* ***Both*** *sisters enjoy cycling.* ***Both*** *of us agree that this is the right decision.* *I took two books out of the library and read them* ***both****.*
neither **and** ***either***	
• *Neither* and *either* are followed by a verb in the singular. ***Neither*** *painting appeals to me.* ***Neither*** *of us knew the answer.* ***Neither*** *Chris nor his sister reads a great deal.*	***Either*** *of the plans suits me.* ***Either*** *colour can be used for the walls and ceiling.* *Don't ask for my opinion; I don't like* ***either****.* ▶ A plural verb is often used in spoken English.
no **and** ***none***	
• *No* and *none* are used with singular, plural and uncountable nouns and with a singular verb. ***No*** *progress* ***has*** *been made.* ***No*** *politician* ***dares*** *to speak out on this issue.* ***None*** *of the songs* ***was*** *any good.* *Half a bar of chocolate* ***is*** *better than* ***none****!*	▶ In informal English, a plural verb may be used. ***None*** *of my friends* ***have*** *been to see me.*

Advanced grammar points

Grammar point 1

1 The words in bold in five of the sentences below are grammatically incorrect. Which ones?

- **a** Did you hear that awful noise that **any** street musicians were making outside the office this morning?
- **b** Would you like to listen to **any** new cassettes I've recorded?
- **c** She refuses on principle to lend **anyone** money.
- **d** **Some** authors are exceedingly wealthy, but the majority struggle to make ends meet.
- **e** Have you got **some** tickets left for the concert on Saturday night?
- **f** I'd be grateful for **some** help you could give me.
- **g** If **someone** phones when I'm out, could you take a message please?
- **h** **Some** five per cent of adults are severely tone deaf.
- **i** That was **some** performance!

2 Correct the sentences which contain errors and explain the reasons for your choices.

Any and the related pronouns *anyone*, *anybody* and *anything* are used:

- in positive sentences to refer to each one or all members of a group, saying it does not matter which.
  The charity appreciates donations of ***any*** *books or clothes.*
- in general questions.
  Did you see ***anyone*** *we know at the theatre last night?*
- in negative sentences and following verbs or adjectives which are implicitly negative.
  She is reluctant to watch/doesn't enjoy/hates ***any*** *films which have been dubbed.*
- in conditional clauses.
  If you have ***any*** *free time on Friday, drop in and see me at the gallery.*

Some and the related pronouns *someone*, *somebody* and *something* are used:

- to refer to a number of people or things or an amount of something but not all.
  I find it hard to believe that ***some*** *people actually like rap music.*
- to refer to a person or thing, when you do not know or say exactly which.
  Something *tells me this is going to be my lucky day.*
- in questions which are requests or offers, or which expect the answer '*Yes*'.
  Would you like ***something*** *else to eat?*
- *some* can also be used to say that something was very good or very impressive.
  That was ***some*** *dinner you cooked for us last night!*
- *some* can also be used as an adverb before a numeral to mean 'approximately'.
  Despite the rain, ***some*** *two thousand people turned up for the open-air concert.*

Grammar point 2

Match the beginnings of the sentences (1 – 4) to the endings (a – d) which would logically complete them.

1 Few people appreciated
2 A few people appreciated
3 Little of the money raised by the charity
4 A little of the money raised by the charity

a reached the people it was intended to help.
b the poetry reading, but the majority left during the interval.
c went on administration, but most of it was spent on blankets and food supplies.
d the work of Van Gogh during his lifetime.

- *A few* (used with countable nouns) and *a little* (used with uncountable nouns) mean a small quantity or number of something.
- *Few* and *little* used without '*a*' mean a quantity or number that is less than expected or less than desirable.

Practice A

Circle (an) appropriate word(s) to fill each gap below. In some cases, more than one word may be suitable.

A: Have you read (1) .... good books lately? I'm looking for (2) .... to take with me on holiday, but (3) .... new authors really appeal to me these days.
B: Well, I always enjoy (4) .... by Ian Rankin as a holiday read, but maybe you're not keen on crime novels.

1	**a** some	**b** any	**c** a few
2	**a** something	**b** anything	**c** a few
3	**a** some	**b** a few	**c** few
4	**a** any	**b** anything	**c** something

A: What did you think of the end-of-term show at the art college this year?
B: Well, (5) .... of the sculptures were quite original, I thought, but I didn't think much of (6) .... of the paintings. It seems to me that they take (7) .... care to teach them the fundamentals of painting or drawing these days. (8) ...., even a child of five, could have produced most of the pictures they had on show.

5	**a** some	**b** a few	**c** any
6	**a** some	**b** any	**c** a few
7	**a** some	**b** little	**c** a little
8	**a** Someone	**b** Anyone	**c** Anybody

A: Would you like (9) .... more cake?
B: Yes, please. It's really good. Did you make it yourself?
A: Yes, I did. I got the recipe from (10)........... website. I don't remember exactly which, but there are quite (11) .... where you can get food tips and recipes.
B: Really? That sounds useful. Could you give me (12) .... addresses? I can never think of (13) .... new to cook.

9	**a** a little	**b** any	**c** some
10	**a** one	**b** any	**c** some
11	**a** some	**b** a few	**c** few
12	**a** some	**b** any	**c** a few
13	**a** a little	**b** something	**c** anything

Practice B

Work with a partner and rewrite the second sentence in each pair of sentences below so that the meaning is similar. Then compare your ideas with the rest of the class and decide which are the best solutions.

1 **a** My mother isn't keen on abstract art and my father doesn't like it either.
b Neither ....

2 **a** Ten actors auditioned for the part but the director felt that none of them was really suitable.
b The director felt that every ....

3 **a** Although she only ever made two films, each of them is considered to be a classic.
b Both ....

4 **a** I don't mind which play we go to – both of the ones you've suggested sound quite appealing.
b Either ....

5 **a** All the writers shortlisted for the prize are women.
b Each ....

Practice C

Complete the gaps in the text with one word only. All the words you need to write are either determiners or pronouns. The first one has been done as an example. (0)

In the 1980s, architects Richard Rogers and Norman Foster rescued the reputation of their profession in Britain. Nowadays **(0)** ..*these*... two men are responsible for more than half of the landmark buildings currently under way. No **(1)** .... firms of architects come close to matching **(2)** .... extraordinary range of new building projects – from bridges and art galleries to airports and corporate headquarters. Although several commercial practices specialise in office blocks and shopping malls, these companies have **(3)** .... of the scope, invention or cultural drive of the two most influential firms British architecture has ever known.

Their dominance is **(4)** .... new. Nearly 15 years ago the Royal Academy included their work in a glamorous show of the most influential British architects of the time. Foster was represented by the headquarters of the Hongkong and Shanghai Bank in Hong Kong and Rogers by the Lloyd's Building in the City of London. These buildings were as distinctive then as they are now: **(5)** .... was controversial and has since been acclaimed a masterpiece. **(6)** .... proved that, at the time, Foster and Rogers could produce more inventive and memorable buildings than almost **(7)** .... else.

In some ways **(8)** .... Foster and Rogers are outsiders from the middle class mainstream of British architects, who tend to find it hard to let go and let their imaginations rip. And, unlike such architects, **(9)** .... of them ever made a distinction between cultural and commercial architecture. Lloyd's and the Hongkong Bank linked their fortunes to **(10)** .... of mega-finance and they have not looked back since. Yet even if Foster and Rogers were merely efficient, businesslike architects these factors would not be enough to explain their dominance of the architectural top twenty. What matters is that they have created – consistently, convincingly and with only a **(11)** .... mistakes along the way – **(12)** .... of the most exciting, memorable and enjoyable buildings of the past 20 years.

Vocabulary

Verbs used with reflexive pronouns

1 Many verbs may be followed by reflexive pronouns. They can be divided into three categories, as below.

- Verbs which are used only with reflexive pronouns.
  My sister ***prides herself on*** *her accurate use of English.*
- Verbs which may be used with a reflexive pronoun or with another structure, with very little change in meaning.
  Some children seem unable to ***amuse themselves*** *for even half an hour.*
  The children love Uncle Bob because he always ***amuses*** *them with jokes and conjuring tricks.*
- Verbs which may be used with a reflexive pronoun or with another structure, with a complete change in meaning.
  The panel agreed that it was the third candidate who ***deported herself*** *best at the interview.*
  The government has ***deported*** *more than three hundred illegal immigrants this year.*

2 Put the verbs below in the correct part of the chart. If necessary, use a dictionary to help you. The first two have been done as examples.

abandon absent (from) acquit apply avail (of) cloister comport contain count deceive deny distinguish enjoy force forget ingratiate (with) justify pace perjure resign (to) steel suit support treat

Only with a reflexive pronoun	With or without reflexive pronoun; little change in meaning	With or without reflexive pronoun; complete change in meaning
absent (from), ...	....	abandon, ...
....	....	....
....	....	....
....	....	....

3 Work with a partner and think of at least one extra verb to add to each column of the chart. Share your ideas with the rest of the class, and add their suggestions to the chart.

4 Complete the second sentence so that it has a similar meaning to the first sentence, using the word given. Do not change the word given. You must use between three and eight words, including the word given.

1 We were surprised that John didn't turn up at the meeting as agreed.
from
To our surprise, ... meeting.

2 As a child, I tried to win the favour of my teacher by taking her flowers.
ingratiate
As a child, I used gifts of flowers to try .... teacher.

3 She has finally accepted the fact that her novel will never be a best-seller.
resigned
At last she .... sales of her novel.

4 Their tutor couldn't understand why, with so many reference resources available, the students hadn't chosen to consult any of them.
themselves
Their tutor couldn't understand .... any reference resources.

5 The witness lied in court in an attempt to help his friend.
himself
The witness .... would help his friend.

6 One of the best cures for depression is to find an activity which absorbs all of your attention.
lose
Finding an activity .... be one of the best cures for depression.

Set phrases including determiners

5 A number of set phrases which include determiners exist in spoken English. Some of these are listed below. Work with a partner and try to work out where each phrase would be used in the conversations and the extract from a book review below. Use each phrase only once.

a all the more
b all the same
c all too often
d at any rate
e by all means
f by any chance
g every bit as
h every once in a while
i in any case
j much as
k on the whole
l second to none

A: Aren't you enjoying the play?

B: Well, **(1)** .... I think it's pretty disappointing. The plot's weak and a lot of the dialogue is wooden. The writer should have stuck to what he's good at and not tried experimenting with a futuristic theme.

A: Yes, I see what you mean. **(2)** ...., I admire him for trying something different. It's easy to keep on producing the same sort of light comedy that goes down well with the public.

B: That's true I suppose. Well, the male lead's very good, **(3)** ...., so that makes up a bit for the rest of it.

C: Are you going into town this evening **(4)** ....?

D: Yes, why?

C: Well, I'm going to a recital at the Guildhall, but my car's broken down, and I wondered if you could give me a lift.

D: **(5)** ...., I'd be happy to. I'm going to visit my mother at the hospital and I go past the door of the Guildhall **(6)** .... Who's giving the recital?

C: A young opera singer called Maria Romanescu – she's not very well-known yet but I think she's **(7)** .... when it comes to singing Verdi.

D: Oh, that sounds wonderful. I adore Verdi's music.

C: Well, why don't you join me? I'd enjoy your company.

D: Thanks, but **(8)** .... I'd love to, I don't want to disappoint my mother.

(9) ...., the authors of successful first novels find it difficult to live up to the precedent they have set. Some fail to get a second book published at all; others find their second work goes largely unnoticed by the critics and the buying public. **(10)** ...., however, an author manages to produce a second novel which is **(11)** .... refreshing and enjoyable as her first. This is the case with Beryl Samson, winner of the 2001 Goldberg Prize for Literature, whose second novel *Twilight Tonality* has just been published to great critical acclaim. Ms Samson's achievement is **(12)** .... impressive when you consider that she is now in her late sixties and did not start writing until after she had retired.

6 Now match each phrase in exercise 5 to a phrase in the list below which could be substituted for it.

1 anyway ....
2 at least ....
3 certainly ....
4 even more ....
5 even though ....
6 in general ....
7 just as ....
8 nevertheless ....
9 occasionally ....
10 perhaps ....
11 the best there is ....
12 unfortunately very frequently ....

Word formation: more noun suffixes

7 Put the five noun suffixes below in the correct column of the chart.

-age -ee -er/-or(-itor/-ator) -ist -ship

Abstract concepts	Objects / abstract concepts	People
....	....	....
....	....	....

8 Which two suffixes are added mainly to verbs or verb stems?

9 If these suffixes are added to the same verb, e.g. *employ*, what different meaning does each suffix carry?

10 Put the words below in the correct part of the chart, adding the suffix and making any necessary spelling changes. The first two have been done as examples.

animate block caricature censor citizen coin comment court diary divorce evacuate exhibit foot flute front ideal mile philanthropy piano sentimental spill succeed train vocal

-age	-ee	-er/-or (-itor/-ator)	-ist	-ship
blockage, ...	....	animator, ...	....	....
....	....	....	....	....
....	....	....	....	....
....	....	....	....	....
....	....	....	....	....
....	....	....	....	....
....	....	....	....	....

11 The suffix *-ship* can also be added to nouns which already have a suffix relating to people, for example:

read + er + ship = readership sea + man + ship = seamanship

12 Form nouns with two suffixes based on the words below and add them to the *-ship* column of the chart in exercise 10.

crafts dictate horse lead music relate work

13 Complete the gaps in the text with a word formed from the word given in the margin. All the words you need to write are nouns. The first one has been done as an example.

Until the end of the eighteenth century, most artists worked on the basis of carrying out specific commissions for churches, royal courts or wealthy private **(0)** ...*collectors*..., and thus enjoyed a measure of financial security. This form of **(1)** .... declined in the following century, however, and painters and **(2)** .... were increasingly obliged to try to sell their works on the open market, with their main outlet being large official exhibitions in which their work was displayed along with that of their **(3)** .... This made life hard for many artists, especially for **(4)** .... whose style did not coincide with public taste.	COLLECT PATRON SCULPT COMPETE INNOVATE
Since the second half of the nineteenth century the rise of small commercial galleries under private **(5)** .... has given artists better opportunities to display their work, but nevertheless many artists still go through periods of considerable financial **(6)**	OWN HARD
Recently company **(7)** ...., especially in the form of prizes, has begun to partially fill the gap left by the demise of private patrons. For example, the high-street bank NatWest offers an annual art prize worth a total of £36,000 – including 11 awards of £1,000 to all **(8)**	SPONSOR FINAL
However, unlike **(9)** .... for literature prizes such as the Booker, who usually enjoy increased sales as a spin-off from appearing on the shortlist, artists do not necessarily benefit from the media **(10)** .... generated by winning a prize. One recent winner of the controversial Turner Prize found that galleries did not offer her subsequent exhibitions, as she had hoped, because they felt she was 'too obvious a candidate for invitation'.	NOMINATE COVER

Study tip

Recording new vocabulary effectively is very important, but this alone will not mean that you have learnt it. Most people need to see, hear or use words several times before they remember them. Use these strategies:

- Look through your vocabulary notebook regularly to revise new words.
- It is more helpful to revise for five minutes every day than for five hours before an exam!
- Use new vocabulary you have learnt in compositions you write or during classroom discussions.
- Get together with friends from your class to revise vocabulary by playing word games together, such as the one below or the ones on pages 26 (Unit 1), 40 (Unit 2), 51 and 52 (Unit 3), 96 (Unit 6) or 115 (Unit 7).

Use your English

1 Work in pairs. Each pair chooses one word (a noun, verb, adjective or adverb) from any of the units you have studied so far.

2 Write all the words that have been chosen on the board.

3 Each pair writes a short dialogue or passage which includes all the words on the board. You have a time limit of ten minutes for this.

4 Read out the dialogues and passages and vote for the one you like best.

Gapped sentences

14 Think of **one** word which can be used to complete all three sentences in each group below. Follow the example.

- The young man devoted his life to the *pursuit* of pleasure.
- I have to admit that hill walking is a *pursuit* which doesn't interest me at all.
- The flustered mother ran out of the supermarket in hot *pursuit* of her absconding toddler.

All the words in this section have appeared earlier in this unit, but not necessarily in the same context or in the same grammatical form.

1

- Unfortunately, the first poet's dreary and depressing verses set the .... for the rest of the reading, resulting in a dull and melancholy evening.
- I can't get a dialling ....; are you sure you've got it plugged in?
- The residents' association feels that opening a pub in the street would lower the .... of the neighbourhood.

2

- The government has set up a .... to investigate why so much public money was spent on a building which nobody wants to use.
- The lift is out of .... so we'll have to use the stairs.
- She doesn't get a salary but they give her twenty per cent .... on everything she sells.

3

- Think .... lucky you didn't manage to get tickets for the concert; it was so awful that we left at the interval.
- After so much hard work, you owe it to .... to take a short holiday.
- You have only .... to blame for not being shortlisted; you should have got your entry in on time.

4

- After twenty years touring the provinces as a stand-up comedian, Bill Ryder has at last achieved a .... of success with his own TV show.
- He's been a heavy smoker most of his life, so I imagine his sense of .... must be fairly diminished.
- I turned down his invitation to the concert since Stravinsky's music has never been to my ....

5

- I'm happy to play a few tunes for you if you want, but I'm warning you I'm very out of ....
- There's no reason at all why conductors shouldn't be women but, in ...., very few are.
- Our son's just been invited to join a very distinguished legal .... in London.

15 Using a dictionary, check the exact meaning of any words, set phrases or usages that were unfamiliar to you. With a partner, write your own sentences to illustrate the usage and meaning of the new items.

Summary

Reading

1 Skim-read these two texts. In terms of subject-matter, what do they have in common?

Text 1

Traditionally, photography involved a fair amount of technical expertise – without an ability to focus and a basic understanding of shutter speeds and f-stops, the result were rarely aesthetically pleasing. The advent of the cheap auto-everything camera overcame these technical problems, but has meant that now pictures rarely truly represent what was seen on the scene – faces are carefully framed, colours are bleached by flash and eyes are reduced to red, unblinking pinpricks.

The antidote to this blandness is the Lomo Compact-Automat – a small, automatic camera originally developed by the KGB and produced in St Petersburg. It is a squat hunk of metal which is simple to operate and can be used in low-light situations without the need for a flash. Thanks to its manual focus the camera frequently produces blurred images, but the high-quality lens and automatic exposure allow for the occasional accidental piece of sharp-shot brilliance.

In the early Nineties an Austrian student picked up a Lomo camera in a junk shop in Eastern Europe and took it back to Vienna. He was entranced by the pictures it produced with their profusion of colours and quirky combination of sharp edges and blurs. The Lomo became the object of his friends' and his friends' friends' desires, more cameras were obtained, exhibitions were mounted and a society inaugurated.

In 1994 the Lomo factory decided to discontinue the camera. A Viennese representation went to St Petersburg and offered to promote the Lomo in return for its worldwide distribution rights. As a result the factory recommenced manufacturing the camera, the price increased and a cult was born.

Text 2

The famous French photographer Cartier-Bresson expressed his intention as being 'to record, in a fraction of a second, the emotion of a subject, and the beauty of form'. Lomo users also aim to capture the essence of a subject, but for them this is not done by waiting patiently for Cartier-Bresson's 'decisive moment'. On the contrary, the manifesto of the Lomographic Society encourages Lomographers 'not to think – you don't have to know beforehand what is captured on your film'. To facilitate the taking of spontaneous pictures it further suggests that you should shoot from the hip – looking through the viewfinder is frowned on.

Aficionados of the Lomo camera claim that this results in pictures which look more realistic as the subjects are not aware that they are being photographed and thus do not act up for the lens. As one devotee put it 'Lomography is not about perfection. It's a document of the surface of the world. It's about the capturing of a moment in time as you experience it.'

By following the tenets of Lomography, you will never be sure what's lurking on your film but, for good or bad, you are sure to be surprised by your results. After a day out at the Notting Hill carnival during which I shot off 72 pictures at random on my new Lomo camera, I was delighted to find when I got my films back, that the camera had absorbed all the colour and frantic energy of the carnival in a way which more carefully studied shots with a conventional camera and technique could never have achieved.

Summary section: practice

Questions on the texts

2 In the first and second paragraphs of Text 1, what impression does the writer give of photographs produced by inexpensive fully-automatic cameras?

Reminder: Look back at Unit 4, page 75, for a summary of strategies for dealing with this type of question.

3 What is meant by 'became the object of his friends' and his friends' friends' desires'? (Text 1, line 16)

Reminder: Look back at Unit 3, page 55, for a summary of strategies for dealing with this type of question.

4 What 'results in pictures which look more realistic'? (Text 2, lines 9 – 10)

Reminder: Look back at Unit 2, page 43, for a summary of strategies for dealing with this type of question.

5 Which word in Text 2, paragraph 2 reinforces the idea introduced in the first text that Lomography is 'a cult'?

Reminder: Look back at Unit 1, page 31, for a summary of strategies for dealing with this type of question.

Summary writing

In a paragraph of between 50 and 70 words, summarise, in your own words as far as possible, the appeal of Lomography as opposed to conventional photography.

6 Check that you know what you're being asked to summarise. Re-read the texts, highlighting or underlining all possible content points.

7 Combine any similar points so that you have a resulting list of four content points.

Reminder: Unit 5, page 87 and Unit 6, page 99 have examples of doing this.

8 Rewrite the four content points, as concisely as possible, in your own words.

Reminder: Unit 7, page 119 has examples of strategies for doing this.

9 Travel and tourism

Grammar • Clauses

Vocabulary • Phrasal verbs: travel and transport
• Verb forms and phrasal verbs as connectors
• Word formation: adjectives ending in *-able/-ible, -ous, -less* and *-some*

Summary • Practice

Grammar: Clauses

Grammar overview

Relative clauses	
• If the relative pronoun (*who, which, that, whom*) refers to the subject of the verb which follows it, it may not be omitted. *That is the director* ***who*** *won the Oscar.* *He owns a Picasso* ***which*** *hangs in his bedroom.* • If the relative pronoun refers to the object of the verb it may be omitted. *The holiday (which) I went on was a disaster.* *This is the friend (whom) I was telling you about.* • *Whose* is used for both people and things and cannot be omitted. *That's Anna,* ***whose*** *husband works for Olympic Airways.* *The green house,* ***whose*** *garden backs onto the railway, is for sale.*	• We use *of which* to distinguish between several different things. *There are five restaurants in town,* ***of which*** *only two are worth visiting.* • We can use the relative adverbs *when, where* and *why* to refer to time, place and the reason for something. *That was the day* ***when*** *everything changed.* *Crete is the island* ***where*** *we spent the summer.* *The poor working conditions are* ***why*** *I left my last job.*
Defining and non-defining relative clauses	
• A defining relative clause contains information essential to the understanding of the sentence. Without it, the sentence would be meaningless. *He's the man* ***who lives opposite****.* *Jonathon is someone* ***whom I love dearly****.* '*He's the man.*' or '*Jonathon is someone*', have little meaning if they stand alone. • A non-defining relative clause contains non-essential information which can be omitted without affecting the main meaning of the sentence. The non-essential information appears between two commas. *The island of Skyros,* ***which is packed with tourists all summer****, is becoming increasingly popular.*	• When a preposition is used in the relative clause we can follow these patterns. *'The Doll's House' is the play* ***in which*** *he acted.* *'The Doll's House' is the play (which) he acted* ***in****.* *Here is the gentleman* ***to whom*** *the letter was addressed.* *Here is the gentleman (whom) the letter was addressed* ***to****.*
Clauses of purpose and reason	
so as not to – *I didn't ask for a second helping* ***so as not to*** *seem greedy.* to infinitive – *I came* ***to see*** *if you needed any help.* in order (not) to – *He must spend five years training* ***in order to*** *be able to practise medicine.*	for + -ing – *This gadget is* ***for getting*** *oysters out of their shells.* because of – *I'm leaving* ***because of*** *his unacceptable behaviour.* as, since – *We'll have to use the other phone box* ***as*** *this one's broken.* ***Since*** *it's your last night here why don't we go out for a meal?*

Clauses of result	
therefore – *The manager considered the accident to be his personal responsibility and* ***therefore*** *tendered his resignation.* consequently – *The baggage handlers strike has not yet been resolved and* ***consequently*** *all outgoing flights will be subject to delay.* thus – *Mr Jarrold's visa was found to be invalid and* ***thus*** *he was obliged to return home.*	hence – *Fuel prices are subject to sudden rises,* ***hence*** *airlines may be obliged to pass a small surcharge on to their customers.* as a result – *She contracted malaria while travelling in India and* ***as a result*** *was hospitalised.* in such a way as to/that – *John worded his letter* ***in such a way as to*** *cause the minimum offence.*
Clauses of concession and contrast	
although – *He travelled to France by air* ***although*** *he doesn't enjoy flying.* but – *The family wanted to book a trip to Paris* ***but*** *there were no tickets left.* however – *I made my suggestion,* ***however****, no-one agreed with me.* even though – ***Even though*** *he never gets any exercise he's very fit.* in contrast to – *Girls were discovered to have a concentration span of 15 minutes,* ***in contrast to*** *just 5 minutes for boys.* despite – *The boss approved the project,* ***despite*** *my objections.*	in spite of – ***In spite of*** *her immaculate references, she didn't get the job.* nevertheless – *The sea was pretty rough.* ***Nevertheless****, the captain decided to make the crossing.* all the same – *I don't think you're entirely right;* ***all the same*** *I see your point.* while / whereas – *Shares in the FirstHouse hotel chain have dropped,* ***while*** *FirstHouse restaurant shares are rising.* yet – *He was warned of the danger* ***yet*** *he insisted on continuing.*

Advanced grammar points

Grammar point 1

Focus

All the sentences below are grammatically correct, but the meaning of one is not logical. Which one? What is wrong with it?

1 When he travels on public transport abroad, Alan carries his passport inside his shirt for fear of it being stolen.

2 When he travels on public transport abroad, Alan carries his passport inside his shirt so that it won't be stolen.

3 If he's planning to travel to remote areas of a country, Alan learns some basic phrases in the local language lest he should communicate with the inhabitants.

4 If he's planning to travel to remote areas of a country, Alan learns some basic phrases in the local language in order that he may communicate with the inhabitants.

- These connectors express purpose in any context.
  so that + modal verb + main verb
  in order that + modal verb + main verb
  I'm packing a couple of jumpers ***so that / in order that I won't feel cold*** *in the evenings.*
  I read a history of the island before I went there ***so that / in order that I could really appreciate*** *the sites we were going to visit.*

- These connectors express purpose only in the context of unpleasant consequences which you are hoping to avoid by your actions.
  for fear of + ing form (active or passive)
  I'm packing a couple of jumpers ***for fear of feeling*** *cold in the evenings.*
  For fear of being robbed *by pickpockets, couples travelling together are advised to divide up money and any important documents between them.*

- *lest* + *should* + main verb (active or passive)
  Lest they should be robbed *by pickpockets, couples travelling together are advised to divide up money and any important documents between them.*
  Make sure that you have had all the necessary vaccinations ***lest you should be refused*** *entry at the frontier.*

▶ This structure is mainly used in formal written English.

Practice A

Work with a partner and complete each sentence below using your own ideas. Then compare your answers with the rest of the class.

1 We've chosen a hotel in the centre of the town so that ....
2 I'm carrying my jewellery and my toiletries in my hand luggage for fear of ....
....
3 Campers are prohibited from lighting fires in the forest lest ....
4 I think you should take a high protection factor sun-cream with you in order that
....
5 Travellers planning to trek in the mountains are advised to take a local guide with them lest ....
6 I always take lots of books with me on holiday so that ....

Use your English

What preparations do you usually make before going on holiday?
What purpose do they fulfil?
What precautions do you take when travelling, and why?

Grammar point 2

Focus

What function do all four sentences below express?

a purpose **b** reason **c** result

1 Our trip to Goa was so enjoyable (that) we've decided to go back again next year.
2 We enjoyed our trip to Goa so much (that) we've decided to go back again next year.
3 We had such fun in Goa (that) we've decided to go back again next year.
4 We had such an enjoyable trip to Goa (that) we've decided to go back again next year.

The structures below are commonly used to link a feeling or event with its result. In spoken English, *that* is often left out. (See Unit 3, page 47, for more examples of these structures used with adjectives.)

- *so* + adjective / adverb *(that)*
  The sea was ***so rough (that)*** *most of the passengers felt ill.*
  The boat heaved up and down ***so wildly (that)*** *most of the passengers felt ill.*
- *such* + noun / noun + adjective .. *(that)*
  That camping holiday was ***such a disaster (that)*** *I vowed never to go camping again.*
  I had ***such a disastrous camping holiday*** *a few years ago* ***(that)*** *I vowed never to go camping again.*

Practice B

Find two different ways to join each pair of sentences below into one sentence which has the same meaning as the original two. An example is given to help you.

The food in Italy was delicious. I put on five kilos during my holiday.
The food in Italy was so delicious that I put on five kilos during my holiday.
I ate such a lot of delicious food during my holiday in Italy that I put on five kilos.

1 I spent a lot of money on my summer holiday. I won't be able to afford a skiing holiday as well.

....

....

2 The coach journey was awful. I'll go by train next time.

....

....

3 My aunt's first ever foreign holiday was a great success. She's now planning to travel abroad every year.

....

....

4 The pool at the hotel was lovely. We only went to the beach a couple of times.

....

....

5 Sam loves the island of Mykonos. He's gone there every summer for the last ten years.

....

....

Practice C

Complete the gaps in the text with one word only. All the words you need to write are either relative pronouns, connectors or part of connecting phrases. The first one has been done as an example.

We all love to be beside the seaside. As **(0)** ....long.... as the seaside in question is not in Britain in August. The exodus to overseas beaches, mainly on the Mediterranean, has reached **(1)** .... huge proportions that the government is launching an investigation. Ministers will visit several British resorts in an attempt to reverse the trend **(2)** .... is hitting these towns **(3)** .... hard that the local economies have become severely depressed.

(4) .... Britain boasts many beautiful and unspoiled beaches, most of these are totally unknown to the hordes of British holidaymakers **(5)** .... make their yearly pilgrimage to overcrowded resorts abroad. **(6)** ...., you hardly need a degree in tourism studies, or a government investigation, to guess the main reason for the annual exodus. Because **(7)** .... the vagaries of the weather at home, Britons enjoy sunshine more than southern Europeans, **(8)** .... take it for granted. **(9)** .... the British head south **(10)** .... their two-week summer break should be spent, like much of the rest of the year is, under grey skies. Most probably, nothing short of global warming will warm Britons to their seaside heritage at home.

Practice D

Complete the second sentence so that it has a similar meaning to the first sentence, using the word given. Do not change the word given. You must use between three and eight words, including the word given.

1 She studied the holiday brochure carefully but was still disappointed with her hotel when she got there.
despite
On her arrival, she was disappointed with her hotel .... detail.

2 For fear of spreading infectious diseases, visitors are prohibited from importing animal products.
lest
Visitors may not .... infectious diseases.

3 The tour guide gave us lots of information and, as a result, we felt really at home in the city.
informative.
The tour guide .... we felt really at home in the city.

4 We missed our connection since our first flight arrived nearly an hour late.
delayed
Our first flight .... we missed our connection.

5 While on holiday in Thailand, he met the daughter of one of the country's most famous artists.
father
While he was on holiday there, he met a girl .... most famous artists.

6 Harry's always so anxious about missing a flight that he gets to the airport three hours before the plane leaves.
not
In .... gets to the airport three hours before the plane leaves.

7 The children got rather bored on the coach journey there, but they loved the visit to the medieval castle.
even
The children loved the visit to the medieval castle .... rather boring.

Vocabulary

Phrasal verbs: travel and transport

1 The newspaper headlines below all contain phrasal verbs related in some way to travel, transport or movement. Match each headline to a definition.

1 Near-miss at Heathrow as plane **takes off** without clearance.
2 Prisoner **makes off** after hitting policeman on head.
3 Teenager **sets out** on solo round-the-world voyage.
4 Father **sees** teenage yachtsman **off** at Portsmouth harbour.
5 Teenage yachtsman **gets off** safely despite fog.
6 British cyclist **catches up with** leaders in Tour de France race.
7 Escaped prisoner believed to be **making for** London.
8 Delayed commuter train **gets in** ten hours late.
9 Missing pensioner was **set down** at wrong bus stop.
10 Teenage yachtsman **turns back** after storm in South Atlantic.

a accompany someone to the start of their journey to say goodbye
b arrive
c depart/begin a journey
d reach someone who is ahead of you/in front of you
e go towards/in the direction of
f leave the ground
g leave/manage to depart
h return in the direction you came from
i run away/off
j deliver a passenger by bus, coach or taxi to their destination

2 Which phrasal verb in the text can also:

1 mean 'move towards someone in a threatening manner'?
2 be used transitively, with a pronoun between the verb and adverb, in which case it means 'tell somebody to go back to where they came from'?

3 Rewrite this extract from a teenager's holiday diary, replacing the words in bold with appropriate phrasal verbs from this unit.

We finally (1) **managed to leave** at 8.00 after Dad had (2) **returned to the house** twice, first to check that he'd turned the gas off, and then to check that he'd locked the front door after checking the gas! We (3) **drove in the direction of** the airport, all squashed up in the car as Grandad had come along to (4) **say goodbye to us** and to take the car back home afterwards. Then we got a flat tyre and had to stop to change it. Luckily, whenever we're going to the airport, Dad always insists on (5) **starting the journey** at least two hours earlier than necessary, so we had plenty of time to spare, but Mum still got in a panic.

When we reached the airport we found needn't have worried, as our flight was delayed and the plane wasn't going to (6) **arrive** for another hour and a half. Dad and Grandad immediately went to the bar, leaving Mum, Rachel and me in an enormous queue to check in. Then a small boy waving a plastic toy sword approached Rachel. He probably just wanted to play with her but she thought he was (7) **trying to attack** her, so she (8) **ran away** at top speed and I had to chase her. She runs pretty fast for a five year old, but eventually I managed to (9) **reach** her just as the passport control officer was (10) **telling her to return to where she'd been**!

Once we'd all found each other again and got checked in, it was nearly time to board the plane. The four of us got on the second bus, so were surprised to find when we got to the plane that no-one from the first bus was there yet. Then it turned out that the driver had (11) **left them** beside a plane bound for Paris instead of Ibiza! It took another hour to sort that mess out, and by the time our plane (12) **left the ground**, nearly four hours late, I was beginning to wish I'd gone to the school camp in Wales instead of on yet another disastrous family holiday.

Verb forms and phrasal verbs as connectors

4 Read the short text below. Which of the phrases in bold:

a links a situation or event to its cause?
b links a situation or event to its result?

> The release of the film 'Braveheart' in 1995 (1) **brought about** an increase in the number of tourists visiting Scotland over the next two years. Thereafter, however, there was a decline in visitor numbers. This poor performance (2) **stemmed from** poor standards of service and inadequate marketing.

5 Write each verb in the appropriate column.

was attributed to **caused** **created** **contributed to**
led to **resulted in** **resulted from** **sparked off**

brought about	stemmed from
....	....
....	....
....	....
....	....
....	....

6 Which verb form in the first column would show that there may have been other situations or events that also helped to bring about the same result?

7 Which verb form in the second column would show that people believe this to be the cause of a situation, but are not absolutely certain?

8 Complete the second sentence so that it has a similar meaning to the first sentence, using the word given. Do not change the word given. You must use between three and eight words, including the word given.

1 Global warming is caused by carbon emissions from aeroplanes, among other pollutants.
contribute
Carbon emissions from aeroplanes and .... global warming.

2 I think that driving at night sparks off my migraines.
stem
My migraines seem .... at night.

3 We believe the strong pound is the reason for the rising popularity of foreign holidays.
to
The rising popularity of foreign holidays .... of the pound.

4 The culture of these islands has changed a lot since the advent of tourism.
brought
Tourism .... in these islands.

5 The coral reef was destroyed to build a new harbour and, as a result, several marine species have been lost.
in
The destruction .... of several marine species.

Word formation: adjectives ending in *-able/-ible, -ous, -less* and *-some*

9 Many adjectives can be formed by adding the suffixes *-able/-ible, -ous, -less* or *-some* to a noun or verb stem, for example:

enjoy**able** comprehens**ible** cauti**ous** taste**less** weari**some**

Which of these four suffixes does not carry the meaning of 'causing or displaying the qualities of' the noun or verb it is attached to?

10 Put the words below in the correct part of the chart, adding the suffix that would be used to change the word into an adjective, and making any necessary spelling changes. Be careful! One of the words can form two adjectives. The first two have been done as examples.

aim	**disaster**	**knowledge**	**permit**	**remorse**	**sustain**
break	**fault**	**loathe**	**prosper**	**space**	**tolerate**
contempt	**glory**	**memory**	**quarrel**	**suspicion**	**trouble**

-able/-ible	-ous	-less	-some
breakable, ...	....	aimless, ...	....
....	....	....	....
....	....	....	....
....	....	....	....
....	....	....	....

11 Which word formed two adjectives? What are the differences in meaning between them? Complete the sentences below with the more appropriate adjective.

1 The man insulted other passengers who complained when he smoked in the non-smoking section of the plane, swore at the air stewardess when she refused to serve him a drink and generally behaved in a rowdy and .... manner.

2 The air stewardess made it clear how .... she was of his behaviour.

12 Several adjectives ending in *-some* have meanings which are not immediately obvious from the stem, or have stems which no longer exist alone as words in English. Can you guess the meaning of these examples? If not, use a dictionary to help you.

cumbersome	**gruesome**	**toothsome**	**winsome**

Can you think of any other adjectives ending in *-some* where the meaning is not clear from the stem?

13 Complete the gaps in the text with a word formed from the word given in the margin. All the words you need to write are either adjectives or adverbs. The first one has been done as an example.

It's over 35 years since travel writer Dervla Murphy set off on her bike from
Ireland and arrived, several months later, in India. She's been pedalling
(0) ...relentlessly.... ever since – not quite so fast now that she's nearly 70, but even RELENT
more **(1)** .... as she sees countries from South America to Asia FURY
despoiled by **(2)** .... development and disfigured by western values. MEDDLE

Travel writing wasn't a **(3)** .... genre in the early 1960s; so, in FASHION
describing her trip, Murphy followed the solitary stars of two other
(4) .... female wanderers whose work she admired: the Victorian DAUNT
Isabella Bird, and Freya Stark, who started writing in the 1930s. Since then, she
has continued to indulge her **(5)** .... appetite for travel and adventure, SATIATE
and to delight her readers along the way.

Unlike other big names in travel writing, Murphy has stayed true to the form: she
doesn't intersperse her narratives with chunks of **(6)** .... and self- TIRE
indulgent autobiography, and is **(7)** .... of authors who attempt to fire CONTEMPT
their readers' interest by starting their narrative with a dramatic incident in the
middle of the jungle. She just tells a straightforward tale of her **(8)** .... CIRCUIT
journeys, from day one through to the last.

The book Murphy is currently working on is about the Balkans. There are prizes
and penalties for ageing authors. In Africa, her white hair earned her
(9) .... respect; the Balkans were frustrating because local people felt BOUND
an Irish grandmother had no business being there. Usually the journey is relatively
easy; the writing more **(10)** .... This time, both were tough going. LABOUR
Happily, there's a Murphy's law that says, come what may, the book will be
finished.

Gapped sentences

Study tip

Part 4 of the Use of English paper (gapped sentences) tests your knowledge of words which have several different meanings or which occur in many different contexts or set phrases. To help you prepare for this:

- Remember that the words which appear in this task are usually quite short, simple words.
- Use an English-English dictionary developed specially for advanced learners, such as the *Longman Dictionary of Contemporary English*, to check words which are already familiar to you for alternative meanings or usages.
- Some dictionaries are also available on CD-Rom. If you have access, at home or at school, to one of these, try using the *text search facility* to look up words you already know. This will allow you to see the word in different contexts and with various collocations.

14 Think of **one** word which can be used to complete all three sentences in each group below. Follow the example.

- The young man devoted his life to the *pursuit* of pleasure.
- I have to admit that hill walking is a *pursuit* which doesn't interest me at all.
- The flustered mother ran out of the supermarket in hot *pursuit* of her absconding toddler.

All the words in this section have appeared earlier in this unit, but not necessarily in the same context or in the same grammatical form.

1

- I've known Sheila for years, but I still find her .... and rather unfriendly.
- I've discovered that a .... ancestor of mine was related to Napoleon.
- Could you pass me the .... control so that I can change the channel, please?

2

- I thought the hotel was excellent .... for money.
- I know that piece of pottery is in rather bad taste, but it has sentimental .... for me.
- I was foolish enough to take her comments at face ...., even though I know she's a compulsive liar.

3

- Sarah's the only person I know who takes the .... to bake her own bread.
- Apparently the clients had .... finding the right exit from the motorway.
- As far as I'm concerned, air travel is more .... than it's worth.

4

- We plan to .... sail for the island as soon as the sun comes up.
- Don't forget to .... your alarm clock, as we've got an early start tomorrow.
- I'm counting on you to .... a good example to our new employees.

5

- It took us an hour to reach the .... of the queue for checking-in.
- All that attention at the party has gone to Paula's ....
- I certainly wouldn't go on that mountain-climbing holiday with her, as I've got no .... for heights.

15 Using a dictionary, check the exact meaning of any words, set phrases or usages that were unfamiliar to you.

16 Look the two words below up in your dictionary. How many entries are there for each word?

1 lead (verb)
2 cumbersome (adjective)

Summary

Reading

1 Skim-read these two texts. In terms of subject-matter, what do they have in common?

Text 1

Tourism is now the world's largest industry, accounting for more than 10% of the world's GDP, and is predicted to double in size every ten years or so. Along with this growth comes a clear sustainability challenge, as moving millions of people around on land, sea and air creates problems of transport emissions and other forms of pollution. Aware of these factors, governments have started introducing new regulations, particularly in the transport sector. Airlines and airports, for example, have been obliged to progressively minimise noise levels and cruise operators have had to establish codes of conduct for waste disposal.

This enforced environmental responsibility is now being augmented by a broader vision. Because it is selling clean air, clean beaches and unspoiled scenery, the travel and tourism sector has realised that by protecting the environment, it preserves its core business assets. Furthermore, effective conservation of energy, waste and water can significantly reduce costs. In 1997, for example, the Scandic hotel chain launched an eco-hotel where sophisticated control systems were introduced to manage energy, waste, air quality and water consumption. The hotel's profits rose since the running costs decreased as a result of this efficient environmental investment. Most importantly, customers loved it.

If people want to travel in ways that are less environmentally damaging and stay in places that are less polluted, they will use companies that practise sustainability, thus creating a virtuous circle of demand and response. That will mean 'wise growth' which retains the economic benefits of one of the world's fastest growth industries and minimises the adverse impacts.

Text 2

Given that 500 million tourists roam the world each year, I cannot disagree with the need to minimise the impacts of tourism – but how should this be done? Critics of mass tourism suggest that only low-volume, 'green' tourism should be allowed. Yet the irony is that green tourists go to some of the most ecologically sensitive spots on earth, where their environmental impact may be just as severe. Others bemoan the social changes that come in the wake of tourism. But do local people want to stay as they are? Why should they not enjoy the fruits of tourism? Tourism is in many places actually keeping alive or even reviving local traditions and crafts. Once, at a South Pacific Tourism Conference, I warned delegates against allowing tourism to spoil paradise. An islander retorted: 'My great grandfather was a cannibal and your Scottish missionaries converted him to Christianity. The social changes that tourism will bring are small compared to that.'

So how should the explosion of tourism be managed? The travel industry can set standards in the areas of energy reduction, waste disposal and water savings. Many hotels now recycle waste and encourage energy efficiency. Increasingly, tourist destinations are realising that inappropriate development may spoil their natural attractions – the Caribbean island of St Lucia recently turned down a scheme to put a cable car and restaurant on top of its beautiful twin mountain peak, the Pitons. A lot of little steps like these can, I believe, combine to create a major change in practices.

Summary section: practice

Questions on the texts

2 What exactly does the phrase 'this enforced environmental responsibility' describe? (Text 1, line 9)

3 Explain in your own words why the author has chosen to use the expression 'a virtuous circle' (Text 1, line 20)

Clues: What does the word 'virtuous' mean?
The author has adapted the usual expression 'a vicious circle'. Why?

4 What opinion of the critics of mass tourism does the author express in Text 2, paragraph 1?

Clues: Focus both on green tourists and people who criticise the social impacts of mass tourism.
Keep you answer concise. The best way to do this here is by using adjectives.

5 Which phrase in Text 2, paragraph 1 refers to the economic benefits of the tourist industry which are mentioned in the first text?

Summary writing

In a paragraph of between 50 and 70 words, summarise, in your own words as far as possible, the reasons given in the texts for being optimistic about the impacts of tourism.

6 Check that you're clear about what you're being asked to summarise. Should you:

1 describe the negative effects of tourism?
2 describe changes and improvements?

7 Re-read the texts highlighting or underlining all possible content points.

8 Combine any similar points so that you have a resulting list of four content points.

Clue: One point appears in both texts.

9 Rewrite the four content points, as concisely as possible, in your own words.

Practice test 3

Part 1

For questions 1 – 15, read the text below and think of the word which best fits each space. Use only **one** word in each space. There is an example at the beginning (0).

Example:

0	W	A	S													

The Great Britain

The *SS Great Britain*, designed by the engineer Isambard Kingdom Brunel, revolutionised ship design when it **(0)** ..was.. launched in 1843. Brunel had already built an enormous wooden paddle ship, but realised he needed **(1)** .... bigger to beat the competition to carry passengers to America. His solution was a propeller-driven iron ship, with sails to save fuel in the right winds. However, it was of **(2)** .... an innovative design that, **(3)** .... the ship's luxurious facilities, only 50 passengers were courageous **(4)** .... to buy tickets for the first journey to New York.

The *Great Britain* had a long **(5)** .... star-crossed working life. In 1846 it ran aground in Northern Ireland. **(6)** .... of the 180 passengers was injured, and a group of clergymen conducted a service to **(7)** .... their nerves. The ship lay on the beach for a year until Brunel **(8)** .... devised a rescue which proved **(9)** .... expensive that it bankrupted the vessel's operators.

The ship was sold in 1850 **(10)** .... £18,000, a fraction of its original cost. Converted **(11)** .... sail, it took thousands of emigrants to Australia. **(12)** .... run aground again in 1886, it spent 50 years as a floating wool store before **(13)** .... abandoned in 1937. The *Great Britain* was not forgotten, however, and **(14)** ...., in 1970, a millionaire sponsored a rescue which resulted **(15)** .... the ship being towed back to Britain.

Part 2

For questions 16 – 25, read the text below. Use the word given in capitals at the end of some of the lines to form a word that fits in the space in the same line. There is an example at the beginning (0).

Example:

0	E	X	P	E	N	D	I	T	U	R	E					

La Tourette Monastery

Great architecture has never been dependent on the **(0)** ..*expenditure*.. of vast sums	**SPEND**
of money. One of the greatest buildings of all time is the monastery of Sainte-Marie	
de la Tourette near Lyon, consecrated in 1960 and built cheaply from that most	
(16) .... of building materials – concrete. Yet here is a building that is at once as	**PRETEND**
poor and as rich as the mendicant monks for whom it was designed and built. Poor	
in terms of cost and the materials used to build it, rich in ideas and **(17)**	**SPIRIT**
Today, much new architecture is slick and polished, erected by teams of **(18)**	**CONTRACT**
working to designs fed through very **(19)** .... computer programs. The buildings,	**RELY**
whether office blocks, shopping malls or schools, are **(20)** .... in absolute terms,	**COST**
yet generally good value for money. Most, however, are **(21)** .... or even cynical.	**SOUL**
La Tourette, by contrast, is a tour de force. Set high on a ridge **(22)** .... the	**LOOK**
vineyards of Beaujolais country, this college and monastery was **(23)** .... from the	**MISSION**
great architect Le Corbusier in 1953. La Tourette marked a profound change in Le	
Corbusier's approach to architecture; a move away from the severe, white geometry	
of his pre-war years. It also **(24)** .... a new architecture for a church trying to come	**PRESENT**
to terms with a world of **(25)** .... and progress.	**MODERN**

Part 3

For questions 26 – 31, think of **one** word only which can be used appropriately in all three sentences. Here is an example (0).

Example:

0 The young man devoted his life to the ...... of pleasure.

I have to admit that hill walking is a ...... which doesn't interest me at all.

The flustered mother ran out of the supermarket in hot ...... of her absconding toddler.

0	P	U	R	S	U	I	T							

Exam tip

Remember these ideas from the Introduction to this book (pages 10 – 11):

- Look first at whichever sentence out of the three you find the easiest.
- Think of two or three words that could fit in the gap in that sentence. *... hill walking is a **hobby/pastime/pursuit** which ...*
- Check each word out in the other two sentences to see if it makes sense.

26

- Karen's had a lot of ...... on her hands since the last of her children went off to university.
- I had the ...... of my life on my holiday in Bali.
- Employers are getting strict with employees who surf the Internet in the company's ....

27

- The British Ambassador ...... us in his villa on the outskirts of the city.
- I can assure you that I never even ...... the notion of trying to lie to you.
- After dinner Paul ...... us with jokes and tales of his travels.

28

- Quite frankly, Kate's theory about caffeine being good for you doesn't hold …… .
- The children were in hot …… after ringing all their neighbour's doorbells then running away.
- Villages in this area often suffer from a …… shortage in summer as supplies are diverted to the coastal resorts which attract tourists.

29

- I've just heard that my novel's been …… by a very reputable publisher.
- It took ten years before she felt she had really been …… into the village community.
- The company has finally …… responsibility for the accident.

30

- Antonia may have a …… tongue sometimes, but she's basically a kind and generous person.
- I think you'd make a good editor, as you have a …… eye for detail.
- The road to the south coast is notorious for its dangerously …… bends and steep descents.

31

- If you're in our area, we'd be very happy to put you …… for a few days.
- There's nothing my daughter likes more than dressing …… for a party.
- Frank says he finds it annoying that his mother still waits …… for him when he goes out even though he's no longer a teenager.

Part 4

For questions 32 – 39, complete the second sentence so that it has a similar meaning to the first sentence, using the word given. **Do not change the word given**. You must use between three and eight words, including the word given. Here is an example (0).

Example:

0 The company's profits appear to be improving significantly this year.
evidence
The company's .... this year.

0	profits show evidence of significant improvement

32 Thanks to Bob, we won the match.
for
Had .... lost the match.

33 He promised never to lie again.
truth
He swore .... now on.

34 The authorities will only withdraw an advertisement if a substantial number of people complain about it in writing.
written
Only if a substantial number of people .... withdraw an advertisement.

35 It is recommended that you take water with you as wells and springs are few and far between in this area.
lest
Travellers to this area are .... unable to find a well or spring.

36 The band's not going to play any more, so why don't we leave?
now
We might .... given their final encore.

37 I've been racking my brains to remember where I've seen that man before.
finger
Try as I .... where I've seen that man before.

38 His logic proved to be irrefutable.
argument
So .... refute it.

39 Getting to work should be much easier once the new underground line is ready.
commuting
The new underground line .... much easier.

Part 5

You are going to read two texts about TV advertising aimed at children. For questions 40 – 43, answer with a word or short phrase. You do not need to write complete sentences. For question **44** write a summary according to the instructions given.

A

It seems that the jury is still out on the question of whether TV advertising influences children. After analysing 20 international studies on children as consumers, Adrian Furnham, professor of psychology at University College, London, found there was no evidence to support calls for stricter controls on the advertising of sweets, toys and other goods aimed at children. The studies he analysed indicated that children are far more sophisticated consumers than is popularly imagined and that there is no esoteric knowledge which advertisers can employ to create, out of nowhere, demands in children. They also showed that authoritative parenting styles – laying down rules and expectations, but explaining decisions and valuing the child's point of view – nurture responsibility in children. Professor Furnham concluded it was not advertising that harms children, but irresponsible parenting.

Four months later, however, research into the impact of TV advertising on under sevens was published by a team of psychologists led by Karen Pine of the University of Hertfordshire. This study discovered an increasing desire to consume in children from as young as three and found that children who watch the most television pester their parents for the greatest number of toys and presents. These researchers also discovered that the letters English children write to Father Christmas contain requests for twenty-five percent more presents than those in Sweden, where advertising to children is banned. The problem of susceptibility to advertising was exacerbated amongst the children who regularly watched television alone – these requested a far greater number of branded toys than those who watched television in the company of their parents.

40 Explain in your own words what is meant by the phrase 'the jury is still out' in line 1.

....

....

41 Who or what indicated that 'authoritative parenting styles ... nurture responsibility in children' (lines 10 to 12)?

....

....

B	There are several reasons why a ban on TV advertising aimed at children would be inappropriate for the UK and the most important of these, to my mind, is the quality of children's television. In Sweden, where advertising to children under twelve is banned, children's television is dominated by cheap American cartoons (many of which, by the way, are linked to merchandising). A ban on children's advertising here would have a catastrophic effect on the funding of commercial children's television programming. If advertising revenue were taken away from independent television channels, children's programmes would be removed, reduced to low-cost shows from elsewhere, or could even become available on subscription only. What we should be paying attention to, and what we in this country do pay attention to, is how best to self-regulate advertising, to make sure that vulnerable audiences aren't exploited. Advertising agencies comply with tough rules about what we can and cannot do. The regulations pay special regard to the child audience and contain provisions to ensure that children are not exposed to inappropriate commercial messages or influence. Of course, some elements of merchandising are excessive and irritating for parents. But advertising helps children to discriminate and to grow up and, just like adults, they know, or they soon learn, that they can't automatically have what they see advertised. Children are going to be joining a commercial world. They have to learn to cope with and interpret the marketing influences that surround them.	

Exam tip

Remember that when answering questions which ask you to identify words or phrases in the text, like question 43 above, you should write down *the exact words* as they appear in the text.

42 What opinion does the author have of Swedish television programmes for children?

....

....

43 What phrase in the second paragraph echoes the problem of 'susceptibility to advertising' mentioned in line 21 of Text A?

....

....

44 In a paragraph of between 50 and 70 words, summarise in your own words as far as possible, the arguments for and against banning TV advertising aimed at children.

10 Health and fitness

Grammar
- Conditionals

Vocabulary
- Phrasal verbs and set phrases: health and fitness
- Noun + noun compounds
- Word formation: prefixes *fore-, hyper-, inter-, pre-*

Summary
- Paraphrasing

Grammar: Conditionals

Grammar overview

Zero conditional

if / when + present tense, present tense
If you jump *the traffic lights,* ***you're breaking*** *the law.*
When you do *aerobic exercise,* ***you burn up*** *calories.*

First conditional

if / unless + present tense, *will / may* + bare infinitive
If you need *to have a blood test,* ***I'll come along*** *to give you moral support.*
I ***won't believe*** *her* ***unless she shows*** *me the evidence.*
If you exercise *too hard without warming up,* ***you may pull*** *a muscle.*

The following pattern can also be used in first conditional type sentences.

when / once / before / as soon as / if / etc. + present perfect, future form / *can* + bare infinitive
Once you've reached *your ideal weight you* ***can give up*** *your diet.*
He'll phone *you* ***when he has received*** *the results.*

Other future forms may also be used in first conditional sentences.
If we don't hurry up*, the yoga class* ***will have started*** *before we get there*

Second conditional

if + past simple, *would / could / might* + bare infinitive
If you went *to the dentist's regularly,* ***you could avoid*** *tooth decay.*
You would be *healthier* ***if you took*** *more exercise.*

Third conditional

if + past perfect, *would/could/might have* + past participle
If my parents hadn't both worked *for the same company,* ***they might never have met.***
My aunt could have died if she hadn't got *to the hospital in time.*

Other phrases used in conditional sentences

The following phrases can also be used in conditional type sentences: *providing/provided that, suppose/supposing, on condition that, assuming that, but for, as long as.*

Provided that *both sides lay down their arms, the treaty will be signed.*

Supposing *he has missed his flight, what are we going to do?*

Children are admitted to the restaurant ***on condition that*** *they don't make a lot of noise.*

Assuming that *Peter comes for the weekend, we will be six for dinner on Sunday.*

But for *my mother's support, I would never have go through this difficult time.*

You can take my lap-top on holiday with you ***as long as*** *you look after it.*

Advanced grammar points

Grammar point 1

Read the sentences below. What meaning (a–c) does the word in bold convey?

1 If you **will** smoke forty cigarettes a day, you shouldn't be surprised that your cough doesn't go away.

2 If you **should** pass the chemist's when you're in town, could you pop in and get some more aspirin?

3 If he **won't** go to the dentist, you can't force him.

a happen to / by any chance **b** refuse **c** insist on

Although *will/won't* and *should* rarely appear in *if* clauses, they can be used in these situations:

- to show that the chance of something happening is fairly small.
  *If you **should** have to stay overnight in the hospital, I'll bring you whatever you need.*
- to show that you disapprove of another person's insistence on doing something.
  *If you **will** eat snacks between meals, you can't possibly expect to lose weight.*
- when someone refuses to do something.
  *If he **won't** have an operation, you'll have to investigate alternative forms of treatment.*

Grammar point 2

1 Match the beginnings of sentences (1–3) to the endings (a–c) which would logically complete each one.

1 Had the clinical trials for this new antibiotic been more stringent,

2 Were any further adverse reactions to this antibiotic to be reported,

3 Should a patient have a history of penicillin intolerance,

a the drug would have to be withdrawn from the market.

b this drug may also cause an adverse reaction.

c the drug would never have gone into production.

2 Which of the resulting sentences is:

1 a type of first conditional structure?
2 a type of second conditional structure?
3 a type of third conditional structure?

These forms are sometimes used, mainly in written English, as an alternative to the *if* clause in conditional sentences. (The main clause follows the usual rules for conditional sentences).

- First conditional: *should* + noun / pronoun / noun phrase + bare infinitive
  ***Should any patient suffer** an adverse reaction to this new drug, please report this immediately to the Medicines Control Agency.*
- Second conditional: *were* + noun / pronoun / noun phrase + infinitive with *to*
  ***Were the government to spend** as much on health services as it does on defence, the nation might be healthier and happier.*
- Third conditional: *had* + noun / pronoun / noun phrase + past participle
  ***Had the junior doctor in question not been** on duty for eighteen hours without a break, this tragedy might not have happened.*

Practice A

Rephrase the *if* clauses below, using appropriate forms from Grammar points 1 and 2 above. Two examples are given to help you.

Example 1: If you happen to see Mike at the party,
You write: *If you should see Mike at the party,*
Example 2: If this new health policy was implemented,
You write: *Were this new health policy to be implemented,*

1 If you insist on eating nothing but fruit,
....

2 If you feel drowsy after taking the pills,
....

3 If the hospital built a new wing,
....

4 If by any chance you find that new diet book on sale at the airport,
....

5 If she refuses to give up smoking,
....

6 If the nutritionist had been properly trained,
....

Practice B

Work with a partner. Together, write main clauses to complete the rephrased beginnings of sentences in Practice A above. Two examples are given to help you. When you have finished, compare your ideas with the rest of the class.

If you should see Mike at the party, *could you ask him to call me?*
Were this new health policy to be implemented, *the number of people dying while in hospital care might be reduced.*

Grammar point 3

Match each sentence below to the function (a – b) it is performing.

1 If her teeth are so decayed now, she can't have looked after them when she was younger.

2 If he hadn't dropped out of university, he would be a qualified doctor by now.

a Linking a hypothetical present situation to an event in the past.

b Linking a real present situation to a deduction about its cause.

- To link a real present situation to a deduction about its cause.
  if + present or present perfect tense, *must* / *can't* + *have* + past participle
  *If she'**s lost** so much weight so rapidly, she **must have been** on a really strict diet.*
  *He **can't have been** as ill as he claimed he was last week if he'**s looking** so well now.*
- To link a hypothetical present situation to an event in the past.
  if + past perfect, *could* / *would* / *might* + verb
  *She **might be** a lot healthier if she **had listened** to her doctor's advice.*
  *I **wouldn't be** fat now if I **hadn't been overfed** as a child.*

Practice C

Combine the two sentences in each pair below into one, using an *if* clause. Follow the examples.

Example 1:
I'm feeling very stressed. I took on too many projects at once.
I might feel less stressed if I hadn't taken on so many projects at once.
I wouldn't be feeling so stressed if I hadn't taken on so many projects at once.

Example 2:
Diana looks exceedingly fit. I expect she's started doing aerobics again.
If Diana's looking so fit, she must have started doing aerobics again.

1 I don't feel very energetic. I forgot to take those vitamin pills you gave me.
....

2 He was probably playing computer games half the night. His eyes are red and puffy.
....

3 Her childhood was very unhappy. She suffers from anorexia now.
....

4 John looks very tanned and healthy. I imagine he's been on another skiing holiday.
....

5 I expect Adam didn't go to the gym after all. He's back home already.
....

6 She's too tired to study. She was out at a club till 4.00am.
....

7 She's put on an awful lot of weight. I suppose she didn't stick to her diet.
....

8 My sister's not very keen on sports. Our gym teacher at school was always sarcastic to her.
....

Practice D

Complete the second sentence so that it has a similar meaning to the first sentence, using the word given. Do not change the word given. You must use between three and eight words, including the word given.

1 If children ate healthier food, there would be fewer cases of adolescent obesity.
healthily
Were ...., there would be fewer cases of adolescent obesity.

2 I fully intended to come and see you before, but I've been incredibly busy at work.
snowed
Had I .... have come to see you earlier.

3 It is only in extremely rare circumstances that this illness proves to be fatal.
die
Were a patient .... considered most unusual.

4 The doctor arrived just as we were leaving for the hospital so we didn't need to take our daughter there after all.
timely
But for the .... our daughter to the hospital.

5 I should be home from work by six o'clock and I'll call you immediately after that.
soon
I'll call you .... work.

6 He said he would take legal action against his doctor if she didn't let him see his own medical records.
unless
He threatened to take his doctor .... see his own medical records.

7 My grandfather was exceedingly fit right up till his death in a climbing accident.
might
My grandfather was so fit that had he .... still be alive today.

8 If the government refuses to drop these plans, the nurses will come out on strike.
go
The nurses will come out on strike .... with these plans.

9 In the event of accidental contact with the skin, wash the affected area immediately.
substance
Wash the affected area .... into contact with the skin.

10 I missed that lesson, so I've no idea how to treat a patient who is in shock.
attended
If .... how to treat a patient who is in shock.

Vocabulary

Phrasal verbs and set phrases: health and fitness

1 The advertisements below contain phrasal verbs related in some way to health and fitness. Match each phrasal verb in bold to a definition.

Finding it hard to (1) **get over** illnesses? Or perhaps the demands of job and family are (2) **tiring** you **out**? People lead hectic lives these days and cannot always find time to eat a balanced diet which contains all the nutrients the body needs to keep it healthy. That's why we have developed ZING!, a unique new vitamin and mineral supplement for busy adults. Just one capsule of ZING! a day will (3) **pep** you **up**, (4) **get** you **back** on top form and (5) **build up** your resistance to stress, infections and viruses.

Put a spring in your step!

Springtime is no fun if you suffer from hay fever – a simple walk in the park can (6) **bring on** an attack of sneezing and itchy eyes. But a solution is no further away than your local chemist's shop. Ask for Nasalclear, the new spray that (7) **clears up** most hay fever symptoms within half an hour.

The Body Beautiful opens next week!

Our new health and fitness centre offers:

- Counselling and dietary advice for ladies who've been (8) **putting on** weight.
- Aerobics classes to help you (9) **burn off** excess calories.
- A fully-equipped gym where you can (10) **work out** alone or with an instructor.

75-year old Sheila Turner felt dizzy when she woke up last Monday morning. She was going downstairs to phone her daughter for help when she (11) **passed out** and fell down ten steps. Sheila (12) **came to** twelve hours later in a hospital ward and learnt that she had fractured a hip in her fall. Sheila was one of the lucky ones – her cleaning lady arrived about half an hour later, let herself in and called an ambulance. Had she not done so, Sheila might have (13) **passed away** before help could be summoned. Near-tragedies like this happen every day and some of the less lucky old people don't (14) **pull through**. At DK Laboratories, we have developed a Personal Alarm System especially for old people who live alone. Should the person fall, a small transmitter worn round the neck or waist emits ....

a cause something bad to happen ☐
b die ☐
c exercise ☐
d exhaust ☐
e faint ☐
f get fatter ☐
g gradually increase ☐
h make more active and full of energy ☐
i make something go away ☐
j manage to survive a serious accident or illness ☐
k recover from ☐
l regain consciousness ☐
m return someone (or something) to their former condition ☐
n use energy through physical effort ☐

2 The phrasal verb *clear up* can be used transitively, as in the text, or intransitively, for example: *My cold has* ***cleared up*** *at last.* We can also use *clear up* intransitively with 'the weather'. What does the verb mean when it is used intransitively?

3 Used transitively, *clear up* could collocate with three of the four nouns below. Which ones?

your toys   this problem   the table   the living room

4 What other things could you *build up*?

5 What other things could you *put on*?

6 The phrasal verbs below could be substituted for two verbs in the texts without any change in meaning. Which ones?

come round = ...
pass on = ...

7 The first advertisement contains two prepositional phrases which mean the opposite of each other. Find them and write them in the appropriate part of the chart below.

healthy, fit	tired, unhealthy, unfit
....	....
....	....
....	....
....	....

8 Add these adjectives and phrases to the chart in exercise 7.

all in **off colour** **full of beans** **in good shape**
in perfect health **run down** **in the pink**
in tip-top condition **under the weather** **washed out**

9 Complete each gap in the text below with a suitable verb, adverb or preposition. The first one has been done as an example.

Ten years ago Julie had a bout of flu which lasted for more than three weeks. Although it finally **(0)** ...cleared.. up, Julie was left feeling permanently tired and run **(1)** .... She tried exercising more regularly, thinking this might **(2)** .... her up, but it only left her even more exhausted. Courses of tonics and supplements also failed to get her **(3)** .... in condition. Finally she went to her GP, who diagnosed her as suffering from ME (myalgic encephalomyelitis). This is a puzzling condition, also known as or Post-Viral Syndrome or Chronic Fatigue Syndrome. It is characterised by muscle pain, depression and exhaustion and is often **(4)** .... on by a viral infection. Unfortunately, there is no one cure for the condition, though some symptoms can be treated. Like other sufferers, Julie found she had to learn her own limits – she could walk to the shops, but walking back again would tire her **(5)** .... She learnt to rest regularly to **(6)** .... up her strength before going anywhere and to turn **(7)** .... her family for help with chores she would normally have done herself. As she was much less active than before, Julie started to **(8)** .... on weight and this got her **(9)** .... even more. At one point she was so depressed that she **(10)** .... to staying in bed all day. Luckily, about two years ago, Julie began to recover – her energy levels increased, her spirits improved and she was able to **(11)** .... up a part-time job working from home. Although she wouldn't say she has completely **(12)** .... over the worst of her ME yet – unfortunately relapses are common with this condition – she has recently started **(13)** .... out gently and has managed to burn **(14)** .... some of her excess weight.

Noun + noun compounds

English frequently combines two (or more) nouns as a way of imparting a lot of information in a short space, for example:

cancer ward = the hospital ward where people suffering from cancer are treated
hospital consultant = a doctor who is a specialist and works in a hospital
health services = doctors, hospitals and other places or people responsible for people's health
blood pressure gauge = an instrument which measures the force with which blood flows through your body

10 What noun compounds would express these ideas?

1 a company which manufactures drugs
2 an operation to transplant a heart into someone else's body
3 a patient who is suffering from cancer
4 an injury sustained in the leg
5 cuts in the amount of money which the government will spend on health
6 a man who enjoys spending time with his family
7 the hospital ward where people are taken when an emergency has occurred
8 a device used for opening bottles
9 waste emitted or discharged by a factory
10 an officer responsible for the safety of people working in a specific place

11 Many common noun compounds have an institution (e.g. school, government) as the first word. Work with a partner and think of three nouns that would commonly follow each of the nouns below, then share your ideas with the rest of the class.

family	government	hospital	police	school

Word formation: prefixes *fore-, hyper-, inter-, pre-*

12 The prefixes below can be added to nouns, adjectives or verbs to alter their meaning. Match each prefix to the meaning it conveys.

Prefixes	Meanings
1 fore as in *forefather, forearm*	**a** more than usual/too much
2 hyper as in *hyperactive*	**b** between/among
3 inter as in *international*	**c** before/at the front
4 pre as in *predate, prearrange*	**d** before/in advance

13 Which of the above prefixes would you guess is the least commonly used?

14 Put the words below in the correct part of the chart, adding the prefix that would be used to alter the word's meaning. The first three have been done as examples.

act cast conception connected critical dependent determined face front ground market marry mature meditate mingle occupy planetary sentiment sight tension thought ventilate warn

fore-	hyper-	inter-	pre-
forecast, ...	....	interact, ...	preconception, ...
....	....	....	....
....	....	....	....
....	....	....	....
....	....	....	....

15 Two words which appear in the same column are specialist medical terms. Which ones? If necessary, check their meaning in a dictionary or with your teacher.

16 Seven of the words in the other three columns are verbs. Which ones? What would be the corresponding noun form for each of them?

Use your English

Work with a partner. Choose two words from the chart in 14 and/or from exercise 16. Write two sentences, each including one of the words you have chosen. The sentences should not be definitions, but should illustrate the meaning of the word. When all pairs are ready, take turns to read your sentences aloud, saying 'beep' instead of the word. The rest of the class must guess what the missing word is.

Example: *Most of my 'beep' about life in Britain were proved wrong when I finally visited the country.*
Answer: ***preconceptions***

17 Complete the gaps in the text with a word formed from the word given in the margin. The first one has been done as an example. Six of the words you need to write include the prefixes you have studied in this unit.

The World Health Organisation says 100 to 150 million people around the	
world are **(0)** ..asthmatic.... and the number is growing by 50% every	ASTHMA
decade. Many theories have been put forward concerning the causes of	
asthma and the reasons why its **(1)** ...., especially among	OCCUR
children, has increased so **(2)** .... in recent years.	DRAMA
Certainly some children have a genetic **(3)** .... towards	DISPOSE
developing it, as asthma, eczema and other allergic conditions, like hay	
fever, are **(4)** .... and run in families. However an inherited	LINK
(5) .... towards a health problem does not necessarily mean that	TEND
a child is **(6)** .... to develop the condition. Some theories to	DESTINY
explain the increase in asthma focus on environmental factors, such as air	
(7) ...., diet or the widespread use of pesticides. One new	POLLUTE
suggestion is that most Western families are **(8)** .... about	ENTHUSIASM
hygiene and that by keeping their homes 'too clean', their children's	
immune systems are no longer given the chance to develop properly	
through **(9)** .... to normal levels of bacteria.	EXPOSE
What is clear is that there is a complex **(10)** .... between	RELATION
hereditary and environmental factors, and thus it is difficult to	
(11) .... which children in a family with a history of allergic	SEE
(12) .... will develop asthma, and which will not. In addition,	ORDER
the triggers for an attack can vary widely; one child may be	
(13) .... to house dust and pet hairs, while his sibling is	SENSITIVE
(14) .... by these but reacts badly to spores or mould.	AFFECT

Gapped sentences

18 Think of **one** word which can be used to complete all three sentences in each group below. Follow the example.

- The young man devoted his life to the *pursuit* of pleasure.
- I have to admit that hill walking is a *pursuit* which doesn't interest me at all.
- The flustered mother ran out of the supermarket in hot *pursuit* of her absconding toddler.

All the missing words in this section are verbs which have appeared in this unit, but in other contexts.

1
- I tried that diet too, but it didn't .... for me.
- If I go cycling I .... up such an appetite that I put back on all the calories I'd burnt off!
- Tony's taken up boxing to try and .... off the stress his job causes him.

2
- You should use water, rather than milk, for .... the tablets down.
- I find it very relaxing to hear the sound of waves .... on the shore.
- Penny says she's .... her hands of the committee as they spend hours talking but never resolve anything.

3
- The council is expected to .... the plans for the new sports centre this week.
- After struggling for three hours to finish his essay Dick went for a walk to .... his head.
- We hope that this meeting will .... the way for future co-operation between our companies.

4
- She felt a sharp pain .... down her left arm as she got out of bed.
- I've put some tissues in your schoolbag in case your nose starts to .... again.
- You'll need more memory on your computer if you want to .... that program.

5
- Hardly a day .... without him regretting the argument they had had.
- Fortunately, it seems that your tactless remark .... unnoticed.
- I've .... your enquiry on to our sales department, who should be able to help you.

19 Using a dictionary, check the exact meaning of any phrasal verbs, idioms or usages that were unfamiliar to you.

Study tip

The most effective way to broaden your vocabulary is by reading widely in English and this can be pleasurable if you are reading on topics which interest you. Try buying a magazine you would normally read in your own language, for example a fashion, sports or computer magazine, in English for a change. Alternatively, if you have access to the Internet at home or school, use a search engine like www.yahoo.co.uk to find English language sites on topics that interest you.

Summary

Reading

1 Skim-read these two texts. In terms of subject-matter, what do they have in common?

Text 1

During a clinical trial, two women with similar blood pressure levels are given the same dose of a new hypertension drug. One woman's blood pressure returns to normal, but the other's crashes to an abnormally low level and remains that way for the next six hours. The telling difference between these two women is a gene which determines how well 25 per cent of prescription drugs will work.

Adverse reactions to drugs account for one in 15 hospital admissions and are a major cause of death, yet many harmful side effects could be predicted. Scientists have found that a substantial number of people have an inactive version of the gene CYP2D6 which produces a liver enzyme that helps the body to process many commonly-prescribed drugs. If this enzyme is deficient, a drug will either be metabolised too quickly and not do the work it was intended to do, or will not be processed at all, thus causing adverse reactions.

A simple test for the gene CYP2D6 is now being developed and should be available to GPs* soon. By administering it, doctors will know whether a patient needs a different dose of a drug, or another medicine altogether. Tests for other genes involved in drug metabolism also exist but are more expensive and complicated to administer and so are currently used in only a few teaching hospitals and specialist academic centres. Nevertheless, many scientists believe the future of medicine lies in establishing and recording each patient's genetic code on a DNA chip, so that all treatments with drugs, either in emergencies or in routine visits to the GP, can be safely tailored to the patient's genetic make-up.

** GP – General Practitioner (family doctor)*

Text 2

Clinical trials of new medicines do not identify problems that may occur in a tiny minority of people. In Britain, a system of yellow cards and black triangles is intended to form a safety net to alert the authorities to unexpected harmful effects of medicines. A yellow card is the form a doctor sends to the Medicines Control Agency if he is concerned that a patient has had a serious side-effect from a particular drug. A black triangle appears on the information sheet sent to doctors by the manufacturer if a drug is less than two years old. Doctors are supposed to report all side-effects of black triangle drugs – not just the serious ones.

In fact, there are major problems with the safety net. A recent survey found that a quarter of information sheets on new drugs did not in fact carry the black triangle symbol. As doctors cannot be expected to know by heart which among the thousands of medicines available are new, the blame for non-reporting of side effects from these drugs lies fair and square with the manufacturers.

There are other weaknesses. Filling in a yellow form is voluntary. Some doctors fill in stacks, some hardly any – the average is less than one a year per doctor. It was recently suggested that patients themselves fill in yellow cards and send them to the MCA. This eminently sensible idea was rejected by the Department of Health, who responded that doctors were better placed than patients to make judgements on side-effects. If they or the MCA have a better solution for improving reporting procedures and thus safeguarding patients' health, they should implement it now.

Skills development: Paraphrasing

2 Read the rubric below, but do not write a summary.

> *Summarise, in your own words as far as possible, the ways mentioned in the texts in which the risks of people suffering serious side-effects from drugs could be reduced.*

3 Work with a partner and decide what the four content points are. Then check your ideas with the rest of the class and your teacher.

4 Read the draft summary below. The four content points have been correctly identified, but the draft is too long and exhibits some other faults.

> Patients could be given a new test to see if they are deficient in the gene CYP2D6 which produces a liver enzyme that helps the body to process many commonly-prescribed drugs. If this enzyme is deficient, a drug may not be processed at all and can cause adverse reactions. In future, everyone's genetic code will be recorded on a DNA chip so that all treatments with drugs can be tailored to the patient's genetic make-up. In addition, companies which produce drugs should be stricter about informing doctors that the medicines which they are selling are new, and the procedures that are used for reporting side-effects should be improved.

5 Choose *Yes* or *No* for each fault below. If you choose *Yes* for a fault, write in the numbers of the lines where this problem occurs.

1	Parts have been copied straight from the texts.	Yes No	line(s) ____
2	More detail than necessary has been included.	Yes No	line(s) ____
3	There are grammatical errors.	Yes No	line(s) ____
4	Ideas could be put more succinctly.	Yes No	line(s) ____

6 Lines 1 to 3 of the draft are too similar to the text and it is not necessary to give so much detail. Answer these questions.

1 What kind of test is it? (use a noun + noun compound)

2 What does the test show a patient may or may not be able to do?

3 Find a synonym in Text 1 for the verb 'process'.

4 Which of the following would be the best synonym for 'commonly-prescribed'?
often prescribed   normally used   frequently used

7 Lines 4 to 5 of the draft are too similar to the text and could be expressed more succinctly. Answer these questions.

1 Rephrase 'everyone's genetic code will be recorded on a DNA chip' by changing 'code' to a verb, and using the gerund of that verb: 'genetic .... on DNA chips'

2 Rephrase 'all treatments with drugs' into two words only, using a noun + noun compound.

3 Find a synonym for the verb 'tailored'.

8 In lines 6 to 8 several words could be cut out. Answer these questions.

1 What noun + noun compound means 'companies which produce drugs'?

2 Cut out the superfluous words from the phrases 'the medicines which they are selling are new' and 'the procedures that are used for reporting'.

9 Insert your answers from questions 6, 7 and 8 into the paraphrased summary below. You should end up with a total of 63 words.

> Patients could be given a new .... which shows whether they may be unable to .... many .... drugs. In future, genetic .... on DNA chips will allow .... to be .... to a patient's genetic make-up. In addition, ... should be stricter about informing doctors that .... and .... side-effects should be improved.

11 Biology and the body

Grammar • Unreal past and wishes

Vocabulary • Phrasal verbs, idioms and set phrases: parts of the body
• Collocations
• Word formation: revision

Summary • Practice

Grammar: Unreal past and wishes

Grammar overview

The present subjunctive

The present subjunctive (the use of the infinitive without *to* in all persons) is rarely used except in formal English. However, it does occur after certain reporting verbs and some adjectives as well as in a number of set phrases.

- report verb + *that* + infinitive without *to*
  She ***insisted that she pay*** *for the damage.*
  He ***suggested*** *that* ***we call*** *the police.*
- adj + *that* + infinitive without *to*
  It is ***advisable that she leave.***
  It is ***essential*** *that the patient* **be** *left in peace until he recovers.*

Other verbs and adjectives which often follow this pattern are: *order, propose, recommend, request, think, desirable, preferable,* etc. In less formal English the following structure could be chosen instead of the subjunctive

- (*that*) + *should* + infinitive without *to*
  She ***insisted that she should pay*** *for the damage.*
- Set phrases – *be that as it may, come what may, suffice it to say, far be it from me, so be it, Heaven forbid! God Save the King!*

See Unit 7, Advanced grammar points, Page 114 for more on reporting verbs and Unit 4, Vocabulary page 71–72 for more on adjectives.

The past subjunctive

The past subjunctive (the use of *were* in all persons) is used:

- in formal English (where spoken English would generally use *was*)
  If ***he weren't*** *so stubborn, they might reach an agreement.*
  (*'If he* ***wasn't*** *so stubborn, they might reach an agreement.'*)
  He wishes ***his mother weren't*** *so strict.*
  (*'He wishes his mother* ***wasn't*** *so strict.'*)
- in the phrase, *If I were you, …*
  I wouldn't set off in this weather ***if I were you.***
- in the pattern, *were* + subject + *to* infinitive. (See Unit 10, Conditionals, page 153.)
  Were the prime-minister to reveal *the truth, there would be a nationwide scandal.*

wish and *if only*

- *wish / if only* + past tense / past subjunctive – to talk about a present situation which you would like to change
  I wish I had *more time to relax.*
  If only I was coming *with you!*
- *wish / if only* + past perfect – to talk about a past situation which you wish had been different in some way
  She wishes she hadn't spoken *so rudely to her boss.*
  If only we had set off *five minutes earlier!*

It's high time

- *it's (high) time, it's about time* + past simple / past continuous / past subjunctive
  It's high time you stopped *moping about the house and got a job!*
  It's time I was leaving.

Advanced grammar points

Grammar point 1

1 One of the four sentences below is grammatically incorrect. Which one?
   1 I wish I could resist cream cakes.
   2 I wish I would be thinner.
   3 I wish my Mum wouldn't eat chocolate bars in front of me when she knows I'm on a diet.
   4 I wish I could come with you to that lecture on binge eating, but I've already made arrangements for Friday night.

2 What would be the correct form of the sentence which is wrong?

3 Match each of the remaining three sentences to a function below.
   a Expressing a wish about the future which cannot be fulfilled.
   b Expressing annoyance about someone else's behaviour.
   c Expressing regret about your inability to do something.

Wish can be followed by *could* + verb:

- when referring to future events or activities which are very unlikely to happen.
  My brother ***wishes he could*** *go to the party too, but he has an exam the next day.*
- when expressing a wish or regret about something you are unable to do.
  I wish I could *swim.*

Wish can be followed by *would / wouldn't* + verb:

- when the person expressing the wish is not the same as the one the wish relates to, and the speaker finds the action or habit referred to annoying or unpleasant.
  I ***wish you wouldn't*** *speak with your mouth full.*
  My sister ***wishes her husband would*** *give up smoking.*

For other structures with *wish*, see this unit, Grammar overview, opposite.

Practice A

Work with a partner and rewrite each sentence below in two different ways. Each rewritten sentence should contain an appropriate form of the verb *wish* followed by a suitable structure. Follow the example.

I never learnt to ride a bicycle, and I've often regretted that I didn't.
I've often wished that I had learnt to ride a bicycle.
I've often wished that I could ride a bicycle.

1 I envy you your ability to pick up foreign languages easily.
....
....

2 Steve really wants to go to university, but his father expects him to join the family business.
....
....

3 I hate being overweight.
....
....

4 I'm sorry I didn't go to university when I had the chance.
....
....

5 I'd really like to go on holiday with you to Spain, but I don't think I'll be able to take any more time off work.
....
....

Grammar point 2

1 What time period do the words in bold in the sentences below refer to? Choose from the past or the present for each sentence separately.

1 I'd rather **you went** outside to smoke.
2 I'd rather **you'd warned** me that she was a vegetarian before bringing her home to dinner.
3 I'd rather **have gone** on a beach holiday, but my husband wanted to do something more active.

2 Now match each sentence to the function (a – c) it expresses.

a Expressing a preference that was not fulfilled.
b Making a firm but polite request.
c Criticising someone politely for something they have done.

- *I'd rather* + *you* + simple past is used to make a polite request in the present.
- *I'd rather* + *you* + past perfect is used to criticise someone's past actions.
- *I'd rather* + perfect infinitive is used to describe something you would have preferred to do in contrast with what you actually did.

See also Unit 3, Advanced grammar points, Grammar point 4, page 47, for other structures with *I'd rather*.

Grammar point 3

Read the four sentences below. In two of them the speaker is making an assumption about someone based on what they can see. In the other two the speaker is describing how someone looks by comparing them to a situation which is probably not true. Mark each sentence A if it is an assumption and C if it is a comparison.

1 Sammy's gone awfully pale all of a sudden. Oh no, he looks as if he's going to be sick.
2 You look as if you were going to a torture chamber rather than a dentist's surgery.
3 You seem to be in a very good mood today, Dr White. In fact, you look as though you'd just won the lottery.
4 That poor young doctor looks as though he's been working all night. He's got huge bags under his eyes.

The phrases *as if* and *as though* are used after verbs like *act, behave, feel, look, sound* and *speak*.

- When you are making an assumption based on what you can see or hear, the verb after *as if/as* though is in a present, present perfect tense or future form.
  I think he must be the manager, as it sounds ***as if he's giving*** *instructions to the others.*
  Look, Tom's giving us the thumbs-up signal. It looks ***as though he's managed to*** *find someone who can tell us the way back to the motorway.*
  It's very overcast. In fact, it looks ***as if it's going to*** *rain.*
- When you are making a comparison, the verb after *as if/as though* is in the simple past, past continuous, past subjunctive, or past perfect tense.
  Lucy behaves ***as if she owned*** *the restaurant, but in fact she's only an employee, just like the rest of us.*
  The man in that shop spoke to me ***as if I was/were*** *a servant rather than a customer.*
  What was that that fell on my head? I feel ***as if I'd been hit*** *by a ton of bricks.*

Practice B

Circle the more appropriate verb to fill each gap below. If both are equally suitable, circle both.

1 I'm worried about my niece. She looks as if she never .... enough.
a eats **b** ate **c** both

2 What did I say? You're looking at me as if I .... from outer space.
a came **b** come **c** both

3 I wish my brother .... in the house.
a didn't smoke **b** wouldn't smoke **c** both

4 I'd rather you .... in the house.
a didn't smoke **b** wouldn't smoke **c** both

5 I don't like the way he speaks to me as though he .... the boss.
a was **b** were **c** both

6 I'd rather you .... my mother that I have to undergo some medical tests.
a wouldn't have told **b** hadn't told **c** both

7 Did you notice the cat's ear is torn? He looks as if he .... again.
a has been fighting **b** had been fighting **c** both

8 From what I've been told, it sounds as though he .... his job.
a has lost **b** had lost **c** both

9 I wish my Grandad .... his false teeth out when he eats.
a wouldn't take **b** didn't take **c** both

10 I'd rather .... biology, but my teachers persuaded me to take physics instead.
a studied **b** have studied **c** both

Practice C

Complete the second sentence so that it has a similar meaning to the first sentence, using the word given. Do not change the word given. You must use between three and eight words, including the word given.

1 The shock of seeing him there could be compared to that of seeing a ghost.
felt
When she saw him .... a ghost.

2 I wish I'd trained as a vet instead of as a doctor.
rather
I'd .... than a doctor.

3 I regret telling her my secret.
confided
If .... her!

4 It was unfortunate that you brought up the subject of politics at dinner.
rather
I'd .... about politics at dinner.

5 At your age, you should have decided by now what job you want to do.
high
It's .... you want to follow.

6 Apparently Sophie now regrets turning down Bob's proposal and marrying Greg instead.
wishes
It seems .... of Greg.

7 I find it hard to concentrate on my work since my boss became so critical.
criticise
I wish my boss .... my concentration.

8 Could you take your shoes off before you come into the house?
removed
I'd .... coming into the house.

Practice D

Complete the gaps in the text with **one** word only. The first one has been done as an example.

A survey has found just one per cent **(0)** ....*of*..... young women are 'completely happy' with the shape of their body. Over 3,000 women, **(1)** .... an average age of 25, responded to the survey on newwomanco.uk, the website of a British women's magazine. Nearly all **(2)** .... respondents wished they **(3)** .... thinner, no matter what weight they were, and most were unhappy with **(4)** .... shape. Eighty per cent believed slim women were more attractive **(5)** .... men and 58% thought they had more success in their careers.

Interestingly, the survey revealed that women were **(6)** .... more likely than men to criticise other women and **(7)** .... pressure on them to have a 'perfect body'. Asked who was most likely to criticise, 85% of respondents said other women, **(8)** .... just 15% said men. Lorraine Eames, editor of newwoman.co.uk, said, 'Women are their **(9)** .... worst enemies when it comes to how they feel **(10)** .... their bodies. The truth is, men are happy with us the way we are – it's the women **(11)** .... point out our flaws. It's **(12)** .... we did ourselves a favour and let go of the unattainable 'perfect' body dream and celebrated the female form in all **(13)** .... uniqueness.'

Commenting on the survey results, a female GP and an eating disorder specialist **(14)** .... pointed out that the media contribute **(15)** .... women's poor body image by giving so much attention to actresses and models who look **(16)** .... if they were famine victims, and said they **(17)** .... rather women's magazines didn't present **(18)** .... thin models as images of female perfection.

Vocabulary

Phrasal verbs, idioms and set phrases: parts of the body

1 Which two of these parts of the body cannot be used as a verb?

back chest ear elbow face finger foot hand head mouth nose shoulder toe

2 Complete the phrases below with an appropriate word from exercise 1. Use each of the remaining eleven words only once. Follow the example.

1 ...head... a committee/investigation
2 .... the burden/responsibility of
3 .... down a tradition/an heirloom
4 .... platitudes
5 .... into someone else's business
6 .... someone up
7 .... the bill
8 .... your hair/the goods on display
9 .... the line
10 .... the music
11 .... through the crowd/your way to the exit

3 Match each completed phrase to a definition

a accept a difficult or unpleasant task ☐
b accept criticism or punishment for something you've done wrong ☐
c be in charge of ☐
d do what you have been told to do ☐
e move using this part of the body to clear your way ☐
f pass something from generation to generation ☐
g pay ☐
h say things that you do not really believe ☐
i show too much curiosity about someone else's life ☐
j support someone in an argument or discussion ☐
k touch ☐

4 Match the words in the columns to make commonly-used phrases. Follow the example.

1 all fingers and	a cheek
2 cheek by	b ear
3 from ear to	c eye
4 from head to	d hand
5 hand in	e jowl
6 neck and	f neck
7 eye to	g thumbs
8 tongue in	h toe

5 Use the phrases from exercise 4 to complete the sentences below. If necessary, use a dictionary to help you.

1 The children were grinning .... about the joke they'd played on their teacher.
2 Don't ask me to fill up that lovely vase for you, I'm .... today!
3 I saw Paula and her new boyfriend walking .... along the beach yesterday.
4 She was covered .... in dust and cobwebs after cleaning out the cupboards.
5 Tim and Bobby were .... as they crossed the finishing line of the race.
6 My brother and I haven't spoken to each other for years, as we don't see .... on several important issues.
7 She says she prefers country life, as in a large city you have to live .... with too many neighbours.
8 You shouldn't take what Mark says so seriously; most of his remarks are entirely ....

6 Several set phrases in English follow the pattern.

have/don't have + a/an (good) part of body + *for* + noun phrase
She ***doesn't have a head for heights***.

Work with a partner and decide what the phrases below might mean.

1 That boy has a nose for trouble.
2 He's got a head for figures.
3 I don't have a good eye for colour.
4 Your daughter seems to have an ear for languages.

7 With your partner, think of some other things you could have *an ear, an eye, a head* or *a nose for* and share your ideas with the rest of the class.

8 Complete the second sentence so that it has a similar meaning to the first sentence, using the word given. Do not change the word given. You must use between three and eight words, including the word given.

1 When his sister died, Jack took on the task of raising her three children.
burden
It was Jack who .... three children when she died.

2 I inherited this clock from my father and it belonged to his father before that.
down
This clock .... father and, in turn, to me.

3 It annoys me the way Harry invites you out for a drink, then you end up paying for everything yourself!
foot
I wish .... you out for a drink.

4 I thought I could count on your support at the meeting.
up
I had hoped .... at the meeting.

5 Anna should become a journalist as she's got an instinctive ability to spot a scandal.
nose
Anna's got .... a good journalist.

6 She and her husband disagree strongly about how their daughter should be educated.
eye
She and her husband .... daughter's education.

7 There were a lot of people waiting at the bar but I managed to push through to the front.
way
I managed to .... and get to the bar.

Collocations

9 Work with a partner and complete the charts below, ticking each box where an adjective can collocate with a noun. One column has been done as an example. If necessary, use a dictionary to help you.

	arthritis	illness/disease	pain	pneumonia
acute				
chronic				
dull				
infectious				
throbbing				

	glands	knee	leg	throat
inflamed				
sore				
swollen				
sprained				

10 What other adjectives do we use in English to describe a pain?

11 What other nouns can the adjective *acute* collocate with? How does the meaning of the adjective change when it collocates with different nouns?

12 What other parts of your body could become *inflamed*?

13 What other parts of your body could become *sprained*?

14 Now complete this chart, ticking each box where a verb can collocate with a noun.

	a cold	a disease	a fever/ a temperature	a rash/spots	an illness	tuberculosis
break/come out in						
come/go down with						
contract						
run						
ward off						

15 Complete the gaps in the conversations below with words from the charts above. You may need to use some more than once.

A: I'm a bit worried about the Susie. She's been complaining of a **(1)** .... throat for a couple of days, and now she's **(2)** .... a rash on her chest. One of her friends **(3)** .... chickenpox a couple of weeks ago, so maybe ..

B: Uh-oh, I think you'd better call the doctor. That's a highly **(4)** .... illness, and the other children might catch it too.

C: Have you heard the latest about Paul?

D: Don't tell me – he's **(5)** .... his wrist playing tennis again and will be taking another week off work.

C: No, not the wrist, though he will be off work. But this time it's really exotic. Apparently he's **(6)** .... a very high fever and the doctor thinks he may have **(7)** .... malaria on his holiday in Thailand last month!

E: Why on earth are you putting lemon and whisky in a mug?

F: Well, I think I might be **(8)** .... the flu. I've got a **(9)** .... in my head and my **(10)** .... are swollen .

E: Poor you. I still don't see what the whisky's got to do with it, though.

F: Oh, right, that. Well, it's an old remedy of my grandma's to **(11)** .... colds and flu – honey, whisky and lemon in hot water, then straight to bed.

Use your English

Work in pairs. Each pair compiles a list of symptoms which might occur together (you may include your own ideas as well as items from exercises 9 and 14 above.) When all pairs are ready, take turns to read out your symptoms, then the rest of the class should offer a diagnosis.

Example: *My eyes are itchy and inflamed, I keep sneezing and my whole face feels as if it's slightly swollen.*

Answer: *I think you must be allergic to something.* or
It sounds like you've got hay fever.

Study tip

At Proficiency level, you are expected to know vocabulary from a wide range of subject areas. An efficient way to help you broaden your subject-specific vocabulary is:

- Club together with some friends from your class to buy an English language newspaper (the ones published on Saturdays and Sundays have the widest range of articles).
- Divide the newspaper up between you, each taking a different section – e.g. sports, health, culture, society, business, finance, science and technology.
- Each student reads *one* article that interests him/her from that section, prepares a brief summary of what the article was about, and picks out ten vocabulary items (idioms, collocations, set phrases or subject-specific words) from the article to present to the rest of the group the next time they meet.

Word formation: revision

16 Complete the gaps in the text with a word formed from the word given in the margin. The first one has been done as an example. All the words you need to write are formed in ways you have studied already in Units 1 to 10. They could include:

- noun suffixes: *-ance/-ence, -cy, -dom, -hood, -ity, -ment, -ness, -tion, -ure, -age, -ee, -er/-or, -ist, -ship*
- negative prefixes: *anti/anti-, dis-, im-, in-, un-, mal-, mis-*
- adjectives ending in *-ful, -ic, -ial , -ical, -able/-ible, -ous, -less, -some* and their related adverbial forms
- prefixes: *over, under, out, pre-, fore-, hyper-, inter-*

Never in human history has a population so **(0)** ...wilfully... and deliberately defied nature as has the present generation. How have we defied it? We have survived. Life **(1)** .... at the start of the 19th century was scarcely 40 years. Over the course of the last half-century, it has continued to increase steadily by two years each decade. Our **(2)** .... survival has produced a revolution in longevity which is shaking the **(3)** .... of societies around the world.	**WILL** **EXPECT** **PRECEDENT** **FOUND**
The idea that the physical **(4)** .... associated with old age is something fixed or **(5)** .... has come to be seen in a new and questioning light. The new realisation is that science no longer dictates that our bodies have to wear out and die according to some **(6)** .... plan.	**DETERIORATE** **MUTATE** **ORDAIN**
Many of our **(7)** .... about why and how we age are beginning to be **(8)** .... by recent advances in genetics and genome research, and it is likely that we will soon understand the ageing process even better than we do at present. We now realise that our bodies are not programmed with some **(9)** .... sell-by date. Indeed, the more we learn about how we age, the more we come to realise that we are programmed for survival. It is by understanding why this programming falls short of allowing us to survive **(10)** .... that we may learn deep lessons that we can turn to our advantage.	**CONCEIVE** **TURN** **AVOID** **DEFINITE**

Gapped sentences

17 Think of **one** word which can be used to complete all three sentences in each group below. Follow the example.

- The young man devoted his life to the *pursuit* of pleasure.
- I have to admit that hill walking is a *pursuit* which doesn't interest me at all.
- The flustered mother ran out of the supermarket in hot *pursuit* of her absconding toddler.

All the missing words in this section are parts of the body.

1

- That girl wraps her father round her little .... and he does anything she asks of him.
- There was something familiar about that man on the bus but I can't put my .... on where I know him from.
- Sally didn't lift a .... to help when we were clearing up after the party.

2

- Tom seems to have a chip on his .... about his lack of education.
- It was marvellous how everyone put their .... to the wheel and helped to repair the damage after the storm.
- Belinda never speaks to me now that she's back with her boyfriend and doesn't need a .... to cry on any more.

3

- The Smiths have been living a .... to mouth existence since he lost his job.
- He no longer competes in tournaments, but he keeps his .... in by playing regular games with friends.
- I don't have a pen to .... at the moment, so I'll call you back later from the office to get the address.

4

- Unfortunately Jake and I got off on the wrong .... from his first day in the company, and our working relationship has been difficult since then.
- When it comes to letting the children go out during the week, their mother always puts her .... down.
- I really put my .... in it when I let slip we'd been to the cinema together before, didn't I?

5

- Would you mind casting your .... over this report before I submit it to the committee?
- I have my .... on a really nice jumper I saw in Benetton last week.
- My manager usually turns a blind .... if I'm a bit unpunctual in the mornings, as she knows I often stay late at the end of the day.

Summary

Reading

1 Skim-read these two texts. In terms of subject-matter, what do they have in common?

Text 1

When the Human Genome Project began, researchers on the project had predicted they might find 70,000 to 140,000 genes. They also believed that one gene contained the code for one protein which would have one function. Instead, the international consortium of scientists discovered that the human genome contained only about 30,000 genes. This is only about fifty per cent more than have been found in the simple roundworm *Caenorhabditis elegans*, which has 19,099 genes, although the human genome is nearly thirty times larger than that of the worm. Given that we are much more sophisticated and intelligent organisms than the roundworm, the proportionately smaller number of genes means that biologists can no longer assume that one gene is a blueprint for one protein that has one function. It seems that nature has found a way of making 'executive' genes that do very sophisticated management work.

Our similarity at a molecular level to other creatures provides confirmation of Darwin's theory of evolution formulated 150 years ago. The same genes, with some adjustments, have been used throughout the 3.8 billion-year story of evolution. What is now clear is that as we move up the ladder of complexity from single cell creatures, through small animals like worms and flies, to human beings, what are added are increasingly varied and subtle control genes. The research also bears out the long-standing theory that modern humans all evolved out of the same three or four groups in Africa; the genome researchers found that the genetic variations between any two individuals in the same population were often greater than those between two people from different ethnic groups.

Text 2

The potentially-poisonous Japanese fugu fish has achieved notoriety among scientists because it has a genome that can be best described as 'concise'. There is no 'junk' DNA, no waste, no nonsense. Now, most people would hardly rate the fugu fish as the acme of creation. If it were, it would be eating us, and not the other way round. But here is a paradox. The human genome probably does not contain significantly more genes than the fugu fish. What sets it apart is that it is more litter strewn than any genome completely sequenced so far

Researchers on the Human Genome Project were somewhat taken aback to find that the genes themselves occupy a mere 1.1% of human chromosomes. A lot of the rest is just rubbish, plain and simple. But at least half the genome is rubbish of a special kind – transposable elements. These are small segments of DNA that contain genetic instructions for enzymes whose function is to make copies and insert the copies elsewhere in the genome. Many contain genes for an enzyme called reverse transcriptase. The chilling part is that reverse transcriptase is a key feature of retroviruses such as HIV-1, the human immunodeficiency virus. The research indicates that at least half of the human genome may consist of DNA that started out as independent viruses or virus-like entities. To make matters worse, hundreds of other genes seem to have been imported directly from bacteria.

If the import of bacterial genes for novel purposes sounds disturbing and familiar, it should – this is precisely the thrust of much research into the genetic modification of organisms in agriculture or biotechnology. All in all, the people dismissed as cranks for believing that humans were genetically engineered by aliens may turn out not to be quite so deranged after all!

Summary section: practice

Questions on the texts

2 Explain in your own words why the author has chosen to use the expression 'executive genes'. (Text 1, line 10)

3 To what or to whom does the word 'those' in line 19 of Text 1 refer?

4 Which two words in Text 2, paragraph 1 relate to the idea introduced in paragraph 2 of the same text about the human genome containing 'rubbish'?

5 In the last paragraph of Text 2, what impression does the writer give of people who believe that humans were genetically engineered by aliens?

Summary writing

In a paragraph of between 50 and 70 words, summarise, in your own words as far as possible, the surprising discoveries made by the researchers working on the Human Genome Project.

6 Check that you're clear about what you're being asked to summarise.

7 Re-read the texts, highlighting or underlining all possible content points.

8 Check your potential content points meet the criteria in the description of the summary task.

Clue: In total five discoveries are mentioned but, according to the texts, one of these did not come as a surprise.

9 Rewrite the four content points, as concisely as possible, in your own words.

10 Check the number of words in your draft summary.

11 Rewrite the summary, paraphrasing it if necessary.

Reminder: Unit 10, page 163, has examples of strategies for doing this

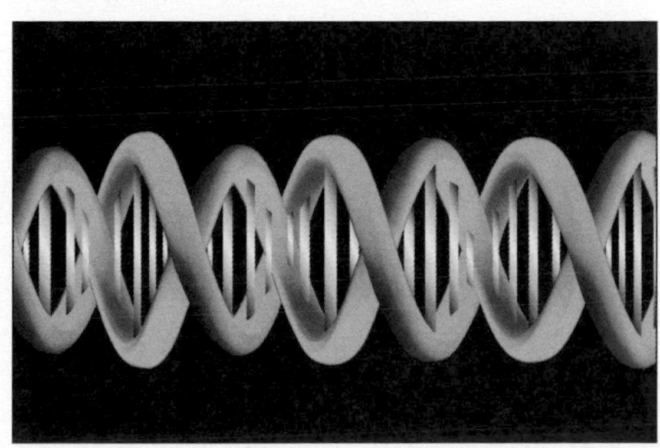

12 The natural world and the environment

Grammar • Passives and causatives

Vocabulary • Phrasal and prepositional verbs, idioms and set phrases: the weather
• Passive verbs with dependent prepositions
• Word formation: prefixes *de-*, *em-/en-*, *re-*

Summary • Practice

Grammar: Passives and causatives

Grammar overview

Passive – tenses

*Man **destroys** thousands of species per year.*	*Thousands of species **are destroyed** every year.*
*The hurricane **caused** millions of pounds worth of damage.*	*Millions of pounds worth of damage **was caused** by the hurricane.*
*The government **is planning** a new offensive on traffic congestion.*	*A new offensive on traffic **congestion is being planned** by the government.*
*The local people **were using** plants and herbs to make traditional medicines.*	*Plants and herbs **were being used** by the local people to make traditional medicines.*
*The government **has set aside** its plans for a nuclear power station after a storm of protest.*	*After a storm of protest the government's plans for a nuclear power station **have been set aside.***
*Even before the advent of the chainsaw, man **had already done** serious damage to the rainforests.*	*Even before the advent of the chainsaw, serious damage **had already been done** to the rainforests.*
*Environmentalists hope their efforts **will halt** the hunting of whales.*	*Environmentalists hope that the hunting of whales **will be halted** by their efforts.*
*Leading nations **will have cut** carbon monoxide emissions drastically by 2010.*	*Carbon monoxide emissions **will have been cut** drastically by 2010.*
*Genetically modified products **may cause** previously unknown allergies.*	*Previously unknown allergies **may be caused** by genetically modified products.*
*Radioactive waste **could have killed** the fish.*	*The fish **could have been killed** by radioactive waste.*
*The rescue workers **ought to take** certain precautions.*	*Certain precautions **ought to be taken** by the rescue workers.*
*She **loves people giving** her flowers.*	*She **loves being given** flowers.*
*He remembers **somebody taking him** to the zoo as a child.*	*He remembers **having been taken** to the zoo as a child.*

Verbs uncommon in passive

Some verbs cannot be used or are uncommon in the passive.

- Intransitive verbs (verbs without an object) – *be, grow up, hop, sit, sleep, die*, etc.
- Single-object prepositional verbs – *apologise to, belong to, compete with, glance at, laugh about, listen to, participate in, smile at, wait for* etc.
- Verbs unusual in passive – *exclaim, hesitate, joke, pretend, reply, resemble, wonder, yell* etc.

Agent and instrument

- In order to talk about the person or thing that performed an action (the agent) we use *by*.
  *The nature reserve was opened **by** Lord Carmarthen.*
- In order to talk about the instrument with which an action was performed or the material from which something is constructed we use *with*.
  *The new house was built **with** recycled, eco-friendly materials.*
  *The victim seems to have been struck **with** a heavy object.*

- It is not necessary to include the agent when the identity of the agent is unknown, irrelevant or when the agent's identity is self-evident from the context.
  The young vandals were arrested.(by the police)
  He was educated at Oxford University. (by his tutors)
  Ten elephants have been shot in this area this year. (we don't know who shot them)
- We do include the agent if that information seems important however.
  If the head finds out that the window was broken ***by his own son****, he'll be furious.*

Reporting opinions

- We use the following patterns with verbs *think, believe, report*, etc. in order to report people's opinions.
  It is thought that *by the end of this century, the sea level will have risen by one metre.*
  He is believed to be *an expert in his field.*
  See Unit 7, page 111 for more on this pattern.

Verbs with two objects

- Sometimes a sentence has more than one object.
  The Mayor awarded the 'best-kept-village' prize to Little Hampton.
  Depending on which piece of information we wish to give emphasis to there are two patterns we can follow:
  Little Hampton was awarded the best-kept-village prize.
  The best-kept-village prize was awarded to Little Hampton.

Causative

- subject + *have* + object + past participle
  The scientist ***will have the test results checked*** *by an expert.*
  We're ***having our garden designed*** *by a famous landscape gardener.*
- In informal English, we can use *get* instead of *have*.
  Where did you ***get your hair done****?*

Advanced grammar points

Grammar point 1

Match the beginnings of sentences with the ending (a – h) which would complete each one, both grammatically and in terms of meaning.

1 Someone must have helped the child
2 The child must have been helped
3 The dogs were made
4 The trainer made the dogs
5 Someone heard the motorist
6 The motorist was heard
7 You aren't allowed
8 They don't let you

a import meat products into the country.
b jump through hoops.
c threaten the policeman.
d write this composition.
e to import meat products into the country.
f to jump through hoops.
g to threaten the policeman.
h to write this composition.

- When the verbs *hear, help, make, feel* and *see* are used in the passive they must be followed by an infinitive with *to* rather than the bare infinitive. *See* and *hear* may also still be followed by an *-ing* form, as appropriate. (See Unit 13, Grammar overview, page 197 for more on constructions following *see* and *hear*.)
  It is important that the Prime Minister ***should be seen to care*** *about environmental issues.*
  The film ***was*** *widely* ***felt to be*** *in bad taste.*
- The verb *let* can only be used in the passive when it forms part of a phrasal verb or prepositional verb. When it has the meaning of permission, it is replaced by *be allowed to*.
  The dog must have been ***let off*** *its chain.*
  People shouldn't ***be allowed to*** *dump rubbish wherever they want.*

Practice A

Rewrite each sentence below using an appropriate passive construction. Follow the example.

They constructed the factory in the days when they let people build anywhere they wanted.
The factory was constructed in the days when people were allowed to build anywhere they wanted.

1 Someone should make factories reduce the air pollution they produce.
Factories ....

2 They won't let you smoke in here.
You ....

3 It's important that people see public figures behave with honesty and dignity.
Public figures ....

4 Government grants have helped more than fifty businesses in the area implement energy-saving measures.
Thanks to government grants, more than ....

5 They let me down badly when they didn't let me install a solar panel on my roof.
I felt ....

6 Most people who live here feel that traffic congestion in the town centre has reached unbearable proportions.
The traffic congestion ....

7 Someone heard the politician say that environmental problems were of no concern to her.
The politician ....

Grammar point 2

1 Which sentence in each pair below emphasises the negative aspects of the situation described?

1 a My handbag was snatched. **b** I had my handbag snatched.
2 a My suitcase got left behind at the airport. **b** My suitcase was left behind at the airport.

2 In which sentence below could you substitute *had become stuck* for the words in bold?

a A note saying 'Back in five minutes' **had been stuck** on the shop door, but I waited half an hour and no-one came.
b The child fell and broke his leg while trying to rescue his kitten, which **had got stuck** up a tree.

In addition to its causative use (see this unit, Grammar overview, page 177) the structure *have* + object + past participle is used to describe things, frequently unfortunate or unwanted ones, that happen to people. In spoken English, *get* may be used instead of *have* in this construction.

Hundreds of farmers ***have had their livelihoods destroyed*** *by the recent outbreak of foot and mouth disease.*
The dog ***had/got its ear bitten off*** *in a fight.*

The verb *get* is used instead of *be*:

- in passive constructions in conversation, to emphasise the negative aspects of an event.
  My car ***got hit*** *by a bus.*
- in passive constructions in conversation or informal written English, with the meaning *become*.
  I first ***got involved*** *in green issues back in the seventies.* (informal)
  The research was initiated by Professor Wright, who first ***became involved*** *in environmental issues when she was at Oxford.* (formal)
- in set phrases, such as *get married, get engaged, get dressed, get used to.*

Practice B

Read each sentence below. If you think a sentence is more appropriate to a written text, write W beside it; if you think the sentence would be spoken, write S beside it.

1 By the age of six, most children should be able to dress themselves. ☐

2 The wedding of Robert Mills and Shona Grant will take place on St Valentine's Day. ☐

3 Tom got his licence taken away for six months as he got caught speeding. ☐

4 Investigations are under way to discover why five people were trapped in a lift for more than three hours yesterday. ☐

5 They say the climate is getting warmer so we'll just have to get used to regular flooding in this area. ☐

6 Travellers are strongly advised to ensure they have had all the necessary vaccinations before visiting the Amazon basin. ☐

Practice C

Now convert the sentences from Practice B from written to spoken style, or vice versa. The beginnings and endings have been given to help you and you should use the word(s) given in bold in the new sentence. Follow the example.

By the age of six, most children should be able to dress themselves.
get
Carrie's six now; it's time *she learned to get dressed* on her own.

1 The wedding of Robert Mills and Shona Grant will take place on St Valentine's Day.
are
Rob and Shona .... on St Valentine's Day.

2 Tom got his licence taken away for six months as he got caught speeding.
suspended/arrested
The defendant .... after .... for speeding.

3 Investigations are under way to discover why five people were trapped in a lift for more than three hours yesterday.
find/stuck
They're trying .... those poor people .... in the lift for so long.

4 They say the climate is getting warmer so we'll just have to get used to regular flooding in this area.
accustomed
Inhabitants of low-lying regions .... regular flooding resulting from global warming.

5 Travellers are strongly advised to ensure they have had all the necessary vaccinations before visiting the Amazon basin.
ourselves
The doctor said we have to .... before we go on our cruise up the Amazon.

5 Work with a partner and use the idioms and set phrases below to complete the sentences. If necessary, use a dictionary to help you.

a face like thunder	**a storm in a teacup**
a sunny disposition	**get wind of**
head in the clouds	**on cloud nine**
stole my thunder	**took the wind out of my sails**
under the sun	**weather the storm**

1 The whole idea was mine in the first place, so I was furious when he .... by presenting it as if he had thought it up.

2 Life was hard for us after my father went bankrupt, but thanks to my mother's hard work and patience, we managed to ....

3 I don't think this is the moment to raise the question of a pay rise with your boss – she's had .... since she saw the report on our monthly sales figures.

4 Pay no attention to Peter's complaints – he always makes a fuss about everything but it usually turns out to be ....

5 I was doing really well in the oral exam until they asked me a question about the ozone layer which I couldn't answer and that really ....

6 Ian's the man to ask – he's a self-styled expert on everything ....

7 Say nothing of what I've told you; I don't want anyone to .... of my plan before I'm ready to put it into action.

8 She's been .... since she heard she's been accepted for university.

9 That child's got such .... that it's a pleasure to be in his company.

10 If you didn't have your .... most of the time you'd find it easier to concentrate on your homework.

Passive verbs with dependent prepositions

6 Several verbs which are frequently used in the passive voice, especially in academic written texts, are followed by prepositions. Rewrite each verb in the correct part of the chart, according to the preposition it would be followed by. Some of the verbs may be followed by more than one preposition. Two examples have been given to help you.

be aligned	**be confined**	**be included**	**be regarded**
be applied	**be coupled**	**be intended**	**be related**
be associated	**be defined**	**be involved**	**be situated**
be attributed	**be diagnosed**	**be labelled**	**be subjected**
be based	**be divided**	**be linked**	**be transferred**
be classified	**be extracted**	**be made**	**be used**
be composed	**be grouped**	**be positioned**	**be viewed**

as	....
for	....
from	....
in	....
into	....
of	....
on	....
to	*be applied to,* ....
with	*be aligned with,* ....

7 All of these verbs can be followed by noun phrases. Some may also be followed by clauses containing verbs. What form of the verb do you think should be used?

8 Complete the second sentence so that it has a similar meaning to the first sentence, using the word given. Do not change the word given. You must use between three and eight words, including the word given.

1 People who live in the tropics face several health hazards.
associated
Several health hazards .... in the tropics.

2 The label on that ancient vase should say it comes from Greece, not from Rome.
incorrectly
That ancient Greek vase .... from Rome.

3 People used to think environmental activists were eccentric, but this is not the case nowadays.
viewed
Environmental activists are no .... eccentrics.

4 After giving him several tests, doctors finally came to the conclusion that Paul had contracted malaria.
diagnosed
Paul .... malaria.

5 There is a connection between the hole in the ozone layer and chemicals which are present in aerosol propellants.
linked
The hole in the ozone layer can .... propelling aerosols.

6 In this research centre we study the results of global warming, rather than the causes.
confined
Our research .... the results of global warming.

Study tip

Dependent prepositions exist with verbs, nouns and adjectives. Unfortunately, it is not always possible to deduce which prepositions go with which words, so you need to memorise the correct combinations. Here are two strategies:

- If you like learning things by heart, use the alphabetical list of adjectives, nouns and verbs with their dependent prepositions in the Appendix of this book. Memorise a few combinations each day.
- If you prefer a more active approach, go through texts you have already read in your course book or in the summary sections of this book, pick out typical combinations and make your own list.

In each case, daily practice of about ten items is likely to be more helpful than trying to learn fifty combinations at a time a few days before your exam!

Word formation: prefixes *de-, em-/en-, re-*

9 The prefixes below can be added to verbs, nouns and, less frequently, adjectives, to create new verbs. Match the prefixes to the meanings they convey. Two of the prefixes have two separate meanings.

Prefixes

1 ***de*** as in *desalinate, decode*
2 ***em/en*** as in *empower, enrich*
3 ***re*** as in *rewrite, reunite*

Meanings

a do again, sometimes in a new and better way
b make something less than it was or the opposite of what it was
c make someone or something become/have
d return to a former state
e remove something or remove things from something

10 Put the words below in the correct part of the chart, adding the prefix that would be used to alter the word's meaning. The first two have been done as examples.

able	**close**	**courage**	**large**	**place**
arrange	**compress**	**frost**	**louse**	**state**
bitter	**contaminate**	**fuel**	**motivate**	**try**

de-	em-/en-	re-
....	enable, ...	rearrange, ...
....	....	....
....	....	....
....	....	....

11 Most of the words you have formed can be further transformed into nouns. Write the corresponding noun forms in the chart below. Follow the example.

de-	em-/en-	re-
....	enable (x), ...	rearrange (rearrangement),
....	....	....
....	....	....
....	....	....
....	....	....
....	....	....

Use your English

Work with a partner. Using the meanings given in exercise 9 above to guide you, choose one word from each column of the chart in exercise 10 and write a mock dictionary entry for the word, then share your ideas with the rest of the class. An example is given to help you.

Example: ***enable*** (verb) make someone or something able to do something
His university degree ***enabled*** *him to get a better job.*

12 A number of words can have both *de-* and *re-* added to them. These include:

form	**generate**	**value**	**vitalize**

What would the resulting eight words mean? If necessary, use a dictionary to help you.

13 Complete the gaps in the text with a word formed from the word given in the margin. Eight of the words you need to write include the prefixes you have studied in this unit. The first one has been done as an example.

In January 2001 the **(0)** Intergovernmental Panel on Climate Change (IPCC) issued its latest report on climate change. Climate models worked out by giant super-computers had become far more reliable since the previous report in 1995 and allowed them to **(1)** .... the earlier projections for global warming. Their conclusions were that something very serious is happening and that it cannot be a natural process. The 1990s was the hottest decade for 1,000 years and the Earth is warming faster than at any time in the last 10,000 years. According to the report, human activities are **(2)** .... to blame for the temperature rise. The burning of fossil fuels releases carbon dioxide and, due to **(3)** ...., there are fewer trees to absorb this gas and **(4)** .... it back into oxygen. Methane concentrations have also gone up dramatically because of increases in rice culture and cattle-rearing, both of which generate methane from **(5)** .... vegetation. These greenhouses gases trap heat in the Earth's atmosphere and cause the temperature to rise.	GOVERNMENT APPRAISE EQUIVOCAL FOREST CYCLE COMPOSE
The IPCC reported that, in the worst case, the average temperature could rise by 5.8°C this century, 2°C higher than their original predictions. The resulting melting of ice-caps and glaciers would cause sea levels to rise by up to 88cm, **(6)** .... the homes and livelihoods of tens of millions of people who live in low-lying regions.	DANGER
Unfortunately, there is far greater **(7)** .... among the world's scientists over the issue than among politicians. As long ago as 1990, the IPCC recommended a 60% reduction in carbon dioxide emissions, as the basic level required to return the planet's climate to a healthy level.	UNANIMOUS
Governments globally failed to **(8)** .... these proposals. Now that the dangers have been **(9)** .... by the latest report, it is high time that governments took an active interest in exploring alternative, **(10)** .... energy sources.	ACT AFFIRM NEW

Gapped sentences

14 Think of **one** word which can be used to complete all three sentences in each group below. Follow the example.

- The young man devoted his life to the *pursuit* of pleasure.
- I have to admit that hill walking is a *pursuit* which doesn't interest me at all.
- The flustered mother ran out of the supermarket in hot *pursuit* of her absconding toddler.

All the missing words in this section are nouns or verbs based on animals.

1
- I'm surprised Sheila was so supportive when your mother was ill as I've always thought she was rather a cold ....
- Stan felt like a .... out of water when he first went to work for the company.
- Jane may have a fancy job title, but really she's just a big .... in a small pond.

2
- Nobody's going to take your plate away from you, so there's no need to .... your food like that.
- They're certainly not well-off, but at least they manage to keep the .... from the door.
- He seemed charming at first, but he turned out to be just another .... in sheep's clothing.

3
- As usual, Paul has managed to .... out of attending the monthly committee meeting.
- She may not want to tell me why she's not coming to the party, but I'll .... the reason out of her sooner or later.
- I know you've been lying to me, so there's no point in trying to .... your way back into my favour by bringing me flowers and chocolate!

4
- My father thinks the country's been going to the .... since the last government was elected.
- If I were you I wouldn't interfere; sometimes it's better to let sleeping .... lie.
- Take an umbrella as it's raining cats and .... out there!

5
- Their house is so tiny that there's no room to swing a .... in it.
- She promised to keep it a secret, but then she went and let the .... out of the bag.
- I think my boss is playing .... and mouse with me, as the promotion he promised me three months ago still hasn't come through.

Summary

Reading

1 Skim-read these two texts. In terms of subject-matter, what do they have in common?

Text 1

Seventy per cent of the world's fish stocks are now either fully exploited, overfished, depleted, or rebuilding from previous over-fishing. Marine pollution has also adversely affected fish populations. As a result, world catches have levelled off since their peak in 1989, when 85 to 95 million tonnes of fish were harvested. It seems unlikely they will start rising again until concerted efforts are made to allow stocks to recover and then to fish them in a sustainable way.

Some scientists argue the solution to the fish shortage could be aquaculture. This is another term for fish farming, that is cultivating fish in controlled conditions, rather than catching whatever swims in the sea. However, there are fears that aquaculture will create more problems than it will solve.

Much fish farming relies heavily on fish feed, that is, capturing small fish like mackerel and anchovy and feeding them to carnivorous farmed fish. In the production of the ten most commonly farmed fish, roughly 2kg of wild fish feed are required for every kilogram of farmed fish produced. This means that at the moment fish feed is further draining wild fish stocks, without even producing an equivalent mass of farmed fish.

It is not only through changes in food chain interactions that aquaculture depletes wild fish stocks, but also by spreading diseases from farmed to wild fish. It's difficult to persuade farmed fish to keep to their pens, as is shown by the fact that nearly half of the salmon caught by North Atlantic fishermen are of farmed origin. A further worry is that farmed fish may spawn with wild fish and dilute the genetic makeup of their offspring, making them less well-adapted to their environment than their wild parents.

Text 2

Perhaps the cruellest irony of the growth in fish farming is that it has come close to driving wild fish, the very creatures it was designed to save, to the brink of extinction. In the past 10 years, wild salmon stocks have declined to all-time lows, and in the north-west Highlands, centre of the Scottish aquaculture industry, stocks have been devastated. The cause is infestations of sea lice caused by the proximity of farmed salmon. These are kept in cages, usually situated at the mouths of lakes which open onto the sea. The cages are vast, but the fish are packed in tight, with up to 250,000 of them battling for survival in each one. At these densities, the fish are at the mercy of disease and parasites are rife. Although sea lice are a naturally occurring parasite found in wild fish and a healthy adult fish would normally carry five or six, in the wild fisheries close to the fish farms, salmon and sea trout have been found with up to 500 lice on them.

The solution for the farmed fish is the use of vaccinations and toxic pesticides. As their cages are open to the environment, these chemicals seep into the surrounding water and can damage the habitats around the cages. The intensive feeding regimes also carry a heavy cost. In many farms, the fish are fed automatically, and much of the feed drops straight through the cages to gather on the bottom of the lake along with the ammonium-rich salmon excreta. It is estimated that a 1,000-tonne salmon farm – small by current industry standards – produces sewage waste equivalent to a town of 20,000 people. The resulting mix disturbs the chemical balance of delicate marine habitats.

Summary section: practice

Questions on the texts

2 Which word in Text 1, paragraph 1 reflects the information given about wild salmon stocks in line 3 of Text 2?

Clue: Remember to read the relevant line in Text 2 before *searching for words which convey a similar idea in Text 1.*

3 Explain in your own words what is meant by 'changes in food chain interactions' (Text 1, line 16).

4 Why does the writer use the phrase 'battling for survival' in line 7 of Text 2?

Clue: Note that you are not being asked to explain what the phrase means, but to show how the phrase relates to the content of the surrounding text.

5 What exactly is it that 'disturbs the chemical balance of delicate marine habitats'? (Text 2, line 19.)

Summary writing

In a paragraph of between 50 and 70 words, summarise, in your own words as far as possible, the definite and potential drawbacks of aquaculture.

6 Check that you're clear about what you're being asked to summarise.

7 Re-read the texts, highlighting or underlining all possible content points.

8 Combine similar points so that you have a final list of four content points.

Clues: Three causes are mentioned which all create the same effect – group these together.
Check that you have included any potential drawbacks as well as drawbacks which are known to exist.

9 Rewrite the four content points, as concisely as possible, in your own words.

10 Check the number of words in your draft summary.

11 Rewrite the summary, paraphrasing it if necessary.

Reminder: Unit 10, page 163, has examples of strategies for doing this

Part 3

For questions 26 – 31, think of **one** word only which can be used appropriately in all three sentences. Here is an example (0).

Example:

0 The young man devoted his life to the …… of pleasure.

I have to admit that hill walking is a …… which doesn't interest me at all.

The flustered mother ran out of the supermarket in hot …… of her absconding toddler.

0	P	U	R	S	U	I	T								

26

- Since they re-routed heavy goods traffic down our street you take your …… in your hands every time you step out your front door.
- Tony's been living the high …… since he had that lottery win.
- The portrait is interesting, but it isn't very true to …… .

27

- Paula said to …… her in too if we go to the seaside tomorrow.
- You can …… on me to support you at the meeting.
- You should …… yourself lucky that you left the island the very day before the volcano erupted.

28

- Our trip to the theme park wasn't that expensive as we had been given a coupon which ...... the children free of charge.
- Maeve's feeling a bit upset because her mother's just been ...... to hospital.
- After their third unsuccessful attempt to scale the north face of the mountain, the climbers finally ...... defeat.

29

- The manager felt they needed new ...... in the department, so most of the old staff have been transferred to other jobs.
- Merely trying to find out if Roger had spent a good day at work was like getting ...... out of a stone.
- Bad temper runs in that family's ....

30

- After working so hard to finish their house, Bob and Clare were ...... for a holiday.
- Mark is popular at parties because of his ...... wit.
- My daughter says she doesn't feel ...... to get married yet.

31

- When a job opening in Hong Kong came up, Ben ...... at the chance of it.
- Being the jealous type, Steve immediately ...... to the wrong conclusion when he saw his girlfriend in a cafe with another man.
- The child ...... with joy when he heard he was going to visit the zoo..

Part 4

For questions 32 – 39, complete the second sentence so that it has a similar meaning to the first sentence, using the word given. **Do not change the word given**. You must use between three and eight words, including the word given. Here is an example (0).

Example:

0 The company's profits appear to be improving significantly this year.
evidence
The company's .... this year.

0	profits show evidence of significant improvement

32 I'll take you to the village on Sunday provided that the car is in working order by then.
repaired
As .... then, I'll take you to the village on Sunday.

33 Although everything pointed to her having taken the money, she strenuously denied it.
evidence
She strenuously denied .... the contrary.

34 The manager was totally convinced that his deputy was honest.
faith
The manager .... honesty.

35 Local people say the waters of this spring can heal the sick.
said
The waters of this spring .... powers.

36 It began to rain almost immediately after our arrival at the resort.
we
Scarcely .... it began to rain.

37 The critics had expected the play to be better than it was.
up
The play .... expectations.

38 I found the plot of the book too complicated to follow.
head
I .... the plot of the book.

39 I now regret not having completed my studies at university.
dropped
If .... university.

Part 5

You are going to read two texts about whaling. For questions 40 – 43, answer with a word or short phrase. You do not need to write complete sentences. For question **44** write a summary according to the instructions given.

A

In 1982 the International Whaling Commission (IWC) voted for a moratorium on the commercial hunting of all great whales. Estimating whale numbers is notoriously difficult, but many populations are believed to be growing as a result of the moratorium and some, such as the grey whale, have even been removed from endangered species lists. The IWC's scientific committee reckons there are now about 760,000 minke whales in the southern hemisphere, and a further 175,000 north of the equator, numbers which may be the same as, or higher than, they were before whaling began.

When the moratorium came into force in 1986, all the whaling nations stopped hunting. However, using loopholes in the IWC's rules, both Japan and Norway resumed limited whaling in the 1990s and are now lobbying to be allowed to reinstate commercial whaling. Since 1993 Norwegian vessels have killed more than 2,000 minke whales in Norwegian coastal waters, increasing their annual quota by at least a hundred each year. The Norwegian authorities say the species is sufficiently abundant to allow such catches and fishermen claim the whales need to be culled to preserve fish stocks. In addition, as demand for whale meat is low in Norway, the Norwegians would like to be allowed to sell their surplus stock to the Japanese. This is currently banned by another UN treaty, the Convention on International Trade in Endangered Species.

40 What is increasing 'by at least a hundred each year'? (lines 15 – 16)

....

....

41 What word in paragraph 2 of Text A relates to the practice of selective killing in order to maintain an ecological balance?

....

....

B

Demand for whales is much less now than it was during the peak period of commercial whaling from 1870 to about 1935. Whales were then hunted primarily for their oil and wax, which were used to lubricate machinery and make candles. Nowadays their only commercial value is as food, especially in Japan, where whale meat is a traditional delicacy. The Japanese insist they want only to hunt whales that can be harvested without a threat to their future. Commercial whaling is of no economic significance. It is, however, part of their heritage, and a matter of principle.

Setsuo Izumi, a whaler for 37 years, says 'What people eat is different from country to country. It's a cultural thing.' The IWC moratorium has stopped him hunting minke – favoured for its mild taste – but he insists they are not under threat. 'I see more minke out at sea than I used to and fisherman say they are eating all the fish. Why should we not be allowed to catch them in our coastal waters?'

Joji Morishita, deputy director of the far-seas fisheries at the Japanese Fisheries Agency, thinks many western nations have double standards: 'Wildlife for them is something to see and admire, and you should only eat animals such as cows and pigs that are reared. But in the US they catch 5.6 million wild deer a year. And how would the British react if Hindus tried to ban killing and eating cows, which they consider holy?' He also emphasises the question of scale – after all, the Japanese and Norwegians cannot eat all the whales in the ocean.

42 Explain in your own words why Joji Morishita introduced the subject of cows and Hindus into a discussion about whaling.

....

....

43 What impression is created throughout the second text of the Japanese attitude to whaling?

....

....

44 In a paragraph of between 50 and 70 words, summarise in your own words as far as possible, the reasons put forward by Japan and Norway as to why they should be allowed to resume commercial hunting and trading of whales such as the minke.

Exam tip

It is often a good idea to let some time elapse between writing your first draft of the summary and rewriting it. Do something completely different for at least fifteen minutes (longer is better). This way you are more likely to think of alternative, more concise ways of phrasing your ideas. You can do this in the exam too.

- Write your first draft of the summary.
- Go back to earlier parts of the paper and check or complete any items you found difficult.
- Return to Part 5 and re-write your summary.

13 Science and technology

Grammar • Infinitives and gerunds

Vocabulary • Phrasal verbs: science

• Adverbial phrases incl. gerunds and infinitives

• Word formation: verb suffixes *-en, -ify, -ise*

Summary • Practice

Grammar: Infinitives and gerunds

Grammar overview

Forms of the infinitive in active and passive voice

	Active	Passive
Present	*She seems* ***to have*** *difficulties.*	*The problem seems* ***to be*** *solved.*
Present cont.	*She seems* ***to be having*** *difficulties.*	–
Past	*She seems* ***to have had*** *difficulties.*	*The problem seems* ***to have been*** *solved.*
Past cont.	*She seems* ***to have been having*** *difficulties.*	–

Use of the full infinitive

- After certain verbs – *attempt, begin, try, seem, tend, want* etc.
  He ***tends to exaggerate****.*
  (See Appendix, page 252 and Unit 7, page 111.)
- After certain adjectives – *certain, easy, difficult, interested, keen, glad, likely, obliged, unable*, etc.
  We were ***keen to leave*** *early in order to avoid the rush hour.* (See Unit 1, page 22)
- After *wh-* clauses.
  I don't know ***what to do****.*
  We're unsure ***how*** *to begin.*
- To express purpose.
  They have passed the drug through a number of tests ***to see how effective it is****.*
  (See Unit 9, page 132.)
- With *only* to talk about a disappointing result.
  He worked for days on the project, ***only to be told*** *it had been cancelled.*
- As a replacement for a relative clause.
  The next person ***to tell me*** *(who tells me) my theory is far-fetched is in for trouble.*
- With *too* and *enough* (See Unit 3, page 44).
  She's ***too young to have*** *experience in this field.*
  The statistics are not ***conclusive enough to convince*** *the sponsors.*
- After the verbs *help, hear, make, feel* and *see* in the passive in which case it indicates that the action in question was completed.
  (See Unit 12, page 177.)
  He ***was seen to slip*** *the top-secret file into his briefcase.*
- As the subject of a sentence.
  To have given up *after such hard work seems a shame.*

Use of the infinitive without *to*

- After modal verbs (See Unit 4, page 64 and Unit 6, page 88).
  His claims ***may prove*** *to be true.*
  You ***could have been*** *mistaken.*
- After *had better* and *would rather* (See Unit 3, page 47).
  *We'****d better get*** *a move on!*
  *He'****d rather go*** *hungry than accept charity.*
- after the verbs *feel, hear, see, watch, help* and *make* in the active voice in which case it indicates that the action has been completed.
  He ***helped me collate*** *the data.*
  We ***watched them connect*** *the modem.*

Forms of the gerund in active and passive voice

	Active	Passive
Present	*I don't recall* ***reading*** *this book.*	*He resents* ***being imposed upon.***
Past	*I don't recall* ***having read*** *this book.*	*He resented* ***having been imposed upon.***

Use of the gerund

- After certain verbs – *begin, start, keep, see, go, stop, mention, consider, recommend,* etc.
  We ***went sightseeing.***
  Would you ***consider helping*** *us?*
  (See Unit 7, page 114 (reporting verbs) and Unit 2, page 38 (verbs related to crime and punishment) for more on this.)
- After verbs with dependent prepositions – *insist on, confess to, be fed up with, count on, agree to, consist of* etc.
  The scientists' success ***depends on securing*** *financial backing.*
  She ***congratulated him on winning*** *the prize.*
  (For a full list of verbs with dependent prepositions see the Appendix, page 252. See also Unit 2, page 37, Unit 7, page 114 and Unit 12 page 182.)
- After adjectives with dependent prepositions – *capable of, dependent on, good at, reliant on, responsible for, upset about,* etc.
  He was ***annoyed about being*** *overcharged.*
  She was finally ***successful in proving*** *her theory.*
  (For a full list of adjectives with dependent prepositions see the Appendix, page 254.)
- As the subject or the object of a sentence.
  Conducting *experiments is fun.*
  I don't enjoy ***note-taking*** *and* ***report-writing*** *though.*
- After time adverbials – *after, before, since, while, when* and *whenever.*
  Since winning *the prize, he has gained world-wide recognition.*
  They met ***while holidaying*** *in Greece.*
- After certain verbs related to observation – *see, sense, feel, observe, hear,* etc. in both the active and the passive voice. In this case, the action in question was observed while in progress.
  The police ***saw him entering*** *the building but they didn't see him leave.*
  He ***was heard shouting*** *insults at the boss.*

▶ Contrast these verbs followed by an infinitive with or without *to* (as listed above) where the action is completed.
The police ***saw him enter*** *the building.*
He ***was heard to shout.***

Advanced grammar points
Grammar point 1

Choose which ending, a or b, completes the sentences below.

1 We stopped to consult the road map
a when we realised it was totally inaccurate.
b when we realised we'd lost our way.

2 This time I remembered
a getting a receipt for your photocopies
b to get a receipt for your photocopies.

3 I hate
a to spend yet more money on car repairs this month.
b spending money on car repairs.

4 I'm trying
a to get this champagne cork out.
b wrapping a cloth round the cork.

5 I regret to tell
a my boss that I'd applied for another job.
b you that your application has not been successful.

Some verbs like *continue*, can be followed by a full infinitive or a gerund with very little difference in meaning, while the form that follows others depends on their meaning or context.

- Verbs of desire (e.g. *like, love, hate, can't bear, prefer*, etc.) are followed by *-ing* when they express a general state of affairs and are used with an infinitive when they refer to a hypothetical or potential event.
  *I **love travelling** abroad.* *I **would love to visit** Paris.*
  *I **can't bear studying** chemistry.* *I **couldn't bear to re-sit** my chemistry exam.*
- *Stop* is followed by an infinitive when it refers to changing activity for a specific purpose and *-ing* when it refers to ceasing an activity or habit.
  *The police **stopped the football match to clear** the fans off the pitch.*
  *I **stopped playing football** after I left school.*
- *Remember* and *forget* are followed by *-ing* when they refer to an actual event in the past and by an infinitive when they refer to an instruction which has been, should have been or should be carried out.
  *I **remember locking** the back door before I went out to work.*
  *You **never remember/always forget to lock** the back door.*
  *I'll **never forget watching** that lunar eclipse – it was breathtaking.*
- *Try* is followed by an infinitive when it refers to what someone is attempting to do and by *-ing* when it refers to something you do for a while to see if it works/is enjoyable/suitable etc.
  *I've **tried** several times **to get** that wine stain out of the carpet.*
  *I **tried putting** salt on it, but it didn't help a lot.*
- *Regret* is followed by *-ing* in the present or perfect form when referring to something you wish you had or hadn't done and by an infinitive when imparting bad news, usually in written form.
  *I **regret not asking/having asked** my grandma more about her life when I had the chance.*
  *I **regret to tell you** my grandmother passed away last month.*

Grammar point 2

Focus

1 Which, if any, of the sentences below are grammatically incorrect?

- **a** He wouldn't dare tell the boss what he really thought of him.
- **b** He wouldn't dare to tell the boss what he really thought of him.
- **c** She dared him tell the boss what he really thought of him.
- **d** Our physics teacher was excellent at helping us understand complicated concepts.
- **e** Our physics teacher was excellent at helping us to understand complicated concepts.
- **f** I'm trying and find out what happened.
- **g** I'll try and find out what happened.
- **h** I'll try to find out what happened.

2 Why and how would you change any sentences which you marked incorrect?

- *Dare* may be followed by a bare infinitive or an infinitive with *to* when it is intransitive. When followed by an object, however, it can only be followed by an infinitive with *to*
- *Help* may be followed by a bare infinitive or an infinitive with *to*, without any change in meaning.
- When the verb *try* does not have the endings *-ed, -es* or *-ing*, it may be followed by an infinitive with *to* or by *and* + bare infinitive, without any change in meaning.

Practice A

Circle the more appropriate verb to fill each gap below. If both are equally suitable, circle both.

Before Galileo, no-one had dared (1) .... the notion that the sun went round the earth.

1 a to challenge	**b** challenge	**c** both

I remember (2) .... the story of Newton and the apple at school and (3) .... that I could never have come to the same conclusion as Newton did if I'd been in his place.

2 a being told	**b** to be told	**c** both
3 a think	**b** thinking	**c** both

A: How's the physics class going?
B: Well, I'm trying (4) .... the theory of relativity, but I just can't get my head round it.
A: You could try (5) .... what Einstein did – shut your eyes and imagine you're travelling on a sunbeam.

4 a understanding	**b** to understand	**c** both
5 a and do	**b** doing	**c** both

Few people who watched Neil Armstrong (6) .... on the moon will forget (7) .... such a historic moment.

6 a walk	**b** walking	**c** both
7 a to witness	**b** witnessing	**c** both

After their conquest of the moon, the United States stopped (8) .... so much money in space exploration.

8 a investing	**b** to invest	**c** both

In 2001 a Russian team helped an American (9) .... the first fare-paying tourist in space.

9 a to become	**b** become	**c** both

Grammar point 3

Focus

1 What is the function of the *-ing* clauses in the sentences below? Match each sentence to one function (a – c).

1 Having left school at sixteen to get married, she hadn't completed her education.	**a** To indicate an action or event occurring at the same time as the one in the main clause.
2 Hoping to get into university, she went to private schools to study for the necessary qualifications.	**b** To indicate an action or event occurring immediately before the one in the main clause.
3 Trembling with emotion, she opened the letter that contained her exam results.	**c** To explain the reason for the action or event in the main clause.
4 Reading that she'd passed her exams, she leapt up and hugged her husband.	

To which of the sentences 1 – 4 could you add *on* or *upon* at the start of the *-ing* clause?

- Present and perfect *-ing* clauses may be used, in active or passive form, to show the reason for the action or event in the main clause.
  Having had his theories disproved*, he gave up research and went into business.*
- Present *-ing* clauses may be used, in active or passive form, to show two events occurred simultaneously.
  Being coaxed and reassured *by his mother, the child took his first steps.*
- Present *-ing* clauses may also be used, in active or passive form, to show two events which occurred one after the other. The words *on* or *upon* may be added.
  (On/upon) being told *the news, he flew into a rage.*

4 Choose which phrasal verb can be used to complete the gaps in the sentences below. In some sentences more than one verb may be appropriate.

1 We're having our loft insulated to stop heat being .... through the roof.
a given out b let out c let off

2 My pocket calculator .... solar energy.
a runs down b runs on c gives out

3 Terrorists .... a bomb in central Athens.
a set off b let off c let out

4 Wind power is an energy source that never ....
a runs out b gives out c turns off

5 I'll have to buy a new car soon, as the one I've got now is forever ....
a running out b breaking up c breaking down

6 In the Middle Ages, alchemists tried to .... lead .... gold.
a change into b turn off c turn into

7 Would you .... the TV, please?
a set off b put off c turn off

5 Complete the sentences below about inventions with an appropriate phrasal verb.

1 The foam fire extinguisher, which can .... burning oil or petrol, was invented by Professor Alexander Laurent of St Petersburg in 1905.

2 In 1960, the American physicist T.H. Maiman built the first laser, using a cylindrical rod of artificial ruby. It .... brief, penetrating pulses of light, ten million times as intense as sunlight.

3 In 1895 the Italian engineer Giuseppe Marconi .... the first radio signals using home-made apparatus.

4 The idea for .... coffee beans .... a soluble powder came from the Brazilian Institute of Coffee, but it wasn't until 1937, after eight years of research, that Nestle .... a process for doing this.

5 The first fridge to .... electricity was patented by two Swedish engineers in 1923.

6 Gunpowder was invented by the Chinese, possibly as early as in the ninth century AD, and was used for .... fireworks.

7 The first ballpoint pen was invented by two Hungarian brothers in 1938. In 1958 a Frenchman, Marcel Bich, created a cheap plastic version, the Bic pen, which was designed to be .... once the ink had ....

Use your English

Are you surprised by the dates given for any of the inventions above?
Which of the inventions above do you think is the most useful?
What do you think would be the most useful product or system that could be invented?

Adverbial phrases including gerunds and infinitives

Several adverbial phrases include gerunds and infinitives. These are used, mainly in spoken English, to organise what is being said and to provide information about the speaker's attitude to the information being given.

6 Match each phrase to the function (a – k) it performs.

1 bearing in mind that
2 generally speaking
3 joking apart
4 judging from appearances
5 to be perfectly frank
6 to cut a long story short
7 to make matters worse
8 to put it another way
9 to put it mildly
10 to sum up
11 to tell you the truth

a Showing your opinion is based on something you have seen.
b Showing that something is true most of the time.
c Showing that this is your personal opinion or that you are admitting something.
d Showing that your opinion is sincere or your information is correct and that you are aware it may upset the listener.
e Showing that you are about to rephrase something you or someone else said.
f Showing that you are being less critical than you could be.
g Showing that you will move from a humorous topic to a serious one.
h Introducing a further problem or difficulty.
i Reminding the listener of an important fact.
j Showing you are about to summarise points made earlier.
k Showing that you are coming to the end of a narrative and will not go into more detail.

7 For which phrases in exercise 6 above could these other adverbial phrases be substituted?

1 as far as I can see ....
2 in all honesty ....
3 on the whole ....
4 in other words ....
5 frankly speaking ....
6 considering that ....

8 Complete the sentences below with an appropriate phrase from exercises 6 and 7.

1 ...., it was I who broke your vase, not Penny.
2 I would have though she'd know the answer to that question, ... she studied physics at school.
3 We paid the carpenter a lot of money for those kitchen cupboards and yet they're not very good quality, ...
4 ...., more boys than girls take science subjects at school.
5 Anyway, ..., I got the job in the end, and that's all that matters, really, isn't it?
6 ...., I never liked Felicity very much anyway, so I'm quite glad you're not friends with her any more.
7 So I bandaged his knee, cleaned up the mess on the floor and then, ..., a fuse blew and all the lights went out!
8 So, ..., we have agreed that production of the XJ-20 can go ahead in January, as scheduled, and that you, Peter, will have overall responsibility for installing the necessary plant and equipment to ensure that ...
9 I saw him driving a brand new BMW last week so, ..., he must have landed that well-paid job.
10 As you can see from the chart, X is in inverse proportion to Y. ...., as X decreases, Y increases.

Summary

Reading

1 Skim-read these two texts. In terms of subject-matter, what do they have in common?

Text 1

A scientific task force has reported that collisions with 'near-earth objects', such as asteroids and comets, are no longer the stuff of science fiction, but represent a real threat. US and French astronomers recently calculated that 900 asteroids, all 1 km across or larger, are whizzing around the solar system on orbits that cross that of the earth. Although there is no record of any person being killed by a comet or asteroid, a large one could destroy civilisation. According to the task force, governments should aim to detect a potential collision years in advance, thus giving them time to take emergency measures.

Objects from space hit the earth all the time but most burn up harmlessly as shooting stars. However, a 100-metre object crashes into the planet every 10,000 years, triggering an explosion larger than the most powerful bomb ever let off. An object 1 kilometre in diameter scores a direct hit on the planet every 100,000 years. The most famous of these coincided with the extinction of the dinosaurs 65 million years ago. An asteroid of this size that hit solid earth would form a crater ten times its own size and would shower the stratosphere with dust, blotting out the sun, shutting down all plant growth and condemning those who survived to death by cold and starvation.

Unlike asteroids, which are composed of metal or stone, comets are aggregates of ice and dust which are weakly held together so that when they hit the atmosphere they start breaking up. As they get further down the pressure increases and they break up even faster, resulting in an explosion with a brilliant flash and scorching heat. A blast like that over a densely-populated area would kill 1.5 million people.

Text 2

The press and Hollywood often focus on the impact of a large asteroid, say 1 km in diameter, which would wipe out life within proximity of the impact site. More seriously, it would affect the whole world in indirect ways. The dust and/or vapour cloud created by an impact to either the land or the ocean could be big enough to create a 'nuclear winter', like a mini-ice age, and disrupt climate patterns, adversely affecting major food-growing regions of the world and straining world food supplies. However, such an impact is quite unlikely over the next thousand years, at least.

Of much greater concern should be asteroids in the 30 to 200 metre range, which are far greater in number. The Meteor Crater in Arizona, measuring roughly a kilometre in diameter, was caused by a nickel-iron rock only about 30 meters across. That's a very small asteroid which we couldn't see from telescopes until it's right above Earth – when it's much too late to do anything but duck for cover. However, as seventy per cent of the Earth is covered by oceans, an ocean impact is more likely and would also be much more damaging. An asteroid hitting land causes mainly localised damage. An asteroid hitting the ocean could create a tsunami (huge tidal wave) that would inflict catastrophic damage to coastal cities. The effects of an ocean impact would be felt much further away than the effects of a land impact, due to the more effective propagation of water waves. For example, the earthquake-induced tsunami in Chile in 1960 produced ten-metre high waves 10,600 km away in Hawaii, and waves up to 5 meters high in Japan, 17,000 km away from the earthquake's epicentre.

Summary section: practice

Questions on the texts

2 By using the phrase 'are no longer the stuff of science fiction' (Text 1, line 2), what impression does the author give of the risks of collisions with near earth objects?

3 What exactly was it that 'coincided with the extinction of the dinosaurs'? (Text 1, line 12)

4 Explain in your own words what is meant by 'duck for cover'. (Text 2, line 12)

Clues: In this phrase 'duck' is a verb, not a noun.
In this phrase 'cover' is a noun, not a verb.
You may still not know exactly what the verb 'duck' means, but if you saw a comet or asteroid approaching, what would you do?

5 Which phrases in paragraph 1 of Text 2 echo the idea of 'death by cold and starvation' mentioned in line 15 of Text 1?

Reminder: When answering this type of question, you should write down the exact words and phrases given in the text, without any paraphrasing or rephrasing.

Summary writing

In a paragraph of between 50 and 70 words, summarise, in your own words as far as possible, the possible effects of near-earth objects hitting our planet.

6 Check that you're clear about what exactly 'near-earth objects' are.

Clue: See Text 1 for a definition of these.

7 Re-read the texts, highlighting or underlining all possible content points.

8 The content points could be organised in two possible ways, as shown below.

Option 1

1. Possible effects of impacts by large asteroids.
2. Possible effects of impacts by small asteroids on land.
3. Possible effects of impacts by small asteroids on oceans.
4. Possible effects of impacts by comets.

Option 2

1. Possible immediate effects of impacts by large asteroids.
2. Possible longer-term effects of impacts by large asteroids.
3. Possible effects of impacts by small asteroids on oceans.
4. Possible effects of impacts by comets.

Re-read the texts and decide which of these options would better reflect the information given in both texts.

9 Rewrite the four content points, as concisely as possible, in your own words.

10 Check the number of words in your draft summary.

11 Rewrite the summary, paraphrasing it if necessary.

*The rubric for the summary mentions 'possible effects', therefore the most appropriate verb forms to use will be modals such as **would**, **could** and **might**.*

14 Language and psychology

Grammar • Inversion

Vocabulary • Phrasal verbs and set phrases: language and psychology
• Collocations: compound adjectives
• Word formation: prefixes *bi-, co-/con-/com-, sub-, sym-/syn-, trans-, uni-*

Summary • Practice

Grammar: Inversion

Grammar overview

If we want to give additional emphasis to a particular part of a sentence we can change the usual order of subject-verb-object; this is known as 'inversion'. It can be done in a number of ways.

So and *such*

- In the pattern, *so* + adjective + be + subject + *that* clause.
  So bizarre was his behaviour that *his wife called the doctor.*
- In the pattern *such* + be + noun/noun phrase + *that* clause.
  Such was the complexity of the problem that *even the experts were baffled.*
- See Unit 3, Advanced grammar points, page 47 for the following structure with inversion: *so* + adjective + *a/an* + noun + *is/was* + he/she/it + *that* clause
- Inversion also occurs in conditional sentences. (See Unit 10, page 153.)

as

- With *as*.
  We were furious about the noise, ***as were*** *our neighbours.*
  I went into therapy, ***as did*** *my husband.*

Short answers

- In what are often called 'short answers'.

I am upset *I am feeling upset.*	***So am I.***	*I am not upset.* *I am not feeling upset.*	***Neither am I.***
He speaks French.	***So does she.***	*He doesn't speak French.*	***Neither does she.***
He has finished. *He has been studying.*	***So have I.***	*He hasn't finished.* *He hasn't been studying.*	***Neither have I.***
I was angry. *I was laughing.*	***So was he.***	*I wasn't angry.* *I wasn't laughing.*	***Neither was he.***
She helped.	***So did we.***	*She didn't help.*	***Neither did we.***
They had finished. *They had been studying.*	***So had he.***	*They hadn't finished.* *They hadn't been studying.*	***Neither had he.***

Advanced grammar points

Grammar point 1

1 What parts of speech are the words or phrases in bold in the extract below?
2 What do you notice about the order of the subject and verb following the underlined words in the sentences numbered 1 to 7?
3 Why does this construction not appear in sentence 8?

The village square was gaily decorated with flags. (1) **On one side** was a large platform for the mayor and members of the town council. (2) **Along the other three sides** were small stalls selling snacks, drinks and gaudy souvenirs. Suddenly the sound of a brass band could be heard. (3) 'Hooray, **here** comes the procession!' Lucy shouted, jumping up and down. (4) **Rarely** had Delia seen her daughter so excited. 'Can I go to the front of the crowd now?' Lucy asked. (5) '**Under no circumstances** are you to go anywhere alone,' Delia said firmly, 'but perhaps Daddy will let you sit on his shoulders.' (6) Then **round the corner of the church** marched the brass band. (7) **Next** came a group of children dressed in traditional costume. (8) Then, **from high up on her father's shoulders**, Lucy saw something no-one else did: a man ...

Subject – verb inversion occurs:

- when prepositional phrases of place (e.g. *on one side (of the square)*) are put at the start of a sentence or clause. This construction is possible only with intransitive verbs, e.g. *be, stand, sit, hang, lie,* etc.
- when adverbs or prepositional phrases of movement (e.g. *round the corner, in, out, up*) are put at the start of a sentence or clause. It is possible only with intransitive verbs e.g. *go, come, run, appear, jump, march*, etc.
- when time adverbs (*first, next, again, then*) are put at the start of a sentence or clause. This construction appears with a very limited number of verbs, principally *be* and *come.*
- in conversational English, after *here* and *there,* principally with the verbs *be, come* and *go.*
- when negative or restrictive adverbs or phrases (for example *never, rarely, seldom, not only, nowhere, in no way, on no account, under no circumstances, not for one minute*) are put at the start of a sentence or clause. In this construction transitive and intransitive verbs may be inverted.
  In no way did *the report blame her for the accident.*
  Not only does *he have impeccable manners, he's also exceedingly generous.*

Practice A

Complete the sentences below by rewriting the words in the correct order. Use inversion where it is grammatically possible. Follow the example.

Nowhere / he / spare parts / find / for / could / his / motorcycle
Nowhere could he find spare parts for his motorcycle.

1 There / note / last / my / £20 / goes
....

2 Rarely / at a wedding / I / fun / such / have / had
....

3 On no account / lift / after / objects / should / the / you / heavy / operation
....

4 There, at the back of the cupboard, / had / was / ring / lost / the / I
....

5 On the door of the fridge / stuck / Mary / 'I'm leaving' /saying / had / a note
....

6 Down the middle of the road / a torrent / water / ran / of / greenish
....

7 Not for one minute / that story / I / me / you / did / told / believe
....

Grammar point 2

Each sentence below has a grammatical error in it. Identify the error and correct it.

1 Hardly had we got to the party than he wanted to leave.
2 No sooner had she finished one cigarette when she would light another one.
3 Not until reached I the supermarket checkout did I realise I'd left my wallet at home.
4 Hardly wanted any children tickets for the excursion.

- When a sentence starts with the adverbs *hardly, scarcely* or *barely* and has the meaning 'not long after', inversion occurs in the clause immediately after the adverb and the second clause is introduced with *when*.
  Scarcely had we *laid out the picnic things* ***when*** *it began to rain.*
- When a sentence starts with the adverb *no sooner,* inversion occurs in the clause immediately after the adverb and the second clause is introduced with *than*.
  No sooner had I *got in the bath* ***than*** *the doorbell rang.*
- When a sentence starts with the adverbs *not until, only when* and *only after,* inversion occurs in the second clause, not the one immediately following the adverb.
  Only when you've finished *all your exams* ***may you*** *go out again in the evenings.*
- When the adverbs *hardly, scarcely* or *barely* modify a noun or pronoun rather than a verb, inversion does not occur.
  Barely *ten people attended the talk.*

Practice B

Combine the two sentences into one using the adverb given in brackets. Follow the example.

Harry completed a degree in Japanese. He went on to study Korean after that. (no sooner)
No sooner had Harry completed a degree in Japanese than he went on to study Korean.

1 The audience burst out laughing. That was when the interpreter realised he'd made a mistake. (only when)

....

2 The boat left the harbour. Not long after that it began to sink. (barely)

....

3 Susan stormed out the door in a temper. Seconds later she came back to apologise. (no sooner)

....

4 Ask me politely. Then I'll iron your shirt for you. (not until)

....

5 I didn't have time to digest my lunch. They served us afternoon tea. (hardly)

....

6 Finish your psychology course first. Then you can think about training as a child psychologist. (only after)

....

7 We'd only just arrived at our holiday destination. My father phoned to say my mother was very ill. (scarcely)

....

Practice C

Complete the second sentence so that it has a similar meaning to the first sentence, using the word given. Do not change the word given. You must use between three and eight words, including the word given.

1 He's lost the book I lent him and now he says I didn't ever give it to him.
denies
Not only .... that I ever lent it to him.

2 His behaviour and dedication do not at all come up to the standard we expect.
meet
In no way .... standard.

3 This patient must be attended at all times.
circumstances
Under .... unattended.

4 This was the most difficult case of psychological trauma he had ever dealt with.
faced
Never before .... difficult case of psychological trauma.

5 It is estimated that only about 1,000 pandas still exist in the wild.
thought
Scarcely .... in the wild.

6 The woman was so anxious that she could only go outdoors if she took tranquillisers.
by
Such .... tranquillisers could she go outdoors.

7 We found the key we'd been looking for lying under the sofa.
lay
There, under .... key.

8 She underwent years of training in order to become a psychiatrist then almost immediately decided she wanted to do something else.
qualified
No .... she decided she wanted to do something else.

Practice D

Complete the gaps in the text with one word only. The first one has been done as an example.

In countries **(0)** ....where.... two or more languages are spoken, language is frequently a political and highly emotive issue. **(1)** .... Canada is officially bilingual, the mainly French-speaking province of Quebec introduced a law in 1976 which, **(2)** .... other measures, banned languages **(3)** .... than French on commercial signs and restricted admissions **(4)** .... English-speaking schools. In 1988 the supreme court of Canada ruled that some sections of this law were illegal. No **(5)** .... had they done so **(6)** .... thousands of French speakers took to the streets **(7)** .... protest. Under the regime of General Franco, the Basque language, spoken **(8)** .... about 600,000 people in Spain, was forbidden. So strict **(9)** .... this ban that people using Basque in public could be imprisoned.

Linguistic suppression still goes on but, **(10)** .... the whole, governments nowadays are more tolerant of their minority languages. **(11)** .... has this reversal of attitudes been more pronounced than in Wales. Until well into the twentieth century, Welsh was all **(12)** .... illegal, its use being forbidden in schools, the courts and at many places of work. Only **(13)** .... a long campaign of protest and vandalism by Welsh speakers in the 1960s **(14)** .... the British government allow Welsh to become an official language. **(15)** .... twelve per cent of the population of Wales speak Welsh as a first language but the country is now officially bilingual, all public signs are in Welsh as **(16)** .... as English, and Welsh is the language of instruction in schools in predominantly Welsh-speaking areas.

Vocabulary

Phrasal verbs and set phrases: language and psychology

1 These extracts from an article about dealing with toddlers and pre-school children contain phrasal verbs and set phrases related in some way to language and psychology. Match each verb or phrase in bold to a definition.

Discipline

✻ If you need to (1) **tell** a toddler **off** for doing something wrong, do so immediately – threats of 'just you wait till Daddy gets home' are largely ineffective as the child will have forgotten what she did wrong by the time her father gets round to (2) **giving** her **a talking-to.**

✻ Make it clear it is the behaviour that is unacceptable, not the child herself. ('That was a naughty thing you did when you threw your lunch on the floor,' rather than 'You're a bad girl') and (3) **point out** why it was wrong. (Now I'll have to clean the kitchen floor and we won't be able to spend so long in the park as we'd planned.)

✻ Avoid (4) **reeling off** a catalogue of all her other misdemeanours that day; this will only serve to give her the impression that she is basically a 'bad' person.

✻ If your child (5) **talks back** when criticised or given instructions, don't react with another insult – leave the room until you've both (6) **calmed down** and tackle the issue again later when your (7) **feelings are** no longer **running high.** You then have a much better chance of (8) **talking** her **into** doing what you wanted in the first place.

Communication

✻ Pre-school children can (9) **gabble away** for hours despite having a fairly limited vocabulary. This can be tiresome for parents, but it is an essential stage of language-learning. Make some time in the day when you (10) **join in with** his conversations and then he will be more likely to (11) **pipe down** without protest when you need a little peace and quiet.

✻ Avoid (12) **talking down to** your child – answering questions with 'you're too young to understand that sort of thing' stifles a child's curiosity and desire to learn. Young children are capable of (13) **taking in** quite sophisticated ideas, such as why we have night and day, if they are explained in simple enough terms.

✻ Encourage your child to talk about his feelings and let him cry when it's appropriate – if he is not allowed to do so, he will (14) **bottle** his emotions **up** and they may emerge, much more violently, in the form of tantrums.

✻ Make clear rules for what happens when you have visitors – for example, he mustn't expect you to (15) **break off** every two minutes when talking to friends or relatives just because he's bored, but that it is acceptable to (16) **break in** if he feels unwell or needs to be taken to the bathroom.

✻ (17) **Talk** your child **through** any plans you have for his day, especially if these involve new activities, such as his first day at play-school or the arrival of a new babysitter.

a answer rudely ☐
b avoid showing ☐
c be angry or upset ☐
d be quiet/stop talking ☐
e become quiet after being anxious, upset or excited ☐
f explain something in detail so you are sure it is understood ☐
g interrupt ☐
h participate in an activity with someone else ☐
i patronise someone/talk to someone as if they were stupid ☐
j persuade someone to do something ☐
k repeat a list of things that you remember ☐
l stop an activity, especially a conversation ☐
m talk rapidly and continuously ☐
n talk to someone angrily because they have done something wrong (Watch out. This matches two verbs/phrases) ☐ ☐
o tell someone something they did not already know or had not thought about ☐
p understand ☐

2 The phrasal verb below is the opposite of one in the text. Which one?

talk out of ≠ ....

3 The verb *talk* may also be combined with an adverb to make a phrasal verb meaning 'persuade someone to accept your opinion'. What is the adverb?

4 Rephrase the parts of these sentences in bold using phrasal verbs or set phrases from this unit. Make any other grammatical changes that are necessary.

1 After years of **keeping** his emotions **under tight control**, Bob finds it hard to express his affection for his wife and family.

2 The fact that a two-year old may be able to **recite** the numbers from 1 to 100 **easily** is a sign of a good memory rather than of superior intelligence.

3 **People are getting very upset** about the proposed closure of the factory and the job losses this would entail.

4 I didn't really **understand** much of what Tom said as he was **talking very fast** as usual.

5 I don't want you to feel that I'm **patronising you**; it's just that the procedure we're about to perform is complicated so I want to **explain** it **step-by-step** first.

6 Perhaps we should **stop the meeting now** for coffee and after that we may be able to **get them to accept our point of view**.

7 I would **tell** my child **I was very angry with him** if he **answered me as rudely as that** in public.

8 I'd like to **say, just in case you're not aware of it already**, that the temperature can go as high as forty degrees here, so if you want to **participate in** any of our outdoor classes, you should wear a hat and bring a bottle of water with you.

9 Luckily, I managed to **persuade my sister not to ask for a divorce but that she should go** for marriage guidance counselling instead.

10 Would everyone please **relax and be quiet**? We'll never cover all the points to be discussed if you keep **interrupting each other**. So if you could just **not speak** while someone else is talking, we might be able to reach some decisions.

Collocations: compound adjectives

5 Several adjectives which describe people's character or behaviour are formed from two adjectives linked by a hyphen. Complete the chart below, ticking each box where two adjectives collocate to form a compound adjective. The first one (*cold-blooded*) has been done as an example.

	-blooded	-headed	-hearted	-minded	-spirited	-tempered	-willed
cold	✓						
hard							
high							
hot							
level							
strong							
sweet							
weak							

6 Complete the gaps in the sentences below with collocations from the chart in exercise 5. Use each compound adjective once only.

1 He's forever complaining that moral standards are falling, but I know for a fact that he wasn't so .... in his youth.

2 How could you be so .... as to refuse to help your own son when he's lost his job!

3 I don't know why you have any sympathy for the defendant; as far as I can see, he's a .... murderer.

4 I wouldn't say Linda was a naughty child, but she is very boisterous and ...., which can be wearing at times.

5 I'm looking for an assistant who can work under pressure and who will remain .... if there's a crisis.

6 The manager's so .... that he lets his secretary take all his decisions for him.

7 Several people were worried that the minister might bow to political pressure and be persuaded out of making the reforms he had promised, but he turned out to be more .... than anyone had expected.

8 I'm surprised that Verity's decided to go in for charity work; she always seemed to me to be .... and totally lacking in compassion.

9 Magda's a .... child, who loves to make cards and gifts for people, or help them if they're tired or ill.

10 John's the man we should bring in to decide which people we need to lay off; he's a .... businessman and he won't let his emotions cloud his judgement.

11 Mediterranean people are widely believed to be more .... than their less expressive Northern European neighbours.

12 Rudi's so .... that he would invest all his money in some crazy scheme without thinking twice about the possible risks, and so .... that he won't listen to anyone who warns him that he might be doing something unwise.

13 She and her husband are both ...., so they end up fighting almost every day.

7 Which words in the first row of the chart in exercise 5 would the adjectives below collocate with? What does the resulting compound adjective mean?

absent	blue	empty	even	kind	light	narrow	public

8 One of the words in the first row of the chart can also collocate with an adverb or a noun placed in front of it. Which word is it?

academically- .... = able to think in an academic way
fashion- .... = interested in fashion

Can you think of any other adverbs and nouns which could collocate with this word in a similar way?

Use your English

Work with a partner and write a short description of an imaginary person, which could be summarised by one of the adjectives you have studied in this section. When all pairs are ready, take turns to read out your description and the rest of the class must guess which adjective you chose.

Example: *hot-tempered*
You say: *Our Maths teacher gets angry at the slightest provocation and then he shouts at everyone in sight.*

Word formation: prefixes *bi-, co-/com-/con-, sub-, sym/syn-, trans-, uni-*

9 The prefixes below can be added to nouns, adjectives or verbs to alter their meaning. Match each prefix to the meaning it conveys.

Prefixes

1 **bi-** as in *bicentenary, bisect*
2 **co/com/con-** as in *coexist, commiserate, configuration*
3 **sub-** as in *subnormal, subcommittee*
4 **sym/syn-** as in *symmetrical, synergy*
5 **trans-** as in *transcontinental, transaction, transfigure*
6 **uni-** as in *universal, unilateral*

Meanings

a across/between two things or groups/change in some way
b one, single
c together, sharing
d together, with
e twice/double/consisting of two parts
f under or below/part of a whole

10 Some of the above prefixes, especially *sub-*, can be added to a large number of words. Others, particularly *com-, con-, sym-* and *syn-* are more frequently added to a stem, often of Latin or Greek origin, which does not exist as a word. They are therefore less likely to appear in a Proficiency word formation exercise. Put the words below in the correct column of the chart, and for those that go in the second column, write the word from which they are derived. Follow the examples.

bicycle	**compassionate**	**subcontract**	**sympathise**	**translate**
biped	**compel**	**submerse**	**symphony**	**transplant**
coincidence	**compromise**	**subsoil**	**synthesis**	**uniform**
combine	**concentrate**	**symbolise**	**transcend**	**unilateral**
commiserate	**configuration**	**symmetry**	**transcript**	**unique**

Stem is not a complete word	Stem is a complete word
biped, combine, ...	bicycle (cycle), coincidence (incidence),
....	commiserate (misery), ...
....	....
....	....
....	....
....	....
....	....

11 Complete the gaps in the text with a word formed from the word given in the margin. The first one has been done as an example. Four of the words you need to write include prefixes you have studied in this unit.

Freud claimed that his aim through treatment was to **(0)** ....*enable*.... people to work and love effectively. We have come a long way since the days when Freud had to probe the depths of his own **(1)** .... as no-one else was willing or able to analyse him, but the aims of **(2)** .... therapists remain the same.	ABLE CONSCIOUS TEMPORARY
What is hard to quantify is how effective the 'talking therapies' really are. The very nature of the work, which tends often to be part of an **(3)** .... process, is not something that lends itself well to audit. How, after all, do you measure happiness? Indeed, it has never even been established in scientific terms whether the most **(4)** .... aspect is simply the therapeutic value of having the **(5)** .... attention of a rapt listener.	GO BENEFIT DIVIDE
However, what research has been done reveals wide-ranging and positive **(6)** .... The mental health charity *Mind* interviewed 500 people who had had experiences as mental health patients, and the vast majority viewed talking therapies as '**(7)** .... and validating'. People with personality difficulties, who have traditionally been considered **(8)** .... by psychiatric services, are responding well to cognitive **(9)** .... therapies. Research into treatments for depression shows that a combination of drugs and therapy is more effective than either on its own. Many people suffering from **(10)** .... compulsions and fears have had their lives **(11)** .... in a relatively short time by the skilful intervention of therapists. For those who have been helped to **(12)** .... and overcome their problems, for those who have been led to a greater understanding of their motivations, for those who have been helped to work and love more effectively, therapy is **(13)**	COME FIRM TREAT BEHAVE ABLE FORM FRONT REPLACE

Gapped sentences

12 Think of **one** word which can be used to complete all three sentences in each group below. Follow the example.

- The young man devoted his life to the *pursuit* of pleasure.
- I have to admit that hill walking is a *pursuit* which doesn't interest me at all.
- The flustered mother ran out of the supermarket in hot *pursuit* of her absconding toddler.

All the words you need to write are nouns or verbs which have appeared elsewhere in this unit, but in other contexts.

1
- No sooner had his wife been allowed to leave hospital than he arranged for a nurse to .... her at home.
- When I was a child, we had to .... church every Sunday.
- I'll join you for a drink a bit later, but there are a few matters I must .... to before leaving the office.

2
- Apparently this has been the wettest autumn in living ....
- She has set up a charitable fund in .... of her husband.
- Having a photographic ...., she finds it easy to remember faces.

3
- All those late nights she spends in the office must be .... on Margaret's health.
- At this stage, there's no .... who will win the election.
- Dyslexics often have difficulty in .... left from right.

4
- Feeling shy from being surrounded by so many unfamiliar people, the small boy .... back when he was offered some cake.
- The fate of the condemned man .... in the balance for weeks while the court considered his appeal.
- The walls of the castle were .... with rich tapestries.

5
- I would like to take .... with the remark you made in your editorial about Gaelic speakers.
- While thumbing through a back .... of *The Financial Times* in the dentist's waiting-room, Mike came across his dream job.
- Every time he suggests they should see a counsellor, his wife manages to evade the ....

13 Using a dictionary, check the exact meaning of any phrasal verbs, idioms or usages that were unfamiliar to you.

Study tip

As exam time approaches, revision can become stressful. Try this stress-free method of helping you to remember vocabulary or phrases.

- Write the words or phrases you want to remember on separate pieces of paper, using large letters.
- Stick the pieces of paper up in different places around your room/house, roughly at eye level.
- Leave a set of words or phrases there for three or four days, then change them for new ones.

This method accesses the unconscious mind; you see the words/phrases out of the corner of your eye and the brain takes them in without your being consciously aware of 'learning' them.

Summary

Reading

1 Skim-read these two texts. In terms of subject-matter, what do they have in common?

Text 1

A friend of mine once told me of his first halting efforts to speak Japanese. He was working in an American company in Tokyo where all communication in the workplace was conducted in English, so he had no pressing need to learn the language. His wife, however, was taking Japanese lessons and passed on what she had learnt to him. The first few times he aired his Japanese in public, his efforts were met with politeness but he nevertheless got the impression he was doing something wrong. Quite some time went by before one of his Japanese colleagues plucked up the courage to tell him he spoke Japanese 'like a woman' and explained that often different vocabulary is used for the same objects depending on whether a man or a woman is speaking.

Japanese is not the only language which makes such distinctions, and, although the vocabulary doesn't change, research shows that gender can affect speech patterns in English too. Typically women use a higher frequency of softening devices – such as 'I would think ...', 'sort of' or 'a bit/rather' – than men do. This gives the impression of being unassertive, but is in fact intended as a politeness strategy. They also tend to frame requests or suggestions as questions, which can frequently lead to misunderstandings with men, who favour a more direct approach. Thus, when a woman asks her husband 'Would you like to go out to eat tonight?' she is attempting to open up a discussion of the pros and cons of the idea. Frequently, however, she will be met by a disappointingly blunt answer like 'No, I'm tired' as the man assumes she merely wanted to know his opinion.

Text 2

Women are widely believed to be much more talkative than men, but some recent research has challenged this notion. In an experiment designed to measure the amount of speech produced, three pictures by the artist Albrecht Durer were presented to men and women separately. The subjects were told to take as much time as they wanted to describe the pictures. The average time for men was 13.0 minutes, and for women 3.17 minutes. The reasons for this disparity could lie in the fact that, at least historically speaking, men have had a more prominent role in society and in the business world and so it has been more common, and acceptable, for them to dominate dinner-table conversations or give long wordy speeches. Alternatively, it could be that women are loquacious within the context of an intimate conversation with friends, but not when required to hold forth alone on a topic.

What is not disputed, however, is the fact that male verbosity dries up when it comes to expressing emotions. The reasons for this lie more with socialisation than genes, as male babies tend to be more emotionally expressive than female ones. Several studies of gender role development show that both mothers and fathers discourage their sons from expressing emotions such as sadness and fear, while encouraging their daughters to express vulnerability and affection. Peer groups complete this socialisation process; young girls typically play with one or two others in activities that foster the skills of empathy, self-awareness and expression of feelings. Boys, on the other hand, play structured games in larger groups in which stoicism, toughness and competition are learned.

Summary section: practice

Questions on the texts

2 What are the 'distinctions' referred to in Text 1, line 11?

3 Explain in your own words why the writer has used the phrase 'a disappointingly blunt answer' in line 20 of Text 1?

4 Which phrase in paragraph 2 of Text 2 echoes the statistics given in the first paragraph of the same text about talking time?

5 What is the writer's opinion of the relative importance of heredity and environment where language development is concerned?

Summary writing

In a paragraph of between 50 and 70 words, summarise, in your own words as far as possible, the ways in which gender affects language use.

15 Business and industry

Grammar • Emphasis

Vocabulary • Phrasal verbs: business and commerce
• Verbs with 'empty' *it*
• Word formation: revision

Summary • Practice

Grammar: Emphasis

Grammar overview

There are a number of different ways to give more emphasis to certain parts of a sentence.

- By using reflexive pronouns.
  *He managed to repair the kettle **himself**.*
  *They didn't trust me. They wanted to count the money **themselves**.*
- By the use of repetition.
  *They **talked and talked** but still couldn't reach an agreement.*
  *He worked there, **day in, day out**, for over 20 years.*
  *The management board has discussed this question **time and time again** without finding a solution.*
  *The company's profits rose steadily **year after year**.*
- By using *whoever, whatever*, etc.
  ***Whatever** you do, don't mention the report to the boss.*
  *I know that **whenever** I'm in trouble, I can turn to my friends.*
- By using *do* or *did*.
  *I **do** hope you'll come and visit us again!*
  *Oh, I **did** enjoy that!*
- By using *the fact/the problem/the thing/the point is ...*
  ***The fact is that** without this order, the company could go bankrupt.*
  ***The trouble is** I can't remember my bank account PIN number.*
- By using collocations with particular adjectives or adverbs.
  *Every time I go into his office he's got an expression of **complete boredom** on his face.*
  *He couldn't have lied about the price – he's always been **scrupulously honest** in his dealings with us.*

Advanced grammar points

Grammar point 1

Focus

1 Read the short text below.

> Ralph had always dreamed of becoming the managing director of his company. He achieved this by the age of thirty-five, but at great cost to his health.

The second sentence in the text could be rephrased in several different ways.

1 At great cost to his health, he achieved this by the age of thirty-five.
2 By the age of thirty-five he achieved this, but at great cost to his health.
3 This he achieved by the age of thirty-five, but at great cost to his health.

Which sentence would you choose if you wanted to emphasise:

a How young Ralph was when he achieved his dream?
b The price Ralph paid for his success?
c Ralph's achievement?

2 Which of the sentences below (a – c) would you choose if you wanted to emphasise:

1 Ralph's choice in life?
2 The fact that this is your personal opinion?

a I find it rather sad that he placed ambition before his well-being.
b To have placed ambition before his well-being I find rather sad.
c That he placed ambition before his well-being I find rather sad.

- Depending on which part of a sentence you wish to emphasise, the normal order of the clauses can be changed and the one you feel is most important can be brought to the front of the sentence. This technique is called 'fronting'.
- A clause containing the relative pronoun *this, that, these* or *those* is emphasised by bringing the pronoun to the front of the clause or sentence.
  On the whole, she's easy to work for, but never arrive late for a meeting. ***That*** *she will not tolerate.*
- Sometimes when a word or clause is fronted, subject-verb inversion must occur.
  Not even once ***did he regret*** *his decision.*
  Lying on her desk ***was the key*** *she had been looking for.*

▶ See Unit 14, Advanced grammar points 1 and 2 (pages 208 and 210) for explanations and other examples of this.

Practice A

Rephrase the sentences below using fronting to change their emphasis. Make any necessary grammatical changes, as illustrated in Grammar point 1. The beginning of each new sentence is given to help you.

I think it's admirable that she's done so much to foster fair trade.
To have done so much to foster fair trade I think is admirable.

1 I find it astonishing that my old classmate is now the Minister for Trade.
That ....

2 I've been slaving away on this wretched report for the last three days.
For ....

3 I don't have the faintest idea how I can finish the report on time.
How ....

4 Don't dare smoke in my office. I won't put up with that.
Don't dare smoke in my office. ....

5 She got the promotion she wanted thanks to exceeding her sales targets by twenty percent.
Thanks ....

6 It seems odd that he gave up such an interesting and well-paid job.
To ....

7 She had always longed to visit Japan. She finally managed to do this when her company sent her there on a buying trip.
She had always longed to visit Japan. ....

8 Our profits rose last year, for the first time in a decade.
For ....

Grammar point 2

1 Read the short text below.

Both of Ralph's parents were high achievers. (1) **It may have been because of this that he became so ambitious**. However, neither of them expected Ralph to do particularly well since (2) **it was his elder brother Frank who performed better at school**. At the age of sixteen, Ralph left school and got a job selling household goods from door-to-door. (3) **It was then that he discovered he had a head for business**.

2 Which of the clauses or sentences in bold emphasises:
a a time **b** a reason **c** a contrast

3 What do you notice about the structure of the phrase and sentences in bold?

Another way to achieve emphasis is by using a construction known as 'clefting'. This follows the pattern:

it + a form of the verb *be* + emphasised element + clause beginning with *who/that*

The emphasised element can be:

- a pronoun, noun or noun phrase.
  It's ***she*** *who is responsible for after-sales service, not me.*
  It's ***the long working hours*** *that I don't like about this job.*
  It was ***selling things from door-to-door*** *that taught him to be a persuasive salesman.*
- a prepositional phrase.
  It was ***from the press*** *that we first learnt about the proposed closure of the factory.*
- an adverb or adverbial phrase.
  It was ***twenty years ago*** *that we launched this product and it's still going strong.*
  It may have been ***because of this*** *that he became so ambitious.*

Grammar point 3

Focus

1 Match the beginnings of sentences (1 – 7) with the ending (a – g) that would logically complete each sentence.

1 All the shareholders care about is	**a** that they meet lots of different people.
2 What this country needs is	**b** a box of cigars.
3 All I can do now is	**c** cut public spending on health and education.
4 What they like about the job is	**d** that the chairman should resign.
5 What I think is	**e** to start looking for a new job.
6 What they did was	**f** that the company makes a profit.
7 All he got when he retired was	**g** a change of leadership.

2 What does *all* mean in sentences 1, 3 and 7 above?
a everything or everyone **b** the only thing

Another form of clefting follows the pattern:
What/All + subject + verb + *is/was* + emphasised element

The emphasised element can be:

- a noun phrase.
  What she wants is ***some recompense for the extra hours she's put in.***
- an infinitive clause, with or without *to*.
  All I did was ***(to) tell the truth.***
- a *that* clause.
  What they hope is ***that a more modern-sounding name will change the company's image.***

Practice B

Rephrase the sentences below, emphasising the sections in bold. Two examples are given to help you.

Example 1: Bob's in charge of this negotiation, **not you**.
You write: *It's not you who's in charge of this negotiation, but Bob.*
Example 2: You need **a holiday**.
You write: *What you need is a holiday.*

1 I just **pulled** the jammed bit of paper out of the fax machine, and now it won't work.
All ....

2 **The opportunity to travel** attracted me to the job.
It ....

3 The management believe **these measures will make the company more profitable.**
What ....

4 He walked out of the meeting **because he felt unappreciated**.
It ....

5 The union asked for **a five percent wage increase**.
All ....

6 The new factory is to be located **in Malaysia**.
It ....

7 He wants **an office with a view**.
What ....

8 She's motivated by power, **not money**.
It ....

9 Next I'm going to **show you how to repair the machine**.
What ....

Practice C

Complete the second sentence so that it has a similar meaning to the first sentence, using the word given. Do not change the word given. You must use between three and eight words, including the word given.

1 The shareholders think that the company doesn't make large enough profits.
profitable
What the shareholders .... enough.

2 Maybe we didn't get the contract because our price was too high.
competitive
It may have .... we didn't get the contract.

3 I realised that the secretary was the real decision-maker, not the boss.
took
I realised it was not .... decisions.

4 I admire his efficiency more than his ambition.
rather
It .... I admire.

5 The consultant spent three weeks in the company but produced only a short report.
show
After a three-week consultancy all .... a short report.

Practice D

Complete the gaps in the text with **one** word only. The first one has been done as an example.

Some years **(0)** ....*ago*......, small farmers in the Toledo region of southern Belize found it was **(1)** .... worth harvesting their cacao bushes, **(2)** .... low was the price they were being offered. Their situation was not an unusual one. It **(3)** .... the crops produced by small-scale farmers in developing countries, **(4)** .... as bananas, cocoa, honey, sugar, tea and coffee, **(5)** .... are most subject to price fluctuations on the volatile world commodities market. Concerned **(6)** .... this state of affairs, a number of organisations got together in 1994 **(7)** .... establish the Fairtrade Foundation. The first agreement the foundation organised was between the Toledo farmers and **(8)** .... British chocolate manufacturer. This deal cut out the middle men and guaranteed the farmers fair prices for their cacao beans. **(9)** .... was also a condition of the agreement that the premium prices paid for the cacao **(10)** .... be invested in long-term social goals. **(11)** .... to the security the agreement gave them, the farmers were able to plan ahead and money started coming back into their communities.

(12) .... the Fairtrade Foundation found difficult at the beginning was **(13)** .... raise consumer awareness of the issues involved. Not only **(14)** .... few people heard of the concept, **(15)** .... the supermarkets were, at best, indifferent. **(16)** .... after churches, development groups and charities had put pressure on local supermarkets **(17)** .... fair trade goods start to appear on the shelves. There are now more than seventy varieties of **(18)** .... on sale in Britain, and they are selling well, showing that consumers **(19)** .... care where their goods are coming from, and that they are produced in a decent way.

Vocabulary

Phrasal verbs: business and commerce

1 The newspaper article below contains phrasal verbs related to business and commerce. Match each phrasal verb in bold to a definition.

The online sportswear company tracker.com, (1) **set up** two years ago by dotcom entrepreneur Kate Pitt, is to be (2) **taken over** by clothing giant Vantex. Pitt believed that she had (3) **hit upon** a potentially profitable concept by offering high-quality sportswear for sale online, but the public were slow to accept the idea and sales were sluggish. In addition, the company (4) **ran into** problems with distribution and was forced to (5) **pay out** compensation to disgruntled customers whose orders arrived late, or not at all. In an effort to boost sales, Pitt began to (6) **give** free gifts **away** with purchases worth more than £100, but this move failed to (7) **turn** the business **round**. Realising that tracker.com was unable to (8) **break even,** Pitt announced a month ago that she would have to (9) **wind** the company **down** unless a buyer could be found.

Bob Svensson of Vantex will (10) **take over from** Pitt as managing director of tracker.com, which will be renamed vantexonline.com. In a press conference yesterday he said that the idea behind tracker.com was a good one but that Pitt had not been able (11) **sink** enough capital **in** the company to (12) **see** it **through** the tricky start-up phase. He said he was confident that the new company would become profitable with Vantex's financial muscle and brand name behind it. Ms Pitt says she has no definite plans for the future but that she is satisfied with the deal she (13) **pulled off** with Vantex, which will allow her to (14) **pay off** her personal and business debts.

- **a** be bought by/come under the control of ☐
- **b** earn as much as you spend ☐
- **c** establish/start a business, school or organisation ☐
- **d** give back all the money you owe ☐
- **e** give people something to persuade them to buy your products ☐
- **f** gradually reduce something until it stops completely ☐
- **g** have an idea which you think is good ☐
- **h** invest ☐
- **i** support someone or something during a difficult period ☐
- **j** make a failure into a success ☐
- **k** negotiate successfully ☐
- **l** spend money, often unwillingly ☐
- **m** start doing a job that someone else was doing before ☐
- **n** start to experience (usually something bad) ☐

2 Which phrasal verbs in exercise 1 can:

1 have three additional meanings, which are given below?
- Make someone redundant.
- Give someone money to keep them quiet about something illegal or dishonest.
- Be worth it/be successful in the end.

2 also be used intransitively, with the meaning 'become clear/be understood'?

3 also collocate with 'an order', in which case it means 'accept, process and deliver'?

4 also mean 'continue doing a difficult or unpleasant task until it is finished'?

3 Rephrase the parts of the sentences below in bold using phrasal verbs from exercises 1 and 2.

1 No-one but George could have **come up with** such a good idea for the product launch.

2 The fact that Tim had **been given my job** only **became clear to me** when I found him sitting at what had been my desk.

3 After **establishing** his business, Peter felt very optimistic and, feeling sure that he would, at the very least, **make as much money as he needed to spend**, he **spent** the last of his savings **on** a new house. Unfortunately, soon after that, he **began to find he was in** debt, and was obliged to sell the house in order to **give back all** his business loans and to avoid having to **slowly stop his business from trading**.

4 When the company announced that they planned to **make** every worker over 55 **redundant**, Betty went straight to her union. As she'd worked for the company since she was sixteen, the union managed to **negotiate** such a good deal for her that she was given enough money to **support herself** until she is old enough to draw her pension.

5 I was very impressed when I made my first purchase over the Internet – they managed to **process and send** my order within twenty-four hours!

6 That stock market investment was a bit of a risk, but it **was worth it** in the end.

7 Implementing this plan for cutting costs is not going to be easy or popular, but if we can just **keep going until we've done** it, we stand a good chance of **making** the company **succeed instead of failing**.

4 Four of the phrasal verbs you have studied in this unit can be made into business-related nouns. What are they? The first one has been done as an example. Be careful, 4 and 5 are the same word but with different meanings.

1 the act of getting control of a company ......takeover......

2 a large payment of money, often in compensation or in payment of an insurance claim ....

3 something given to you when you buy a product ....

4 a payment made to someone to stop them causing you trouble, or when they have been made to leave their job ....

5 a positive result of a particular series of actions ....

5 Use the nouns you identified in exercise 4 to complete the sentences below.

1 My promotion was a totally unexpected .... of my involvement in that project.

2 The company is expected to have to make a .... in the region of £2 million to customers whose health was impaired as a result of using the product.

3 If you like the bowl so much, you're welcome to have it – it was a .... with a giant packet of soap powder I bought.

4 The management resisted the .... for as long as they could, but in the end the financial problems became so acute that they had to agree to it.

5 Workers on the night shift gave the security guard a regular .... so that he wouldn't reveal that they were stealing materials and components from the factory.

Verbs with 'empty' *it*

6 A small number of English verbs contain the word *it* as part of the verb, as in the examples below. The *it* is an 'empty' object, in other words it has no meaning and does not refer to anything else in the sentence. What do you think both verbs mean?

When they heard the police coming, the thieves ***beat it.***
When they heard the police coming, the thieves ***legged it.***

7 Sometimes verbs of this type look like phrasal verbs used with a pronoun. However, again the *it* does not refer back to a previous part of the sentence. One of the sentences below contains a phrasal verb; the other contains a verb with *it* as an 'empty' object. Which is which?

Luckily, all the members of the new project team ***hit it off*** *immediately, so a good working relationship was established from the start.*

The negotiation with the Japanese was long and complicated, but we ***brought it off*** *successfully in the end.*

Can you guess the meaning of the verb with *it* as an empty object?

8 Match the verbs in bold in the sentences below to a definition.

1 I don't know why you and your colleague are so antagonistic towards each other, but it's spoiling the working atmosphere in our team. So this afternoon you're both coming into my office so that you can **have it out** in front of me.

2 If you don't discuss your problems now in a civilised manner, the way things are going you'll end up **slugging it out**.

3 I've told you already I want the floor cleaned, so **jump to it**!

4 Lots of people think that managers who go on business trips abroad **live it up** on the company's money.

5 Many self-employed people **toughed it out** during the recession by working longer hours for less money.

6 The building's going to collapse! **Run for it**!

7 What is it you want to tell me? I won't bite your head off, so **spit it out**!

8 You want to become an actress? Then **go for it**!

9 You're forever talking while I'm trying to work. **Cut it out**!

a do everything you can in order to get what you want

b do something immediately

c fight physically and hard

d have fun/enjoy themselves

e persevere/manage to survive

f run away/escape

g say what you want to say

h settle a disagreement by talking

i stop doing something

9 Complete the second sentence so that it has a similar meaning to the first sentence, using the word given. Do not change the word given. You must use between three and eight words, including the word given.

1 She and her husband disliked each other on their first meeting.
hit
Her husband and she .... met.

2 After years of having fun and spending his money freely, his funds ran out.
up
He .... until his money ran out.

3 The new manager persevered until her staff came to respect her.
toughing
The new manager gained .... out.

4 My son and I discussed our disagreements yesterday and now we're both much happier.
out
We .... and I are much happier.

5 I find the physical violence involved in boxing matches quite sickening.
boxers
I find it sickening to .... out.

Word formation: revision

10 Complete the gaps in the text with a word formed from the word given in the margin. The first one has been done as an example. Most of the words you need to write are formed in ways you have studied already in Units 1 to 14. They could include:

- Noun suffixes: *-ance/-ence, -cy, -dom, -hood, -ity, -ment, -ness, -tion, -ure, -age, -ee, -er/-or, -ist, -ship*
- Verb suffixes: *-en, -ify, -ise*
- Negative prefixes: *anti/anti-, dis-, im-, in-, un-, mal-, mis-*
- Adjectives ending in *-ful, -ic, -ial , -ical, -able/-ible, -ous, -less, -some* and their related adverbial forms
- Prefixes *over, under, out, pre-, fore-, hyper-, inter-, de-, em-/en-, re-, bi-, co-/com-/con-, sub-, sym/syn-, trans-, uni-*

At the turn of this century, perhaps inspired by some of the **(0)** ...fanciful... names chosen by the newly-emerged dotcom	**FANCY**
enterprises, it became **(1)** .... fashionable for companies to	**INCREASE**
change their names. A survey conducted by a firm of brand consultants showed that, in 2000, no fewer than 250 British companies did so. Slightly over half of these chose a new name	
because of a merger or **(2)** .... However, that left 47% who changed their names with no clear reason for doing so, other than	**TAKE**
to **(3)** .... their reputation. Even the Post Office	**GRADE**
(4) .... itself under the new name Consignia, claiming this would help it to expand abroad, where its original name would have	**INVENT**
been even more **(5)** .... than the new one it had chosen. This assertion proved to be highly contentious, but perhaps one should	**MEAN**
be **(6)** .... towards organisations which seek to boost their image through a name change or to market new products	**PATHOS**
(7)	**NATION**
With **(8)** .... continuing apace, it is becoming ever harder to find company names and brand names which are neither	**GLOBE**
(9) .... nor, something which is equally important,	**PRONOUNCE**
ridiculously **(10)** .... in another language. General Motors found this out when they tried to launch the Nova in Spain, only to find that 'no va' means 'doesn't go' in Spanish. Hence the need for brand consultants, whose role is not only to devise names that	**APPROPRIATE**
promote a **(11)** .... corporate image but also to	**FAVOUR**
(12) .... their clients about brand names that might be embarrassing in other parts of the world.	**LIGHT**

Gapped sentences

11 Think of **one** word which can be used to complete all three sentences in each group below. Follow the example.

- The young man devoted his life to the *pursuit* of pleasure.
- I have to admit that hill walking is a *pursuit* which doesn't interest me at all.
- The flustered mother ran out of the supermarket in hot *pursuit* of her absconding toddler.

All the words you need to write are nouns or verbs which have appeared elsewhere in this unit, but in other forms or contexts.

1
- Having made some money on the stock market, he decided to leave his job and .... out into property development.
- The man screamed in terror as the enraged dog .... itself towards his throat.
- The railway company has .... an enquiry into the causes of the accident.

2
- The airbags were included with the car at no extra ....
- I learnt to my .... that Darryl was not always to be trusted.
- She's now counting the .... of not taking out travel insurance before she went to America on holiday.

3
- In the very first year of operation, the company .... over £100,000 each month.
- I thought he would have no head for business but he's .... out to be rather good at running his own company.
- The first two or three years were hard but I think the business has .... the corner now.

4
- The gallery .... mainly in contemporary abstract paintings.
- The new corporate tax has .... a hard blow to many small businesses.
- It was somebody in the distribution department that I .... with last time.

5
- If you feel that unwell, I think you should .... a doctor.
- In principle I think the suggestion is good, but I'd need to .... with my boss before I can give you a final decision.
- She speaks French fluently, but needs to .... a dictionary to check spellings when it comes to writing a letter.

12 Using a dictionary, check the exact meaning of any phrasal verbs, idioms or usages that were unfamiliar to you.

Summary

Reading

1 Skim-read these two texts. In terms of subject-matter, what do they have in common?

Text 1

Twenty years ago, a girl would have got her first Barbie doll at seven or eight and would have played with her almost into her teenage years. Today, most three-year-olds own at least one. At six, a girl is deemed too sophisticated for an ordinary Barbie, so she is lured by a range of street-smart topical dolls. At eight, she diversifies into Barbie clothing, toiletries, electronics and computer software.

The Barbie fatigue shown by those aged over eight is not an isolated phenomenon – the toy industry says that is when traditional toys of any kind lose their appeal. Nowadays there are too many other things competing for children's attention and pocket money: computer software, fast food, pop music and clothes. In an effort to hold on to their increasingly sophisticated young customers, many toy companies are resorting to gimmicks, such as a new trading card series for girls featuring pictures of real boys. As well as trading the cards, little girls can pick out the perfect boyfriend for themselves or their chums.

Arguably, being supply-led, not demand-led, the toy industry is partly to blame for its own troubles. As with fashion, the industry decides what is going to be in the shops eighteen months down the line. No matter how much is spent on marketing or how carefully supply is controlled, children don't always do what toymakers want or expect. The industry was initially taken by surprise by the Pokemon craze and the fact that it was the trading cards which proved much more popular with children than the Nintendo electronic game.

Text 2

Films are important toy-sellers. Representatives of the toy trade were at final script meetings of the Star Wars movies and characters would have their roles expanded, reduced or even cut depending on how 'sellable' they were expected to be. Shameless movie merchandising is now so accepted that film scriptwriters can even share a knowing joke with the audience. In *Toy Story 2*, the heroes enter a toy warehouse and gasp at the shelves filled with thousands of Buzz Lightyear dolls. Their Barbie tour guide comments 'In 1995, manufacturers failed to anticipate demand, so this time round we're prepared'. We laugh, but Disney and toymaker Mattel hope we will buy one anyway.

Merchandising can be tremendously profitable for the licence-holders, but is nevertheless a gamble. Although Disney has had some very lucrative merchandising successes, notably *The Lion King*, others, such as *Mulan*, had toys gathering dust on the shelves. US toymaker Hasbro got the licence for the latest Star Wars movie, *The Phantom Menace*, and in the expectation of making at least $750 million, spent a fortune on promotion. In the event, they made only $600m – not exactly a flop, but certainly a disappointment.

For the retailers, however, even successful merchandising is a mixed blessing. Although toys sold on the back of successful films, books or TV programmes bring customers into the shops, profit margins, never big at the best of times, are especially low on 'hyped' goods. Furthermore, if a toy which is the current fad has sold out, customers feel resentful, which is bad for future business.

Summary section: practice

Questions on the texts

2 What impression does Text 1 give of children over eight?

3 Explain in your own words what is meant by 'supply-led, not demand-led'. (Text 1, line 13)

4 What two things is the word 'others' in Text 2, line 11 contrasting?

5 What word in the last paragraph of Text 2 echoes the one used to describe the Pokemon phenomenon in Text 1?

Summary writing

In a paragraph of between 50 and 70 words, summarise, in your own words as far as possible, the problems faced by manufacturers and retailers in the toy industry.

Study tip

By now you should be familiar with the types of task which appear in the Proficiency Use of English paper and the strategies for carrying these tasks out. Before you sit the exam, however, it would be a good idea to look through the Exam factfile and Introduction of this book (pages 4 to 19) again. Make sure that you are clear about:

- how much time is allocated to doing the whole paper.
- the exact number of items in each task.
- how much time you should allow for each task.

Practice test 5

Part 1

For questions 1 – 15, read the text below and think of the word which best fits each space. Use only **one** word in each space. There is an example at the beginning (0).

Example:

0	T	H	R	O	U	G	H									

Time travel

Perhaps inevitably, it was **(0)** through. science fiction that serious scientists finally convinced themselves that time travel, **(1)** .... difficult, was not theoretically impossible. Carl Sagan, a **(2)** .... known astronomer, had written a novel in which his characters used a 'wormhole', a form of black hole, to travel from a point near the Earth to **(3)** .... near the star Vega. Sagan was aware that he was bending the accepted rules of physics, but this was, **(4)** .... all, a novel. Nevertheless, he wanted the science in his story to be as accurate as **(5)** ...., so he asked Kip Thorne, an expert in gravitational theory, to **(6)** .... it out and advise **(7)** .... how it might be improved. After looking closely at Sagan's equations, Thorne realised that **(8)** .... a wormhole through space-time actually could exist and be used to travel through space. What **(9)** .... Sagan nor Thorne realised at first **(10)** .... that the wormhole they had described would **(11)** .... work as a shortcut through time. It was **(12)** .... when Thorne attended a symposium a year after the publication of the novel **(13)** .... one of the other participants casually pointed **(14)** .... that a wormhole that took a shortcut through space-time could **(15)** .... as well link two different times as two different places.

Exam tip

Remember that:

- All your answers must be transferred to the answer sheet at the end of the Proficiency Use of English exam. Allow yourself enough time to do this.
- The answers to Parts 1, 2 and 3 must be written in capital letters.

Part 2

For questions 16 – 25, read the text below. Use the word given in capitals at the end of some of the lines to form a word that fits in the space in the same line. There is an example at the beginning (0).

Example:

0	A	C	C	E	S	S	I	B	I	L	I	T	Y			

Britain online

In a drive for greater **(0)** accessibility and efficiency, the British government has	ACCESS
announced that it plans to make all public services, from filing tax returns to	
ordering repeat medical **(16)** ...., available online within the next five years.	SCRIPT
Already competitions between different government **(17)** .... are being used to	PART
encourage civil servants to **(18)** .... their websites and to present information in	LIVE
a user-friendly fashion. The government's new information portal, UK Online, will	
be **(19)** .... tailored to life events, such a having a baby, dealing with crime or	SPECIFY
moving house. Eventually it will incorporate **(20)** .... services, such as the ability	ACT
to register the birth of a baby online.	
The greatest challenge facing the UK Online project is to **(21)** .... that its services	SURE
can reach everybody. Currently only about a quarter of UK households have	
Internet access, so the threat of a **(22)** .... digital divide is real. With this in mind,	WIDE
the government is setting up centres in public libraries, schools and shopping malls	
to give Internet access to those who do not have it at home.	
Computer and Internet training courses will be heavily **(23)** ...., while the	SUBSIDY
(24) .... will be able to attend courses for nothing and will be offered free	EMPLOY
(25) .... computers.	CONDITION

Part 4

For questions 32 – 39, complete the second sentence so that it has a similar meaning to the first sentence, using the word given. **Do not change the word given**. You must use between three and eight words, including the word given. Here is an example (0).

Example:

0 The company's profits appear to be improving significantly this year.
evidence
The company's .... this year.

0	profits show evidence of significant improvement

32 Matthew says he was in no way responsible for the financial miscalculation.
all
Matthew .... the financial miscalculation.

33 Immediately after the management announced the job cuts, the workers came out on strike.
been
No .... the workers came out on strike.

34 Nothing annoys him more than people discussing politics over dinner.
political
What .... over dinner.

35 The young painter had no idea at all that she would be awarded a prize.
came
The news of .... the young painter.

36 Your idea of trying to repair it yourself is out of the question.
account
On .... it yourself.

37 Neil is very proud of his ability to pick up languages easily.
himself
Neil .... learning languages.

38 His wife's looking for a part-time job, because they're having financial difficulties.
ends
Since .... his wife's looking for a part-time job.

39 Nobody expected it of him but Sam became the most successful student in his year.
turned
Against .... the most successful student in his year.

Appendices

Idioms

*Items included in this book are marked with an asterisk.**

A

above all most important of all; especially.

above and beyond greater than; more than.

the acid test a test that gives proof that cannot be doubted.

an acquired taste something, especially food or drink, liked only after it has been tried several times.

across the board from or to everyone or everywhere equally.

actions speak louder than words a person is judged more by what he does than by what he says he will do.

add insult to injury to cause offence to someone after one has already caused harm to him in some other way.

after all when all things are considered.

against (all) the odds in spite of the difficulties which would usually make something impossible.

airs and graces proud behaviour, especially in order to impress other people.

alive and kicking still living and active.

all along from the beginning; all the time.

all and sundry every person without exception.

all ears keen to listen to what is about to be said.

***all fingers and thumbs** to lack the ability, especially for a short time, to use your fingers to do something practical.

***all in** tired after work, exercise, etc.

all in all when everything is considered.

all of a piece of the same kind or quality (as something).

***all the more** even more.

***all the same** but in spite of that; nevertheless.

all told including everything or everybody.

***all too often** more often than you would like.

all well and good fine; quite acceptable.

all's well that ends well when something difficult ends happily, there is no need to complain or be disappointed about any trouble it may have caused.

argue the toss to oppose or argue with a decision that has already been taken and that cannot be changed.

***at any rate** at least; whatever else is true.

at arm's length far away, so that you do not have to touch something or become friendly with someone.

at the double as quickly as possible; immediately.

avoid something like the plague to do everything possible to keep away from someone or not be concerned with something.

B

***back and forth** repeatedly in one and then in another direction.

the back of beyond a place far away from a centre where many people live.

back to the grindstone back to work.

bag and baggage with everything a person owns (used especially when a person is leaving a place.

the ball is in someone's court it is someone's turn to take action.

bang your head against a brick wall it is someone's turn to take action.

bark up the wrong tree to direct your efforts, complaints etc. in the wrong direction; to have the wrong idea about something.

(not) bat an eyelid not to show any signs of emotion, e.g. of fear, surprise, etc. in your face.

be anybody's guess (of an event, result etc.) to be uncertain.

be at someone's beck and call ready or forced to obey the orders, wishes, etc. of another person.

***be in care** (of a child) to be looked after by the state (in an orphanage, temporary home, etc.).

***be on cloud nine to** be very happy, ecstatic.

***be snowed under** to have so much work to do that you can't manage.

beat around the bush to delay talking about the most important part of a discussion, subject, etc.

beat someone at their own game to do better than a person in his own work or activities.

a bee in your bonnet an idea or subject that one cannot stop thinking or talking about, especially that is not shared by others.

behind someone's back without the knowledge of the person concerned.

behind bars in prison.

behind the times not fashionable, usual, etc. at the particular time.

bend over backwards make a great effort.

(as) blind as a bat unable to see at all.

break the back of to complete or do the most difficult or largest part of a job, etc.

bring home the bacon to succeed in doing something, for example, earning enough money to support your family.

***bring out the best in someone** to cause the best part of someone's character to be displayed.

*** bring someone down a peg or two** to cause someone to become more humble.

in broad daylight in the daytime, when an act that is unlawful, especially robbery, is able to be seen or discovered.

***butter wouldn't melt in his mouth** someone has the look of a well-behaved, honest person (usually used when the speaker thinks that the person is not so harmless as he looks).

***by all means** certainly; yes (used to give permission or agree to a request).

***by any chance** perhaps.

C

call a spade a spade to speak plainly and directly.

call it a day to finish or stop doing something, especially to stop working.

call someone's bluff to tell someone to do what they threaten because you believe they have no intention of doing it and you want to prove it.

call the shots to be in a position of authority so that you can give orders and make decisions.

chance your arm to take a risk, especially something you have not experienced before.

***cheek by jowl** if people live or work cheek by jowl they live or work very close together.

come to a bad end to come to some misfortune, especially an unpleasant death.

cost an arm and a leg to cost a large amount of money.

curiosity killed the cat used to tell someone not to ask questions about something that does not concern them.

***cut and dried** a decision or result that is cut and dried cannot now be changed.

***cut someone dead** to pretend that you have not seen someone you know, usually because you are angry, upset, etc. with them.

***cut someone off without a penny** to not leave any money, property, etc. in your will to someone (who was expecting to receive an inheritance).

D

(as) daft as a brush (of a person) very silly; not at all sensible.

dance attendance on someone to give much attention to a person, especially in an effort to please.

a dark horse someone who does not tell people much and who has surprising qualities or abilities.

day after day every day; for many days, one after the other.

day in, day out (of repeated actions) for several days together; one day after another.

(as) dead as a dodo completely dead or out of date.

(as) dead as a doornail completely dead; not living or operating.

the dead of night the quietest darkest part of the night when everyone is asleep.

(as) deaf as a post completely deaf (unable to hear).

***(as) different as chalk and cheese** used to describe two people or things which are completely different from each other.

do someone a good / bad turn to do something that is helpful, unhelpful, etc. (to someone).

donkey's years a very long time.

a dose of your own medicine the same treatment as one gives to other people, especially when it is unfair or unpleasant.

down and out without a job or other means of support; homeless and living on the streets.

down-at-heel (of a person's appearance) untidy, uncared for, especially because of a lack of money.

drag your feet to deliberately go slowly or delay something.

draw a blank to fail to discover something after searching hard and asking many questions.

draw the line to set limits, especially when you refuse to go beyond these limits.

***drink like a fish** to be accustomed to drinking a great deal of alcohol.

drive a hard bargain to try to get results very favourable to yourself, especially in a business agreement.

***(as) dull as ditchwater** very boring.

E

eagle-eyed very attentive; watchful.

the early hours very early in the morning, usually before the dawn.

easier said than done it is easier to tell someone how to do something than to do it.

(as) easy as pie very easy; requiring no effort at all.

eat like a horse to eat a great deal.

eat your words to admit that something you have said was wrong.

the eleventh hour at the last possible moment.

the end justifies the means if a result is good, it does not matter if the methods used to get this result are unfair, unjust, violent, etc.

the end of your tether to be so worried, tired etc., that you feel you can no longer deal with a difficult or upsetting situation.

***every bit as** used when saying strongly that someone is just as good, important as someone else.

***every once in a while** occasionally.

F

***a face like thunder** looking very angry.

***face the music** to accept criticism or punishment for something you have done.

face to face in the actual presence (of another person).

***fair and square** honest, correct or proper.

fall between two stools to be concerned with two aims and to fail with regard to both of them.

fall foul of to do something that annoys or offends (another person).

fall on deaf ears (of request for help, etc.) to be or remain unnoticed or disregarded.

far and away by far; absolutely.

far and wide over a large area.

***fast and furious** suddenly and quickly in great quantity or numbers.

***first and foremost** before everything else.

first things first used when th speaker thinks that a more important subject must be discussed or agreed first.

fit like a glove to fit (a person) perfectly.

fly in the face of to show opposition to (a person, idea, etc.), especially in a violent way.

(a) fly in the ointment someone or something that spoils, causes trouble, or lowers the value of something.

a flying start an excellent start.

***foot the bill** to pay the bill, especially when the bill is very large.

***from ear to ear** (of someone's smile) broadly or widely.

***from head to toe** from the top of your body to the bottom.

***full of beans** very lively; full of vigour, health, etc.

G

gain ground to get an advantage and become more successful.

get a word in edgeways to get a chance to speak.

get away from it all to escape from the difficulties and worries of daily life, work, etc.

get even with to harm someone just as much as they have harmed you.

get in on the act to take part in something started by others, in order to get the same success.

get off someone's back to leave a person alone; stop annoying, arguing with, etc.

get off the ground (of a business, plan, etc.) to become successful.

***get on someone's nerves** to cause someone to feel irritated.

***get on like a house on fire** to have an excellent relationship or friendship with someone.

***get wind of something** to hear or find out about something secret or private, especially if you learn it accidentally or unofficially.

***get your own back on someone** to do something that will harm or offend a person who has caused you some harm or offence.

the ghost of a chance the smallest possible chance.

the gift of the gab an ability to speak confidently and to persuade people to do what you want.

give yourself airs to behave as if your are more important, grander, etc. than your are, especially to impress others.

give something up as a bad job to stop trying to do something because the situation is not productive.

go begging to be unclaimed.

go from bad to worse to become worse.

great minds think alike all people who are very clever think in the same way (often used humorously).

grin and bear it to accept and bear an unpleasant or difficult situation without complaining, usually because you realise there is nothing you can do to make it better.

H

a hair's breadth a very short distance or small amount (used to indicate how close something is to something else).

***hale and hearty** in good health; fit and well.

hand in glove in close association or partnership.

hand over fist (earning money) in large amounts.

***hand in hand** holding each other's hand, especially to show love.

handle with kid gloves to treat someone very carefully because they easily become upset.

***hard and fast** firmly; without moving or being changed.

***(as) hard as nails** very hard; not feeling any emotions, especially fear or sympathy.

hard up having little or no money.

hate like poison to hate (someone) very much.

***have a good eye for colour** to have a talent for combining, choosing, etc. colours.

***have a head for heights** to not be afraid of heights.

have a nodding acquaintance with to have only a slight knowledge of (a subject or person).

***have a nose for trouble** to be interested in and good at discovering problems, trouble, etc.

***have a(n) (good) ear for** to have a (good) understanding of music, languages, etc.

have got something down to a fine art to have learned to do something perfectly.

***have the courage of your own convictions** to be brave enough to say or do what you think is right even though other people may not agree or approve.

have your cake and eat it to try to enjoy or get advantage from two things when using or doing one of them makes the other impossible.

***have your head in the clouds** to spend too much time thinking about things that you would like to do.

***high and mighty** talking or behaving as if you think you are more important than other people.

(a) home truth a fact or true statement about someone that is unpleasant when he is told about it.

hustle and bustle confused and busy activity.

I

the icing on the cake a desirable addition, often unnecessary and used simply as an attraction.

***in any case** whatever the situation; whatever may happen or has happened.

***in good shape** fit; in good health.

***in perfect health** with no health problems at all.

in someone's bad books to not be in favour with someone.

in the bag certain; sure.

in the balance in an undecided or uncertain state, especially one between two opposite possibilities.

***in the pink** feeling very well, in good health.

***in tip-top condition** in perfect condition.

the ins and outs the small details, often difficult to explain or understand, of a system, operation, etc.

to all intents and purposes in all important ways or as far as you can see, judge, etc.

J

a Jack of all trades a person who has the ability to do many different kinds of work, although not necessarily very well.

jockey for position to try to get into the best position or situation.

jump in at the deep end to choose to do or be made to do a very difficult job without having prepared for it.

jump to conclusions to decide that something is true too quickly, without knowing all the facts.

jump to it to show immediate and rapid willingness, e.g. to obey an order.

just my luck typical of someone's usual fortune, usually used after an unfortunate event has taken place.

K

keep a low profile to behave quietly and avoid doing things that will make people notice you.

keep an eye on to watch carefully in order to look after.

keep an ace / card up your sleeve to have an idea, plan etc. that you keep secret in order that it may be used at the best possible moment.

keep up appearances to continue to do what is expected in public, especially in order to hide something that you do not want others to know about or that may not be approved of.

(a fine/pretty/etc.) kettle of fish a state of affairs that is confused, difficult, different from expected, etc.

(not) know someone from Adam (not) to know someone at all.

kick your heels to waste time waiting for something.

know like the back of your hand to know something very well indeed.

know no bounds something has no limits.

L

(in the) lap of luxury having an easy, comfortable life with plenty of money, possessions etc.

leading light a person who is very important and famous, especially an important member of a group.

let the cat out of the bag to accidentally reveal a secret.

lie through your teeth to tell lies in an open and unashamed manner.

like a bear with a sore head bad-tempered, impatient or discontented.

***like a bull in a china shop** to keep knocking things over, dropping things, breaking things etc.

***like a red rag to a bull** very likely to make someone angry or upset.

like water off a duck's back if advice, warnings, or rude remarks are like water off a duck's back to someone, they have no effect on them.

look a gift horse in the mouth to look for faults or other things to complain about in something that is freely offered.

look daggers at someone to give fierce or angry looks to a person.

***look like mutton dressed as lamb** an offensive expression meaning a woman who is trying to look younger than she really is.

look on the bright side to see the good points in something that is bad in other ways.

lose your bearings to become suddenly confused and not know where you are or what you should be doing.

lose your grip to become less confident and less able to deal with a situation.

lose your temper to become angry.

lose your touch to lose your ability to do something.

loud and clear very clearly; with strong emphasis.

***love at first sight** when two people fall in love with each other the first time they meet.

***little love lost between two people** there is great dislike.

M

(as) mad as a hatter very mad or silly.

***meek and mild** extremely quiet and gentle.

make a killing to make a lot of money in a short time.

make a mountain out of a mole hill to treat a problem as if it was very serious when in fact it is not.

***make allowances for** to take into consideration (certain facts or conditions).

***make amends** to put something right, for example by saying you are sorry or by being kind to someone you have offended.

make both ends meet to have just enough money to buy what you need.

make light work of to do something easily and without much effort.

make or break to cause either the complete success or ruin (of a person or thing).

meet your match to find yourself opposed by someone that is likely to beat you in an argument, at some activity, etc.

***a mixed bag** a thoroughly varied mixture (of people or things).

be music to someone's ears (of a piece of news, an event, etc.) to give someone pleasure.

the more the merrier a gathering of people becomes more lively as more people join it (usually said to invite others).

move heaven and earth to try very hard to achieve something.

muddy the waters to make things more complicated or confusing in a situation that was simple before.

N

the naked eye without the help of any instrument.

the name of the game the main idea; exactly the right idea.

a narrow shave a situation in which you only just avoid an accident or something.

a nasty piece of work someone who is dishonest, violent, or likely to cause trouble.

a near miss a narrow escape, especially when two moving objects nearly hit each other.

nearest and dearest your family or closest relatives.

***neck and neck** level or even in a race.

(as) neat as a new pin very neat, tidy and clean.

a new broom a person who has just been put in charge of an organisation and makes many changes.

a night owl a person who stays up late at night.

nip something in the bud to prevent something from becoming a problem by stopping it as soon as it starts.

nuts and bolts the basic practical details.

O

an object lesson a very clear example, e.g. of how to do something which others should learn from.

odds and ends articles of differing types, especially ones that have been forgotten about.

***off and on** with interruptions; irregularly.

***off colour** not feeling very well.

off limits beyond the area where someone is allowed to go.

off the hook to no longer be in a difficult situation.

***off your own bat** without asking for the help, advice, permission, etc. of any other person.

***(as) old as the hills** very old.

an old hand to have a lot of experience of something.

an old wives' tale a foolish, old-fashioned belief or story.

***on balance** considering everything.

***on no account** in no case; not for any reason.

***on the ball** very lively and attentive.

***on the cards** possible; likely to happen.

***on the whole** generally.

***once and for all** now and for the last time.

once in a blue moon extremely rarely.

one and all everybody (used when talking to a crowd or a group of people).

***out of action** not able to work for a certain time because of damage or illness.

out of harm's way not in a position to cause or suffer any danger.

***out of thin air** from nothing; from nowhere.

***over and above** in addition to.

overstep the mark to do or say more than you should, and offend people or make them angry.

P

***pack your bags** to leave, especially because of a disagreement, etc.

paddle your own canoe to depend on yourself and no one else.

paint something in glowing colours to describe something using a lot of praise.

par for the course not different from what you would usually expect; typical.

parrot fashion repeating certain words or ideas without really understanding their meaning.

***a piece of cake** something that can be done or obtained very easily.

***play something by ear** to deal with matters as they arise, without making plans in advance.

***play your cards right** to act in a correct or clever way in order to gain an advantage in a particular situation.

pop the question ask someone to marry you.

practise what you preach to do yourself what you have advised others to do.

***(as) pretty as a picture** very beautiful.

pride of place a high or leading position.

pull a fast one to deceive or cheat.

pull someone's leg to make a joke by telling someone something that is not actually true.

***put all your eggs in one basket** to depend completely on one thing or one course of action in order to get success.

***put someone's back up** to annoy a person by saying or doing something bad or offensive.

***put in an appearance** to go somewhere or attend a party etc., especially because you feel it is your duty to attend.

***put your back into** to make the greatest possible effort to do something.

pure and simple and nothing else (used to give emphasis to an answer which the speaker believes to be the correct and only one.

Q

(as) quick as lightning / a flash very quickly.

quick off the mark to be quick to understand things or react to situations.

quick on the uptake to be fast at learning or understanding things.

(as) quiet as a mouse very quiet.

R

the rat race the struggle for success in your job, business, etc., especially in a large town or city.

raise the roof to make a very loud noise when singing, celebrating etc.

read between the lines to guess someone's real feelings from something they say or write.

(as) red as a beetroot red in the face from feeling awkward or ashamed.

red-handed when someone is caught doing something unlawful.

rhyme or reason meaning, understandable cause, explanation.

(as) right as rain quite alright, especially when compared to what might be expected.

rise to the bait to act in exactly the manner that someone else hoped you would.

rise through the ranks to obtain a high position in an organisation after long experience in lower positions.

round the clock all day and all night without stopping.

***run down** tired, lacking in energy.

run the gauntlet to be criticised or attacked by a lot of people.

run to ground to manage to find someone or something after searching hard.

a running battle an argument that continues or is repeated over a long period of time.

S

***safe and sound** safe and unharmed.

(as) safe as houses very safe.

***save the day** to bring success when failure seems certain.

scare you out of your wits make you extremely frightened.

scrimp and save to be very careful about how you spend your money, especially in order to save money.

***second to none** better than all others.

***(not) see eye to eye** to always disagree with someone.

***see the back of** to get rid of or be finished with someone or something.

***set the ball rolling** to start an activity, conversation, discussion, etc. going.

set your sights on to decide that you want something and will make a determined effort to achieve it.

settle a score to get revenge for a wrong or injury that one has suffered.

shake in your shoes to tremble with fear.

a shot in the dark a guess that is made with little direct knowledge and is therefore not likely to be right.

shrug your shoulders to lift up your shoulders in a gesture of refusal, disappointment, disinterest, etc.

***(as) similar as two peas in a pod** very similar to (something); almost exactly the same.

***sing like a lark** to sing beautifully.

at sixes and sevens confused, in a mess.

smart aleck a person who has a very high opinion of himself and thinks that he knows everything.

snap someone's head off say something to someone in a very angry way.

spill the beans to reveal or make known (a secret, piece of information, etc.)

steal someone's thunder to get the success and praise someone else should have got, by doing what they had intended to do.

step by step gradually, one bit at a time.

(a) storm in a teacup an unnecessary expression of strong feelings about something that is very unimportant.

T

take advantage of to make use of (a person) for your own good or profit.

take something amiss to be offended by something, often because you have misunderstood.

take something in your stride to not allow something to annoy, embarrass, or upset you in any way.

take into account to think about or consider something or someone when making a judgement or decision.

***take the wind out of someone's sails** to make someone lose their confidence, especially by saying or doing something unexpected.

***take to something like a duck to water** to learn how to do something very easily.

teething troubles problems which occur at the beginning of a project, opening of a business, etc.

think twice to reconsider a decision you have already taken or think carefully before doing something.

throw good money after bad to spend more money while attempting to regain what has already been lost.

throw someone off their balance to cause a person to become confused or annoyed.

throw your weight about / around to give orders, especially to impress other people.

tip the balance to influence the result of an event in one particular way when several results are possible.

***to and fro** first in one direction and then another.

to no avail without success.

***toe the line** to do what other people in a job or organisation say you should do, whether you agree with them or not.

***tongue in cheek** if you say something with your tongue in your cheek, you say it as a joke.

***(as) tough as old boots** very strong and able to bear pain, hardship, etc.

tread on someone's toes to offend someone, especially by becoming involved in something that they are responsible for.

***tried and tested** used for something which has been checked and about which there is no doubt.

turn a blind eye to pretend not to see something, especially something immoral, unlawful etc.

turn the tables to change a situation so that one gains a position of advantage, after being at a disadvantage.

***turn your hand to something** to begin or try to do a job, task, etc.

in the twinkling of an eye within a very short time; very quickly.

twist someone's arm to force or persuade someone to do something, for example, by threats.

U

an ugly duckling a dull, ordinary child, plan, etc. that develops into a very interesting and successful one.

***under the weather** not feeling very well.

under someone's thumb under the control or influence of someone.

under your breath (to say something) quietly so that other people can't hear you.

under way in progress.

an unknown quantity a person whose intentions, abilities, etc. are unknown.

up against in opposition to or in competition with.

up and about able to walk and function normally after an illness, accident, etc.

up and down variable, e.g. in health.

an uphill battle a very difficult struggle.

the upper hand the position of power or control; the advantage over someone.

V

vanish into thin air disappear completely, as if by magic.

a vicious circle a situation in which a cause produces a result that itself produces the original cause.

in view of after taking something into consideration.

W

walk of life type of work, trade, profession or social position.

walls have ears even the most secret and private conversation may become known to other people.

(as) warm as toast very warm, especially as compared to the cold outside.

***washed out** tired and lacking energy.

waste your breath to speak without effect, especially when you are trying to persuade someone of something.

watch someone like a hawk to watch someone very closely, especially to catch him doing something wrong.

wear and tear damage or loss of quality or valued suffered during usual or daily use.

***weather the storm** to manage to get through a difficult period.

***well and truly** completely.

a whale of a time a very good or enjoyable time.

whet someone's appetite to make someone eager to obtain, learn, see, etc. more.

win hands down to win without difficulty, very easily.

by word of mouth spoken and not written.

the worse for wear very tired; lacking energy, especially after working hard.

would give your right arm to be willing to give up something of great value.

Y

year in, year out (always the same) one year after another.

the year dot the beginning of time; a long time ago.

Phrasal verbs

The definitions in this list are based on the *Longman Phrasal Verbs Dictionary*. We recommend that you use this dictionary for further reference and study.

A

act out to perform the events in a story, play, or a situation.

act up to behave badly, used especially about children.

angle for to try to get something, by asking or talking about it in an indirect way.

answer back to answer someone rudely or say that you disagree with them, when you should obey them and be polite to them.

answer for if you have to answer for something bad that you have done you are responsible for it.

ask after to ask about someone, especially about their health or what they have been doing.

B

back down to accept that you cannot win an argument and stop trying to win, or accept that you are wrong and change your decision.

back off to stop trying to influence or force someone to do or think something.

***back someone up** to support someone by saying that they are telling the truth.

bail someone out to help someone to get out of trouble, especially by giving them money when they have financial problems.

bang on to talk continuously about something in a boring way.

bear out to support what someone has said or written and so help to prove that it is true.

bear up to remain cheerful and not be badly affected by a bad situation, illness etc.

beef up to improve something by making it stronger, more powerful more effective, etc.

black out to suddenly become unconscious.

blow over if an argument or unpleasant situation blows over, it is forgotten or no longer seems important.

***blow up** to destroy something using a bomb.

***boil away** if liquid boils away, it disappears and changes into steam because it has been boiled for a long time.

boil down to if a situation, problem, discussion, etc. boils down to something, that is the main part or cause of it.

***bottle something up** to keep a strong feeling such as anger or unhappiness hidden and not talk about it or show it.

bow out to give up an important position or job, so that someone can take your place.

bowl over if you are bowled over by something, you are very impressed by it because it is so beautiful, exciting, etc.

***break down** 1) if a substance breaks down, it changes as a result of a chemical process; 2) if a machine breaks down, it stops working because there is something wrong with it.

***break even** if a business breaks even it makes the same amount of money as it spends and so makes neither a profit nor a loss.

***break in** 1) to get into a building by using force, usually to steal something; 2) to suddenly say something when someone else is speaking, so that they have to stop talking.

***break off** if you break off something that you are doing, you stop doing it.

***break out** to escape from prison.

***break up** 1) to break into smaller pieces or parts; if a marriage breaks up, it ends; 2) if a school breaks up, classes end and the holidays begin.

***bring about** to make something happen, especially a change or better situation.

***bring in** 1) to include or mention something, especially for a particular purpose; 2) to earn a particular amount of money.

bring off to succeed in doing something that is very difficult.

***bring on** to make a problem, illness or pain start to happen.

***bring out** to make a particular quality or taste more noticeable.

***bring up** to mention a subject or start to talk about it during a conversation or discussion.

***bring someone up** to charge someone with a crime and make them appear before a court of law.

***build up** to gradually increase in size, amount or strength.

***burn up** to use energy or get rid of unwanted fat from your body by doing physical exercise.

burst out to suddenly start to laugh or cry.

butt in to interrupt a conversation in a rude way, by saying something when it is not your turn to speak.

C

call by to stop and visit someone for a short time, especially when you are on your way to somewhere else.

call in to make a short visit to a person or place, especially when you are going somewhere else.

call off 1) to stop an event that has been arranged from taking place, especially because of a problem; 2) to order an animal or person to stop attacking someone.

call on 1) to visit someone for a short time; 2) to formally and publicly ask someone to do something.

call round to go to someone's house for a short time to visit them.

***calm down** to stop feeling angry or upset.

carry off to succeed in doing something different, especially when there is a good chance that you will fail.

***carry out** to do something that you have organised or planned.

cash in on to make a profit from a situation or get an advantage from it, especially in a way that other people think is unfair or dishonest.

***catch up** 1) to gradually get closer to a moving person or vehicle, by moving faster than they move; 2) to improve so much that you reach the same standard as someone else who was better than you.

***change into** to become something completely different.

***change over to** to stop doing or using one system or thing, and to start doing or using a different one instead.

***clear up** 1) if an illness or infection clears up, or if medicine clears it up, it gets better and disappears; 2) to put things back where they are usually kept and make a place clean and tidy; 3) to solve a problem or deal with a disagreement; 4) (intransitive) if the weather clears up, it stops raining and becomes more pleasant.

***come across** to find something or meet someone by chance, when you are not expecting it.

***come across as** to seem to be a particular type of person or thing.

***come before** to be brought to a person or group in authority in order to be judged.

***come between** to spoil the relationship between two or more people, by causing problems or arguments.

***come out** if the true information about something comes out, it becomes known, especially after being kept secret.

***come round** to become conscious again, for example, after an accident or an operation.

***come to** to become conscious again, for example, after an accident or an operation.

***come up** if a subject, name, etc. comes up in a conversation or meeting, it is mentioned or discussed.

***come up with** to think of an idea, plan or answer.

***come upon** to meet someone or find something by chance or when you do not expect it.

***cut across** to interrupt someone by saying something.

***cut someone off** to take away someone's right to receive your money or property when you die.

D

***delve into** to try to find more detailed information that is not well know.

die away if something such as sound, light, or the wind dies away, it gradually becomes weaker and then stops.

***dig up** 1) to discover hidden or forgotten information by careful searching; 2) to dig and remove something from the ground that is buried there.

dip into 1) to use part of an amount of money that you had intended to keep; 2) to read short parts of a book, magazine etc., without reading the whole thing.

***do someone out of** to cheat someone by not giving them money that they are owed, or something that should belong to them.

do up to repair or decorate a building, so that it looks much better.

drag on if an event drags on, it continues for too long.

drag up to mention an unpleasant event or story about something that happened in the past, even though it is embarrassing or upsetting.

draw on to use knowledge, information or your personal experiences to help you do something.

draw something out to make something continue for longer than is usual.

draw up to prepare a contract, or a list or plan.

E

egg on to encourage someone to do something, especially something that is not sensible or safe.

eke out to make money, food or supplies etc. last as long as possible by using them carefully because you only have a small amount available.

end up to be in a situation that you did not intend or want to be in, because of something that has happened to you or something you have done.

even out to make something become more equal, by sharing or spreading something more equally.

F

fall apart if an organisation, relationship etc. falls apart, it is not working successfully any more and may fail completely.

fall away if land, a road etc. falls away, it slopes down, especially suddenly.

fall back on to use something because other things have failed or because there is no other choice left.

***fall for** 1) to suddenly feel very attracted to someone and feel that you love them; 2) to be tricked into believing something that is not true.

fall in with to accept someone else's plan,suggestion, etc. and not try to change it or disagree.

fall off if the amount, rate, etc. of something falls off, it decreases or becomes lower.

***fall out** to have an argument with someone and stop being friendly with them.

fall through if a plan falls through, something prevents it from happening or being completed successfully.

fan out if a group of people fans out, they move forwards and away from each other and spread over a wide area.

fill someone in to tell someone about things that have happened recently.

fit up provide someone or something with the equipment, furniture, etc. they need.

fizzle out to gradually become less strong, successful, etc. and then end or disappear.

flag down to make a vehicle stop by waving at its driver.

flake out to suddenly fall asleep because you are very tired.

flare up if something such as violence, or anger flares up, it suddenly starts or gets much worse.

fob off to stop someone asking questions by giving them explanations, excuses etc. that are not true.

G

***gabble away** to talk quickly for a long time in a way which is boring or difficult to understand.

gang up to join together in a group to attack or oppose someone.

gear up to prepare for something that is going to happen soon.

get about to be able to move around a place.

***get something across** (to) to succeed in making someone understand an idea or message.

***get ahead** to be successful in your job so that you can progress to a more important job.

***get along** (with) if two or more people get along, they have a friendly relationship.

get at to criticise someone in an unfair and annoying way.

***get away with** to not be noticed or punished when you have done something wrong.

get back at someone to do something to hurt or harm someone, in order to punish them for hurting or harming you.

*get (your own) back on someone** to do something to hurt or harm someone, in order to punish them for hurting or harming you.

get by to have enough money to buy the things you need to live, but no more.

***get someone down** if a situation gets you down, it makes you feel tired and unhappy.

get down to to finally make a serious effort and start doing something.

***get in** if a train, ship or plane gets in at a particular time, it arrives at that time.

***get off** 1) to leave the place where you are, or to start a journey; 2) to not be punished for a crime or something you have done wrong.

***get on** 1) to be successful in your job so that you can progress to a more important job; 2) to continue doing something that you were doing before; 3) if two or more people get on, they have a friendly relationship.

get out of to avoid doing something you have promised to do or are supposed to do.

***get over** to begin to feel better after a shock or an experience which upset you.

get something over to succeed in communicating ideas so that other people understand them.

get something over with to finish something unpleasant of difficult that you have to do.

***get through to** to succeed in making someone understand something, especially when this is difficult.

get up to to do something, especially something that other people do not approve of.

***give away** 1) if a company gives away a product, they give it to people for free in order to attract more customers; 2) to let someone know about something that should be a secret, especially by mistake.

***give out** 1) to produce something such as heat, a smell, light, etc; 2) if a machine gives out, it stops working.

***give yourself up** to allow the police or enemy soldiers to make you a prisoner when they have been trying to catch you.

go along with to accept a particular idea or plan, especially because it might cause trouble if you do not.

***go down** if a computer goes down, or the telephone lines go down, they stop working because of a fault.

***go in for** to do, use, have, etc. a particular type of thing, because you like it.

go off 1) to stop liking someone or something you used to like; 2) if food goes off, it is not good to eat, because it has been kept too long; 3) if a bomb goes off, it explodes.

go under if a business goes under, it has to close because it does not make enough money.

grind on to continue for a long time in a slow and boring way.

H

hammer away (at) to work hard at something for a long time in a determined way.

hammer out to get an agreement with another person, organisation, etc. after a lot of discussion.

***hand down** to give or teach something to someone, especially a younger member of your family, so that they will have it or know about it after you have died.

hand over to give something to someone, especially after they have asked for it.

hang back to not move forward, especially because you are shy, nervous, etc.

hang together if a book, film, etc. hangs together, it is good because it is well-organised.

hang up to end a telephone conversation by putting the receiver down.

***happen on** to find something or meet someone when you do not expect it.

hide out to stay somewhere secret, especially in order to escape from your enemies.

***hit upon** to think of an idea or a plan, especially one that is successful.

hold off 1) to delay doing something; 2) to prevent someone from being successful when they are attacking you.

hold on to wait for a short time.

hold out for to refuse to accept anything less than what you have asked for.

hold something over someone to use information about someone to make them do what you want, especially by threatening them.

***hold up** 1) to stop a vehicle or go into a bank, shop etc. with a gun and demand money from people; 2) to delay someone or something.

home in on to direct your attention towards a particular subject.

***hunt down** to search for a person or an animal by chasing them until you catch them.

I

iron out if you iron out small problems, you deal with them.

J

jabber away to talk quickly and for a long time in a way that is difficult to understand.

***join in (with)** to start doing or becoming involved in something with other people.

join up to become a member of the armed forces.

jot down to quickly write something on a piece of paper so that you do not forget it.

jut out to come out beyond the edge of something.

K

keel over to fall over sideways, especially because you feel weak or unsteady.

***keep up with** to write to, telephone, or meet a friend regularly, so that you do not forget each other.

knit together 1) if people or things knit together, they work together well; 2) if broken bones knit together, they join and grow together again.

knock something down to reduce the price of something.

knuckle down to start to work more seriously than you have been doing.

knuckle under to agree to do what someone is trying to force you to do.

L

***lash out** (at) to suddenly speak angrily to someone or suddenly try to hit or attack someone.

laugh something off to pretend that you are not upset by criticism by laughing and making jokes about it.

***lay off** to stop employing a worker because there is not enough work for him or her to do.

***lead to** to cause something to happen, especially some time later.

***let someone down** to fail to do something that someone is relying on you to do, in a way that is disappointing.

let someone in on something to tell someone about a secret.

***let off** 1) to not punish someone when they have done something wrong; 2) to make something such as a bomb explode.

***let out** to allow someone to leave somewhere.

let up if bad weather or an unpleasant situation lets up, it stops or becomes less bad.

live up to to be as good as people expect or hope.

***look ahead** to think about what will happen in the future, so that you can make plans for it.

***look down on** to think that you are better than someone else, for example because you are more successful, or of a higher social class than they are.

look in to visit someone for a short time.

look into to find out more about something by getting all the necessary information.

look on to watch something while it is happening and do nothing to stop it.

***look through** to read something quickly and not very carefully.

***look up** to try to find information about something in a list, book,etc.

***look up to** to admire and respect someone, for example because they are older than you or have more experience.

***loom ahead** if an unpleasant or worrying situation looks ahead, it is going to happen soon and people are worried or frightened.

M

***make away with** to steal something and escape with it.

***make for** to move towards something.

***make off** to leave quickly, especially in order to escape.

***make off with** to steal something and escape with it.

make something out to manage to see or hear something, but with difficulty.

make something over to someone to officially give money or property to someone.

***make up** 1) if two people who have had an argument make up, they talk to each other and agree to become friends again; 2) to think of something new using your imagination, for example a story or a song.

make up for to do something good for someone after doing something bad to them, so that they forgive you.

mess up to spoil something, make it dirty or untidy.

mount up to increase and become large, usually about debts and costs.

move up to move a little, especially in a row of seats, etc. so that there is more space for others.

muddle through to succeed in doing something even though you are not organised or do not know what you are doing.

N

nail someone / something down to make something final and definite, especially by making someone agree about specific details.

narrow down to reduce the number of things or people you can choose from, by getting rid of those that are not suitable.

nod off to begin to sleep when you do not intend to.

O

opt out to decide not to join a group or take part in a system.

own up to admit you have done something wrong.

P

pan out if an idea or plan pans out, it is successful.

***pass away** to die.

pass something off as to make people believe that something is better or more valueable than it really is.

***pass on** to die.

***pass out** to lose consciousness.

pass up to not take an opportunity when it becomes available.

patch something up if you patch up a relationship or friendship, you stop arguing and agree to be friends.

***pay off** 1) to stop employing a worker after paying them the wages you owe them; 2) to give someone money so that they will not tell other people about something, especially something dishonest or illegal; 3) to pay all the money you own someone; 4) if something that you do pays off, it is successful or worth doing.

***pay out** to pay money to someone because they are owed it.

***pep someone up** to give someone more energy and make them feel less tired.

perk up to become more cheerful or have more energy.

peter out if something peters out, it becomes less and less strong and finally disappears.

pick on someone to treat one person badly in a way that seems unfair.

pick someone out to choose one particular person or thing from a group.

pick over to examine a group of things carefully in order to choose the ones you want.

pick up if a situation picks up, it gets better.

pick something up to learn how to do something by watching others rather than being taught.

pick up on to notice something and realise it is important.

***piece together** to put together all the information that you have about a situation in order to try to understand the truth.

pile in to enter a place or vehicle together with a lot of other people.

***pipe down** to talk more quietly or to stop complaining.

pitch in to help other people to do work, especially in a willing and cheerful way.

***play along** to pretend to agree with someone or to do what they want you to do, in order to avoid annoying them.

***play someone along** to deliberately encourage someone to believe something that is not true, especially that you intend to marry them.

***play down** to try to make people believe that something is less important or serious than it really is.

***play on** to deliberately use an idea or an emotion in order to do or get what you want.

***play up** (intransitive) if children play up they behave badly and cause trouble for the adult they are with, especially as a way of having fun.

***play something up** to emphasise a quality or a fact, in order to attract people's attention to it or to make it seem more important than it really is.

*__plough through__ to read, write or deal with all of something when there is a lot to do and it takes a long time.

*__point out__ to tell someone something that they need to realise, because it is important in a particular situation.

polish off to finish food and drink, or work, quickly and easily.

*__pore over__ to read or study something very carefully for a long time.

press ahead (or press on) to continue doing something in a determined way, especially when it is difficult.

*__pull in__ 1) if the police pull someone in, they take them to a police station in order to ask them questions, because they think the person may have committed a crime; 2) if a train pulls in, it arrives; 3) to attract people in large numbers.

*__pull off__ 1) to succeed in doing or achieving something difficult; 2) if a vehicle pulls off the road it leaves the road.

pull out 1) if a vehicle pulls out it moves forward onto a road; 2) if a train pulls out it starts to leave the station; 3) to stop being involved in something.

pull over if a vehicle pulls over, it slows and moves to the side of the road and stops.

*__pull through__ to succeed in staying alive and gradually get better after you have been seriously ill or injured.

pull up if a vehicle pulls up, it stops somewhere.

push ahead (or push on) to continue doing something even though it is difficult.

push someone around to tell someone what to do in a rude way.

*__put something across__ to explain your ideas, opinions etc. clearly so that other people can understand them.

put back to arrange for something to happen at a later date than was planned.

put (an animal) down to kill an animal without causing it pain because it is ill.

put someone down to criticise someone in an unkind way which makes them seem stupid or unimportant, especially when other people are present.

*__put in for something__ to make an official request to be allowed to do something or have something.

*__put something off__ 1) to make a light stop working by pressing a switch; 2) to delay something until later.

put someone off 1) to stop someone from liking something; 2) to distract someone.

*__put on__ (a play etc.) to arrange for a performance, competition, etc. to take place.

*__put on__ (weight) to become fatter and heavier.

*__put something out__ to make a fire, candle or cigarette stop burning.

put someone out to cause extra work or trouble for someone.

*__put up with__ to accept an unpleasant situation or someone's annoying behaviour without complaining.

R

rabbit on to talk for a long time in a boring or annoying way.

rake in to earn a large amount of money.

rake off to get part of the profits of a business dishonestly.

rake up to talk about something unpleasant from the past that other people do not want to talk about.

rattle off to say something quickly without stopping, for example a list that you have learned.

rattle on to talk quickly and for a long time in a boring way.

*__reel off__ to say something quickly and easily, especially a list of names, numbers, etc.

*__result in__ if something results in a situation or event, it causes the situation or event to happen.

rip off to cheat someone by making them pay much more than the usual price for something.

rule out to decide that something is not possible; to make it impossible for something to happen.

run across to meet someone or find something by chance.

*__run down__ if a battery, watch etc. runs down, it gradually loses power until there is none left.

run someone down 1) to drive into and hurt or kill someone; 2) to criticise someone or something, especially in a way that seems unfair.

*__run into__ to meet someone you know by chance when you did not expect to meet them.

*__run on__ 1) to use a particular kind of fuel of power supply; 2) to continue happening for longer than was expected.

*__run out__ if you run out of something you have no more of it left because you have used all of it.

run through to quickly read or look at something, especially in order to check it.

run up against to have to deal with unexpected problems or difficulties.

S

*__sail through__ to pass an examination very easily and successfully, or to deal with a difficult experience without having any problems.

*__scrape through__ to only just succeed in passing an examination, or in winning an election, race or competition.

*__see someone off__ 1) to go to the airport, train station etc. to say goodbye to someone who is leaving; 2) to chase someone away.

see someone out to show a visitor the way to leave a building by walking there with them.

*__see something through__ to continue to do something until it finishes, even if it is difficult or you do not like doing it.

seize up if a machine seizes up, its moving parts stop working and can no longer move.

sell out to do something that is against your beliefs or principles in order to get power, money, etc.

*__send down__ to put someone in prison.

*__send out__ to broadcast a message or to produce sound or light.

*__send someone up__ to make someone seem silly by copying them in a funny way.

set about to start doing something, especially something that needs a lot of time and effort.

*__set someone down__ if the driver of a bus, taxi or train, sets you down somewhere, he or she stops there and lets you get out.

*__set off__ 1) to make something such as an alarm system start operating; 2) to start to go somewhere.

set on (upon) someone to suddenly attack someone.

*__set out__ 1) to start a journey, especially a long journey; 2) to explain ideas, facts, etc. in a clearly organised way.

*__set up__ to start a business or organisation.

settle down to start living in a place with the intention of staying there, often with a husband or wife.

settle up to pay what you owe on an account or bill.

show up to arrive, especially at a place where people are expecting you.

single out to choose someone or something from among a group of similar people or things.

***sink in** (intransitive) if information, ideas or facts sink in, you gradually understand them and realise their full meaning.

***sink (money) into** if you sink money into a business or product you provide a lot of money for it because you think you can make a profit later.

***slave away** to work very hard for a long time without much time to rest.

slip off to leave a place quickly and quietly, so that no-one notices you going.

slip out if a remark slips out, you say it without intending to.

slip up to make a careless mistake, especially when you're doing your job.

snap up if you snap up a chance to do something, you take it as soon as you can before it is too late.

soldier on to continue doing something, even though it is difficult or unpleasant and needs a lot of effort.

***spark from** if an event or situation sparks from something, it is caused by it.

spell something out to explain something clearly and in detail.

splash out to spend a lot of money on something, especially something expensive which you do not need.

spring up to suddenly appear or start to exist.

squeak through to only just succeed in doing something, for example, passing a test.

squirrel something away to save something and put it in a safe place.

stamp something out to completely get rid of something that is dangerous or that you disapprove of.

stand down to agree to leave your job or official position so that someone else can do it instead.

stand for to represent a word or phrase or idea.

(not) stand for to refuse to accept a situation.

stand in to do someone else's job for a short period of time.

stand out to be very easy to see or notice.

start out to begin to go somewhere.

stave off if you stave off something bad or unpleasant, you prevent it from happening.

steal up to move quietly towards someone until you are very near them.

***stem from** to develop as a result of something.

step down to leave an important job or official position, especially so someone else can do it.

step up to increase the amount of effort, pressure, speed etc.

stick out to point outwards or upwards, beyond the end of something.

stick to to continue doing what you have decide or promised to do.

stir up to deliberately cause trouble or bad feeling.

stop by to visit a place for a short time.

stop off to stop during a journey, for example to see something or have a rest.

stow away to hide on a ship, plane etc. in order to travel without paying.

strike out to start moving in a particular direction.

***stumble upon** to discover something, especially something important or interesting, when you did not expect to.

sum up to describe something using only a few words.

T

take after someone to be like your mother, father, etc. because you look like them, or because you have a similar character.

***take against someone** to start to dislike someone, especially without a good reason.

take something down to write something that someone is saying.

***take someone in** to completely deceive someone so that they believe a lie.

***take something in** to understand news and information and realise its meaning and importance, especially bad or shocking news.

***take off** 1) if a bird or plane takes off, it leaves the ground and rises into the air; 2) to suddenly start being successful; 3) if a play or radio or television show is taken off, it is no longer performed or broadcast.

***take someone off** to copy the way someone speaks or behaves in order to make people laugh.

***take something on** to agree to do some work or accept some responsibilities.

***take someone on** to start to employ someone.

***take over** to get control of a company by buying it or buying most of its shares.

***take over (from)** to start being responsible for something or doing a job that someone else was responsible for before you.

***take to** (drink/drugs) 1) to start drinking a lot of alcohol or using drugs; 2) to start to like a person or place, especially when you first meet them or start to go there.

***take up** 1) to start doing a particular activity or kind of work; 2) to start to have a new position of responsibility; 3) to try to make people pay attention to a problem, by complaining or protesting in support of someone's rights.

***talk back** to answer your parent, teacher, manager, etc. rudely after they have criticised you or told you what to do.

***talk down to** to talk to someone as if you believe that they are less intelligent than you are.

***talk someone into something** to persuade someone to do something by explaining to them why they should do it.

***talk someone out of something** to persuade someone not to do something that they were intending to do, by explaining to them why they should not do it.

***talk someone round** to persuade someone to change their opinion and agree with you.

***talk something through** to discuss all the details of a problem, idea etc. in order to understand it better and decide what to do.

***team up** (with) to join together with another person or organisation in order to do something together.

***tell someone off** if someone such as a teacher or a parent tells you off, they speak to you angrily about something wrong that you have done.

***think out** to plan something carefully and in detail before you do it.

***think over** to think very carefully about an idea or plan before you decide whether you will accept it or agree to it.

*think up to find a new idea or suggestion by thinking about it and using your imagination or intelligence.

throw up 1) if something throws up new ideas, it produces them; 2) to vomit, be sick.

***tire someone out** to make someone very tired.

***toil away** to work very hard for a long period of time.

***trace back** to manage to find someone or something by investigating what they have done in the past.

track down to manage to find someone or something after a lot of effort, by searching for them.

***trawl through** to read or deal with all of something when there is a lot to do and it takes a long time.

tune in to listen to or watch a particular programme on the radio or television.

turn against to stop liking or supporting someone.

turn away to not allow someone to enter a place.

***turn back** to stop when you are travelling and start going back in the direction that you came from.

turn down to decide not to accept an offer or opportunity.

***turn yourself in** to go to the police and admit that you are responsible for a crime.

***turn into** to change and become a different type of thing or person.

***turn off** to make a light, machine or engine stop working, by pressing a switch, turning a tap etc.

***turn something round** 1) to make a business, organisation, economy, etc. successful again after it has been unsuccessful; 2) to complete the process of making a product or providing a service.

***turn to (someone)** to go to someone for advice, sympathy or help.

***turn up** (intransitive) to arrive somewhere, especially when you are not expected.

***turn something up** to find something by searching thoroughly for it.

W

***wade through** to spend a lot of time reading or dealing with something that seems very long and boring.

ward off to prevent something from harming you.

waste away to become very thin and weak, especially because you are ill or not getting enough food.

wear away if something wears away, it becomes thinner because it has been used a lot.

wear down to gradually make someone feel tired and less able to do something.

wear off if a feeling or the effect of something wears off, it gradually becomes weaker and disappears.

whip through to do a piece of work or read something very quickly.

***wind something down** if something that people are doing winds down, they gradually do less of it before stopping completely.

***wipe out** to destroy or get rid of something completely.

***work out** 1) to succeed in understanding something by thinking carefully about it; 2) to do physical exercises in order to keep your body fit and strong.

work up to to gradually get ready to do something that seems difficult.

Verbs and prepositions

A

abandon someone to
abbreviate to
abide by
absent yourself from
abstain from
accord with
account for
accuse someone of
acquaint someone with
acquit someone of
act for
adapt to
add on / in
adhere to
adjust to
admire someone for
admit to
admit someone to (a place)
advise against / on
agree to / on / with / over
ascend to
aim for / at
allow for
allude to
amount to
answer to someone
apologise to someone for something
arrest for
appeal to
appear to
apply to someone for something
approve of
arrange for
arrest someone for something
avail yourself of
align with
argue with / about / over / for / against
ascribe something to someone
ask for / after / about
assign something to someone
associate with
assure someone of something
attach to
attend to
attribute something to

B

base something on
ban someone from
be absent from
be absorbed in
be accustomed to
be acquainted with
be ashamed of
be associated with
be attached to
be composed of
be dedicated to
be devoted to
be given to
be intended for
be involved with / in
be made from / of
be opposed to
be suited to
beg something of someone
beg for
begin by / with
believe in
belong to
benefit from
bet on something
beware of
blame for
blame something on someone
boast of / about
borrow from

C

campaign for
care about / for
cater for / to
centre on
challenge someone to
charge someone with (a crime) / for (a product or service)
choose between
classify as
coincide with
collaborate with someone on something
collide with
combine with
comment on
commit to
communicate with / to
compare to / with

complain about / of / to
compensate for
compete against / with (a person) / in (a contest)
complain about something to someone
compliment someone on
comply with
concentrate on
confer with someone about something
confess to
confide in
confine (someone / something) to
conform to
confront someone with
confuse something / someone with
congratulate someone on
conjure up
consent to
consist of
conspire against
contrast with / to
contribute to
convert to / into
convict of / to
convince someone of
co-operate with / in
correspond with / to
count on
couple something with
credit someone with
criticise someone for / on
cure someone of

D

date from
deal with / in
decide about / on / against
defend from / against
define as
delight in
demand from
depart from
depend on / upon
derive from
descend to
despair of
detach from
deter from
determine on / to
diagnose as
differ from / in / on / about
direct at / towards
disagree with / on / about
disapprove of
discourage someone from
discuss something with
dismiss someone from
dispose of / with
disqualify from
dissuade someone from
distance yourself from
distinguish between
divide into / among / by
dress in
drink to
dwell on / upon something

E

economise on
elaborate on
elope with
emanate from
embark on / upon
emerge from
encourage someone in something
end in / with
engage in
enlist in / for
enter into
entitle someone to
equip with
escape from
evolve into
exchange for
exclude someone from something
excuse someone for / from
expel from
experiment with / on
extract from
exult in

F

fail in
familiarise yourself with
feature in
feed on
fight for / against / with / about
focus on
forgive someone for
free from

G

gain by / from
gaze at / upon
giggle at
glance at
glare at
glisten with
gloat over
graduate from / in
grapple with
grumble to / at / about / over
guess at

H

happen to
harmonise with
head for / towards
help yourself to
hesitate over / about
hinder someone from
hint at
hope for

I

identify with
implicate someone in
impose on
impress on / upon
improve on
include (someone / something) in
indulge in
infect with
infer from
inform on / about / of
ingratiate yourself with
inquire into / about
insist on
insure against
intend to
interfere with
introduce to
invest in
involve (someone) in
issue with (a passport)

J

joke about / with
judge from / by

K

knock at / on
know of / about

L

label as
lack in
laugh at / about / with
lead to / into
lecture on / about
lie to / about
limit yourself to
link something / someone to / with
long for / to
look forward to

M

marvel at
meet with
mention to
misinform about
mistake someone for
mix with

N

negotiate with (a person) on (a subject)
nod to / at
notify of

O

object to
occur to
operate on
opt for / against / out of
originate from

P

pardon for
part with
participate in
peck at
persist in
plead guilty to
plead with
point at
pose for
praise for
pray to
prefer to
prepare for
present with / to
press for
prevent from
pride yourself on
profit from
prohibit from
promise to
prosecute someone for
protect someone against / from
protest about / against / at
provide with / for
punish someone for

Q

qualify as / for
quarrel with (a person) / about / over (a subject)
quote from

R

react to / against
reason with (a person) about / on (a subject)
reckon on / with
recommend to / for
recover from
refer to
refrain from
regard someone as
register with / at / for
repent of
relate to
release from

relieve someone of something
rely on / upon
remind of
remove from
replace with / by
reply to
report to / on
reserve for
resign from
resign yourself to
resolve to
resort to
respond to / with
restrict to
result in / from
retire from / to
revert to
revolve around
rhyme with
rob someone of something

S

save from
search for
seem to
send for
sentence to
separate from / into
shelter from
shoot at
shout at / about
signal to
smell of
specialise in
spend (money/time) on
spy on
stare at
steal from
steel oneself to
strive for
subject someone to
submit to
subsist on
substitute (one thing) for (another)
succeed in / at
succumb to
sue for
suffer from / with
supply with
surrender to
suspect someone of
sympathise with

T

tamper with
tend to
testify to
thank someone for
threaten to / with
throw at / to
tie to
trade in
transform into
translate from … into
treat oneself to
treat for (illness) with (medicine)
transfer someone / something from … to
trick someone into
triumph over
trust with / to

U

undertake to
use for / as

V

vary in
view as
volunteer for
vote for / to / against
vow to

W

wait for / on
warn about / against
watch for
wave at
win at / in
wink at
wish for
worry about / over

Y

yearn for

Adjectives and prepositions

A

able to
absent from
absorbed in
acceptable to
accompanied by
according to
accountable to
accustomed to
acquainted with
active in
addicted to
adequate for
adjacent to
afraid of / to
agreeable to
allergic to
amenable to
angry with / at / about
annoyed about / with / at
anxious about / to
apparent from
appreciative of
apprehensive of / about
appropriate to / for
ashamed of / to
astonished by / at
attached to
averse to
aware of

B

bad at
beneficial to
bound to
brilliant at
busy with

C

capable of
careless of / about
certain of / about
characteristic of
clever at / with
close to
combined with
committed to
composed of
concerned about / with
confident about / of
confined to
connected to / with
conscious of
consistent with
content with
contrary to
convenient for
convinced of
crazy about
credited with
critical of
crowded with
curious about / to

D

damaging to
dear to
dedicated to
deficient in
delighted to / with / about
dependent on
deprived of
descended from
destined for
determined to
detrimental to
devoid of
devoted to
disappointed in / about / with
displeased with
dissatisfied with
distressed by
divisible by
doomed to
doubtful about
dressed in
due to / for

E

eager for
efficient in / at
eligible for
engaged in
engrossed in
enthusiastic about
envious of
equal to
equivalent to
essential to / for
evocative of
excellent at / for
excited about / by / at

exempt from
experienced in / with
expert in
exposed to
expressive of

F

faced with
faithful to
familiar with / to
famous for
fatal to / for
favourable to
fearful of
fit for
fluent in
fond of
fortunate in
fraught with
free from / to
frightened by / at / by
frustrated by / in
full of
furious at / with / about

G

generous to sb with (money)
glad of
good at / for / with / to
grateful to sb for sth
guilty of

H

happy at / with
harmful to
honest about / in
hopeless at / with
horrified at

I

ideal for
identical to
ignorant of
immune to
implicated in
inadequate for
incapable of
inclined to
independent of
indifferent to
inexperienced in
inferior to
innocent of
inseparable from
intent on
interested in
involved with / in
irrelevant to
irrespective of

J

jealous of

K

keen on / to
kind to / of

L

lacking in
laden with
liable for / to
limited to / in
loyal to
lucky at / in

M

made of / from
married to
mindful of
missing from
mistaken about / in
modest about

N

native to
necessary for / to
negligent of
nervous of / about
new to
noted for

O

obedient to
obliged to sb for sth
oblivious to
offended at / by
opposed to
optimistic about

P

peculiar to
pessimistic about
pleased at / with / about
polite to
poor in / at
possessive about
preferable to
prejudiced against
preoccupied with
previous to
proficient at / in
prone to
proud of

R

ready for
redolent of
related to
relevant to
reminiscent of
renowned for
respected for
responsible to sb for sth
restricted to

S

sacred to
safe from
satisfied with / by
sensible of
sensitive to
separate from
serious about
shy of / with
sick with
similar to
slow at
soluble in
sorry about / for
subject to
successful at / in
sufficient for
suitable for
suited to
superior to
sure of / about
surprised at / about / by
suspicious of / about
sympathetic towards

T

thankful for
tolerant of
true to / of
typical of

U

unable to
unaware of
uneasy about
unfaithful to
unfit for
unfortunate in
uninterested in
unqualified for
unwilling to

V

valid for
visible to / from
vital to
vulnerable to

W

wary of
willing to
worried about
worthy of

Nouns and prepositions

A
absorption in
abstinence from
abuse of (power)
access to
admission to / of
affinity with
animosity towards
aptitude for
assault on
attachment to
attendance on / at
attitude to / towards
aversion to
avoidance of
awareness of

B
ban on
basis for / of
belief in
benefit of
breach of
break from

C
centre of
choice of / between / in
combination of
concern about
confidence in
confusion about
connection between
consciousness of
control over / of
craving for
crime against
cruelty to
cure for

D
damage to
danger of
death by
decline in
decrease in
delay in
demand for
desire for
deviation from
devotion to
difficulty in
discussion about
dislike of
disregard for
distaste for

E
ease of
emphasis on
encounter with
exception to
exclusion of sb from sth

F
faith in
fear of
flair for
flock of
flow of
fluency in
freedom from

G
generosity towards
grievance against
grudge against

H
heir to
hostility towards

I
impact on
impression of
improvement in
inability to
inconsistency in
inconvenience to
increase in
intention of
interest in
intimacy between

J
jinx on
judgement of / on / about
justification for

K
key to
knowledge of / about

L
longing for
lack of
love of

M
mastery of
mistrust of

N
necessity for

O
objection to
obsession with

P
portent of
possibility of
postscript to
potential for
precaution against
predisposition towards
prelude to
pride in
proof against
propensity for / to
protection against

Q
quality of
quest for

R
receipt for / of
recipient of
reduction in
reference to
refuge from
relief from
remedy for
responsibility for / to
rise in

S
sequel to
shot at
specialist in
stock of
substitute for
successor to
surge in

T
talent for
taste in
tendency to / towards
traitor to
tribute to
trust in

U
undercurrent of
understanding of
unit of
upshot of
upsurge of / in
upturn in